Other South

Illuminations: Cultural Formations of the Americas

John Beverley and Sara Castro-Klarén, Editors

SOUTH

Faulkner, Coloniality, and the Mariátegui Tradition

HOSAM ABOUL-ELA

UNIVERSITY OF PITTSBURGH PRESS

Published by the University of Pittsburgh Press, Pittsburgh, Pa., 15260

Copyright © 2007, University of Pittsburgh Press

Manufactured in the United States of America

Printed on acid-free paper

10 9 8 7 6 5 4 3 2 1

Library of Congress Cataloging-in-Publication Data

Aboul-Ela, Hosam M.

   Other South : Faulkner, coloniality, and the Mariátegui tradition / Hosam Aboul-Ela.

     p.   cm. — (Illuminations : cultural formations of the Americas)

   Includes bibliographical references and index.

   ISBN 978-0-8229-4314-3 (alk. paper) — ISBN 978-0-8229-5976-2 (pbk. : alk. paper)

   1. Faulkner, William, 1897-1962—Criticism and interpretation. 2. Faulkner, William, 1897-1962—Political and social views. 3. Literature and society—Southern States—History—20th century. 4. American fiction—Southern States—History and criticism. 5. American fiction—20th century—History and criticism. I. Title.

   PS3511.A86Z554 2007

   813'.52—dc2   2007025334

CONTENTS

ACKNOWLEDGMENTS

Two of the most basic claims grounding this study are, first, that the global transition to a hegemony of corporatism has had profound effects on contemporary culture and, second, that ideas are always already the products of their local, material, historical contexts. The conditions under which this study was produced are not immune to the ramifications of these claims; indeed, the shape of the text is to some extent a result of the impact of these two phenomena.

This book came into existence in three distinct stages. First, some of its most basic observations regarding the relationship between political economy and culture in Faulkner and postcolonial theory were formed as I worked on my doctoral dissertation. Second, I continued informally to develop these ideas over several years in which I moved frequently in search of jobs and money (an increasingly common academic career stage that might be designated "job-market purgatory"). Although I was not able to work directly on the questions this study explores during this period, I discussed them with friends and colleagues who often graciously agreed to read part or all of my dissertation. I further explored and developed my thinking in the classroom and, when possible, at academic conferences. Finally, the book in its present form was drafted primarily between early 2003 and late 2004—a period during which I was an assistant professor of English at the University of Houston.

In each stage, I was fortunate to have a group of friends and colleagues who were incredibly generous with their intellectual insights and moral support. It is embarrassing and humbling to me at this point to think of how many have contributed to making this book possible. In the end, my final product could never measure up to the standard implied by the talent, intelligence, and character of those who have helped me through its creation.

I owe a great debt to the following friends, who read and commented on my dissertation while I was writing it: Nandi Bhatia, Purnima Bose, Laura Broms, Ayman El-Desouky, Luc Fanou, Zjaleh Hajibashi, Walid Hamarneh, Salah Hassan, E. Christopher Hudson, Rachel Jennings, Kathleen Kane, José Limon, Naomi Lindstrom, Laura Lyons, Luis Marentes, Louis Mendoza, Charles Rossman, and S. Shankar. I must single out my two graduate school mentors, Barbara Harlow and Warwick Wadlington. Their guidance, support, and friendship have extended far beyond what could reasonably be expected of a dissertation advisor. Indeed, their commitment continued unabated and kept me going through subsequent stages of the project.

From the "job-market purgatory" phase, I owe a great debt to the following friends in Cairo, New York, and Bowling Green, Ohio: Sayyid al-Bahrawy, Gaber Asfour, Ellen Berry, Dana Brand, Brian Gemp, Hisham Kassem, Wadie E. Said, Samah Selim, Sabina Sawhney, and Samer Shehata. Special thanks are owed to the late Edward W. Said, whose assistance kept me in academia. I must also single out Doreen M. Piano, a cherished source of companionship and constructive critique.

During the book's final phase, my Houston colleagues—especially Margot Backus, Ann Christensen, Karen Fang, María Gonzalez, Betty Joseph, James Kastely, Rubén Martinez, David Mazella, Lynn Voskuil, and Marc Zimmerman—have made all the difference, as have hundreds of engaged and inspiring students. Among my students, I must single out those who participated in two seminars conducted during the period when this book was written: "Faulkner and the Politics of Space" and "Postcolonial Theory and Third World Intellectuals." Thank you, then, to Julianna Arnim, Miah Arnold, Heather Bigley, Renee Dodd, Barbara Duffey, Mary Gray, Jacquelyn Hedden, Sharmita Lahiri, Kwang Lee, Raj Mankad, Jill Meyers, Keya Mitra, Roberta

Short, Vanessa Stauffer, Chris Villanosco, Gemini Wahhaj, Sasha West, Austin Westervelt-Lutz, and Emily Wolahan.

I am also grateful to the Houstoun Endowment for financial support; to Peter Kracht of the University of Pittsburgh Press; and to John Beverley, Sara Castro-Klarén, Carol Sickman-Garner, and two anonymous reviewers. My parents provided constant support throughout my peregrinations, as well as my most profound context. My final thanks go to them.

Any errors remaining in this text are my own responsibility.

∿

Sections of chapter 1 appeared in an earlier version as "Comparative Hybridities: Latin American Intellectuals and Postcolonialists," *Rethinking Marxism* 16.3 (2004): 261–79. Sections of chapter 3 appeared in an earlier version as "Writer, Text, and Context: The Geohistorical Location of the Post-48 Arabic Novel," *Edebiyat* 14.1–2 (2003): 5–19. Sections of chapter 4 appeared in an earlier version as "The Poetics of Peripheralization: Faulkner and the Question of the Postcolonial," *American Literature* 77.3 (2004): 483–509. I gratefully acknowledge each of these journals.

Other South

Faulkner's Spatial Politics

Comparative critical discussions of William Faulkner's South and what has come to be called the Global South have a long history and are once again in vogue.[1] This most recent critical discourse has emerged at the same time literary and cultural studies are becoming increasingly invested in debates involving "globalization," debates that have their own distinct instantiations among social scientists, politicians, journalists, artists, and activists. This book reads these two critical discussions together in order to expose the blindnesses and insights of each. I argue that we can only discuss globalization if we take into account some of the various regional accounts of history, philosophy, ideas, and culture. A global discussion of the novel must move beyond the historical European mold for the genre, and a global discussion of theory must account for histories of ideas from more than one intellectual tradition. All of these discussions must acknowledge in a fundamental way that the contemporary world is marked by a radically uneven distribution of material wealth and that this uneven development dramatically affects relations among regions in our current global polysystem. As a result, political and economic divisions have become profoundly spatial. Starting from these premises, I emphasize a history of ideas that I call the Mariátegui tradition (after the early twentieth-century radical Peruvian thinker José Carlos Mariátegui [1894–1930]) because I believe that one particular collection of intellectuals, historians, economists, writers, and artists have quite effectively described over the course of several decades the processes of globalization that so interest North American writers today. I know of no other scholarship using the phrase "Mariátegui tradition," but I believe it is important to invent such a phrase to account for the profound influences that travel across space and time in regions whose cultures have been affected by colonialism and imperialism because such non-European linkages are regularly overlooked by North American discourses of critical theory. Perhaps one of my most surprising conclusions is that the novels of William Faulkner include an inherent critique of processes of colonization, a critique that emerges when his novels are examined in light of Mariátegui-tradition thought. I hope initially to begin to persuade the reader that such a reading of America's great modern novelist has always been latent even in more traditional interpretations of his project.

Faulkner might be more traditionally categorized as a modernist. Yet when one actually reads through older accounts of literary modernism, mentions of Faulkner seem sparse and perfunctory. For example, in Maurice Beebe's 1974 "Introduction: What Modernism Was," Faulkner receives only a few references amid substantial discussion of Eliot, Pound, Yeats, Proust, Woolf, Joyce, Mann, Cubism, Existentialism, and other canonical high-modernist cases. In Beebe's most prominent mention of Faulkner, the Mississippian is used to illustrate the modernist writer's detachment: "The Modernists were not only anti-sentimental but detached and aloof in other ways as well. … Though it was presumably pride which made a romantic like Rousseau turn down a pension because it would have meant appearing before Louis XIV in order to receive it, Faulkner turned down dinner at the White House on the simple grounds that to travel from Charlottesville to Washington was a long way to drive just to eat with strangers" (1076). At one level, this anecdote is typical of the many amusing tales of eccentricity widely circulating in Faulkner discourse. Such stories play an important role in attempts to popularize Faulkner and make him more consumable, more familiar and endearing than immediate experience with his difficult writing would allow. But in the specific context of this discussion of high modernism, Beebe tries to demonstrate that Faulkner's lack of engagement is typical of modernist writers. Thus, he couples Faulkner's rejection of the White House invitation with an account of James Joyce roughly telling his brother, "Don't talk to me about politics."

While early Faulkner criticism pressed this reading of him as aloof, eccentric, and fixated on language and form, more recent critical work systematically tries to put him back into a social and cultural context, to put him back, however gradually, into the flow of history. John T. Matthews, a premier voice in contemporary Faulkner studies, states the problem with clarity in a 2004 article dealing with the historical Haitian context of Faulkner's *Absalom, Absalom!* "It is sobering to acknowledge," he writes, "how assumptions of U.S. exceptionalism, imperial indifference to prenational colonial origins, the peculiarization of the slaveholding South by the rest of the country and other forms of self-conceptual insularity carried over into the neglect of what Faulkner's South shares more broadly with new world histories and experiences" ("Recalling" 239). So resistant was the older Southern Agrarian/New Critical discourse of Faulkner to the historical, political, and sociological dimension, that more recent innovations in Faulkner criticism have still, in my opinion, not fully faced how thoroughly the Mississippian's life and work were implicated in a network of spatial inequalities highly comparable to those characterizing the contemporary dynamic of globalization. What was typically read as Faulkner's aloofness had as much to do with the unique situation of the Southern United States in the post-Reconstruction period as with the individual novelist's idiosyncrasies. Beebe reads the White House anecdote with the presumption that Faulkner is being ironic, that he cares little about Washington, but in fact, even in this small story Faulkner emphasizes the uniqueness of the Southern context. After all, his hosts at the White House would be "strangers." This might be read as a statement of Faulkner's separateness from, subordination to, and dissidence against political elites, specifically the national political elite in Washington, D.C. The "long way to drive" is not so much a reference to geography as to a distance that is cultural, psychological, and historical. Faulkner is a Mississippian living in Virginia. The complications of the relationship between the Southern states and the federal government, from Reconstruction to the moment of Faulkner's invitation, are infinite. His acute sensitivity to this fact plays an essential role in his spurning of the Washington political elite.

In the 1950s, C. Vann Woodward examined the post-Reconstruction U.S. South, coming to the conclusion that the region was then still what he called "a colonial economy." As Woodward demonstrated in his classic 1951 study, the post-Reconstruction South's economy was plagued by a constellation of traits that made it resemble more an African or Asian outpost than a region within the United States. These traits included an ongoing transition from agriculture to industry as the foundation of the economy, widespread monopolization of Southern industry by Northern corporate magnates, and the emergence of a class of Southerners willing to do the bidding of this Northern corporate elite.[2] This historical dynamic led to a Faulknerian worldview firmly rooted in "the colonial difference" (the phrase is borrowed from the recent work of Walter Mignolo). The colonial status of the South relative to U.S. metropolitan centers evinced in Faulkner a keen sense of the local community's distinction not only from the federal government, as represented by the White House, the post office, and other entities, but also from New York literary elites, East Coast corporate and industrial interests, and (in a highly complicated relationship) the United States' West Coast capital of the commercial culture industry.

Indeed, regarding Hollywood, anecdotes similar to the one Beebe related abound, including an apocryphal claim that Faulkner once asked a motion picture studio head who was orienting him if it would be acceptable "to work at home." When the studio head acquiesced, legend has it that Faulkner flew back to Mississippi. This apparently fictional story also encodes the theme of Faulkner's spatial and geographical aversion to the metropolitan centers to which his status as a Mississippian forced him to be economically beholden. Although this particular anecdote is untrue, an ample supply of authentic ones depicts Faulkner's distaste for Hollywood. In one involving Clark Gable, relayed by the director Howard Hawks, the screen idol inadvertently slighted Faulkner during a hunting trip. As Hawks and Faulkner discussed contemporary American fiction, Faulkner listed himself among the great writers of the age, and Gable asked, "Oh, do you write?" Biographer Joseph Blotner reports that Faulkner replied, "Yes, Mr. Gable. What do you do?" (787). Again, while the ostensible point of Faulkner's punch line is an expression of his aloof detachment, one should not miss the performance's political significance. Hollywood had become a major—if not the major—commercial-cultural metropole in the United States. Faulkner could make money there that he could not make in his home state or anyplace within driving distance of his home state. He was, then, stuck in California trying to make money, so his assertion of the irrelevance of Hollywood's star system was also a claim rooted in the politics of the unique spatial dynamic from which his worldview sprang. If he could be forced to work in the metropolitan center of commercial culture, he could not be made to acknowledge its pervasiveness by recognizing Clark Gable. Furthermore, his own outsider status is parodically reinforced in his quip, as though he were asking sarcastically, "Where would I, a Mississippian, have heard of Clark Gable?"

Faulkner's understanding of Mississippi as part of a Southern colonial economy had taken root in his household, where in one generation his family had transitioned from landed gentry to banking, then watched the South become increasingly urban and industrial, with economic development dependent on Northern investment and social and race relations increasingly shaped by a local, Snopes-like comprador class. Faulkner seems to have internalized this historical phenomenon early in life, as a sort of class envy that manifested itself more in terms of spatial politics than in terms of traditional Marxist conceptions of social class. As a consequence, he connected elite power centers with his incessant personal indebtedness. He expressed this notion as early as 1923, before he had devoted any time to serious fiction writing. The occasion was his (by all accounts justified) removal as the University of Mississippi's postmaster after three years of near-total disregard for his responsibilities. Faulkner had adopted the habit of playing cards and drinking with his companions on the job instead of sorting mail. He made his own judgments about what mail deserved to be delivered, helped himself to periodicals that captured his artist's imagination, and snapped at customers who had the gall to ask for his attention while he was writing on the job. His cavalier wisecrack on parting ways with the U.S. Postal Service is yet another piece of the lore surrounding the writer. While his declaration that he was happy that "never again will I be at the beck and call of every son of a bitch with two cents for a postage stamp" is widely known, the remark preceding this one, as provided by David Minter, is more telling: "You know all my life I probably will be at the beck and call of somebody who's got money" (44).[3]

That this economic fatalism relates to spatial politics is made even more evident by comparing Faulkner's attitude to that of Rosa Coldfield, who complains to Harvard-bound Quentin Compson at the beginning of *Absalom, Absalom!*: "I dont imagine you will ever come back here and settle down as a country lawyer in a little town like Jefferson since Northern people have already seen to it that there is little left in the South for a young man." Many of Faulkner's characters, with diverse motivations and backgrounds, express exasperation with colonizing Northerners, but this passage's unique connection to Faulkner's personal vision is suggested by Rosa's linkage of spatial political economy to writing: "So maybe you will enter the literary profession as so many Southern gentlemen and gentlewomen too are doing now and maybe some day you will remember this and write about it" (5). By focusing on writing in this passage, the author implicitly delineates his own position, his own implication in the aggravated spatial dynamic that is at play. Such a passage calls for an examination of these same issues in his fiction, reminding us that Faulkner the body is also Faulkner the geopolitical space.

The specific case of the role played by the colonial economy's politics of space in Faulkner's fiction has still not been presented systematically. Furthermore, if, as Warwick Wadlington has argued, "more than most writers, Faulkner benefits from being read as the producer of a *body* of work" (9, emphasis in original), the task of delineating the role of colonial economics in his fiction constitutes a book-length project. Still, a brief example by way of introduction seems worthwhile before the components of the broad argument are laid out, and the themes of the colonial economy and spatial politics are so pervasive in the Faulkner bibliography that almost any work can serve as a preliminary illustration.

Nevertheless, the reception and uses of the well-known story "A Rose for Emily" make it a particularly telling example. This widely anthologized short story provokes incomplete readings if it is taken out of the contexts of Faulkner's other fiction and of post-Reconstruction Southern history. Within an anthology of short stories or of American literature more broadly, the story represents Faulkner's supposed obsession with the decline of the Southern aristocratic class, embodied here in the figure of the deranged yet proud spinster, Emily Grierson. In the context of Faulkner's body of work and the history analyzed by Woodward and later historians, however, Faulkner's emphasis on the stages of Southern history stands out. The story appears as a sort of allegory of subnational political economy, even its formal aspects reinforcing not so much the aesthetics of high modernism as the processes of historical modernization.[4]

Indeed, from the very opening of the story, its narrator emphasizes the stages of Southern history. The second paragraph describes Emily Grierson's street at the time of her death: "It was a big squarish frame house that had once been white, decorated with cupolas and spires and scrolled balconies in the heavily lightsome style of the seventies, set on what had once been our most selected street. But garages and cotton gins had encroached and obliterated even the august names of that neighborhood; only Miss Emily's house was left, lifting its stubborn and coquettish decay above the cotton wagons and gasoline pumps—an eyesore among eyesores" (119).[5] It is important to go beyond the superficial observation that Emily's house represents a faded glory and note that the structure is in "the style of the seventies"; that is, Emily represents a *post*bellum phenomenon. What has replaced the privileged class status of her street includes cotton gins, gasoline pumps, and other symbols of an increasingly mechanized and modernized, if still not completely urbanized, South. The narrator's phrase "an eyesore among eyesores" perfectly captures the Faulknerian view of the Janus-faced nature of the processes of modernization, for the narrative neither idolizes the past nor calls for a return to the ways of the old South, as do those of his Nashville Fugitive contemporaries, nor does it refrain from critiquing the cruelty of the dependent colonial economy and its altered social formations in the new South.

As in many of Faulkner's novels, this ambivalent attitude toward history, which refuses to equate it with progress, is reinforced through the rearranging of the narrative's temporal sequence. The story presents the stages of Emily's life. She is a young girl whose father thinks her too good for all suitors. Then her father dies, and in her loneliness she socializes with a Northerner who is in town to oversee a building project. Soon after this relationship ends, the town must deal with a stench emanating from her house. Thirty years later, they must confront her for tax evasion. After another ten years, she dies. But the order in which the narrator relates these events is systematically altered, the new arrangement suggesting that history unfolds in a less than perfect line. As this narrative structure, with its insistence on the nonlinear, repeats itself in one Faulkner novel after another, it begins to make a historiographical claim: that under the conditions of unequal development, both the present and the past are "an eyesore."

These conditions of unequal development are embodied in the story by the construction company's "foreman named Homer Barron, a Yankee" (124). Bearing a name that is an almost too obvious conflation of "homosexual" and "robber baron," Homer is placed in the narrative as its most political element. He oversees a building project that brings both "mules and machinery" to the town and eventually changes its physical geography. He comes with no class standing at all, yet his status as a Northerner implicates him with the highest social class, as embodied in Emily. It is this complete breakdown of the old class system that the community finds most striking about the strange liaison between Emily and Homer. At this point, the spatial division North/South has completely trumped the old class hierarchy of aristocrat/merchant/laborer. Faulkner's careful short story technique is most prominently characterized here in the way that Homer's sexual preference—a key to the unfolding of the plot—is referred to only once, in a subordinate clause: "because Homer himself had remarked—he liked men, and it was known that he drank with the younger men in the Elk's Club—that he was not a marrying man" (126). But even this key fact reinforces Homer as a political allegory, for while he is willing to fraternize with the old elite, represented by Emily, he is not beholden to this class; he understands that his space-privilege allows him not only to act as a predator among the young men of the community but also to use the old elite as he will. Homer is minimally visible in the text, yet he controls and determines a great deal. This narrational distribution parallels his spatial designation, since Northern corporate elites played a key role in the social, economic, and physical restructuring of the South after Reconstruction even without being physically present.

The most immediate element in the story's narration, however, is its unidentified narrator. Very little may be determined about this identity. It is gender neutral, relaying both the women's and the men's responses to Emily. At times, it seems to identify with the new South's young lions, but its expansive knowledge of the different stages of Emily's life suggests that it is the product of an older generation. Its only discernible characteristics emerge through negative correspondences. Its remarks about Emily make clear that it is not the voice of an aristocrat, as those about Homer make clear that it is not a "Yankee," and those about the characters of African descent—Emily's servant and the workers brought by Homer—make clear that it is not a Black voice. Also significant is the narrator's consistent use of the pronoun "we," this usage asserting the narrator's position as the voice of an imagined community. Whereas Benedict Anderson uses the phrase "imagined community" to refer to the emergence of nationalist discourse within an emergent nation-state, I am borrowing it here to designate a collective political consciousness that resembles the ideological self-conception he critiques, even though it is not given the official imprimatur of nationhood and excludes certain key groups within the community. It is a subnational formation. The members of this community distinguish themselves from the old South, embodied in Emily, to whom they feel no allegiance or connection. They also insist on their enduring race privilege over people of African descent, whom the narrator never gives voice or agency. Finally, they are keenly aware of the spatial politics that privilege the Yankee in their midst. Thus, in a simple story, this voice arranges a narrational distribution of emphasis that reflects three nexuses of power in the post-Reconstruction South: socioeconomic class, the color line, and last (but for Faulkner never least) space.

I should make clear from the start that I believe the importance of the colonial economy for Faulkner's fiction goes far beyond issues in Faulkner studies. My main interest is in the practice of reading literatures of colonialism. Clearly, the post-Reconstruction Southern United States does not bear precisely the same colonial relationship to the industrialized Northern states that, say, Kenya bore to England between the two World Wars. And yet it is equally true that no two colonialisms are exactly the same, so if the situation represented by Faulkner's South is not exactly Kenya, neither is Kenya exactly the same as India, Ireland, Egypt, or any of the nominally independent nations of Latin America in the early twentieth century. Thus, the very anomaly of the U.S. South's situation forces upon us a precise and nuanced conception of colonialism, so that to study Faulkner in connection with colonial economics is to hone a more specific understanding of colonialisms, and subsequently postcoloniality. To read the U.S. South as postcolonial in this specific sense is to redefine postcoloniality as an outgrowth of political economy, as well as to insist that any use of the category be historically specified rather than presumed as a transcendental signifier.

Furthermore, the insertion of the U.S. South's post-Reconstruction experience sheds light on coloniality's specific character after World War II. In the early twentieth century, Northern industry in the United States managed to reintegrate the South into the nation, succeeding where the Northern military, during the Civil War, and the federal government, during Reconstruction, had failed. This would set a precedent that the United States would continue to follow throughout the twentieth century. After the colonial economy took hold in the Southern states, similar practices spread to the Global South. First, the United States built on its expanded influence in Latin America, begun during mid- and late-nineteenth-century wars through expanded investment in Latin American economies and influence over Latin American politics. By the post–World War II period, the United States was ready to brush aside Britain's traditional claim to its spheres of influence, as it did in Iran, where it played a leading role in the 1953 coup that would eventually establish an American interest in the formerly British-dominated Iranian oil industry. U.S. influence in the *Arab* Middle East would be established soon thereafter, when the Eisenhower administration rejected the military victory of England, France, and Israel in the 1956 Suez Crisis (known in Arab countries as the "tripartite aggression"), diminishing the former colonial rulers and thereby asserting its hegemony over the region. A projection of American power rooted in political economy and culture was replacing Old World colonialisms, with their heavy administrative and policing elements overlaying colonial ideology. This new American hegemony would be used to reinforce privileged U.S. access without ever bothering with official colonization of any of the region's countries.

This global dissemination of the practice of the colonial economy explains the need to use intellectuals from Latin America and the Middle East to read Faulkner: thinkers from these regions saw in full flower the ends of the processes initiated in the Mississippi of Faulkner's youth.

Thus, I start from the fundamental presumption that a model of postcoloniality that sees colonial hegemony as an outgrowth of political economy cannot be generated without some resort to the ideas and intellectual histories of the Global South. In this other South, the economic dynamic tested within the borders of the United States during the post-Reconstruction period came to fruition. Not surprisingly, then, the intellectuals of this other South have offered more complete analyses of this dynamic. Even though I have already called attention to economics and material history, I agree with Walter Mignolo that the phrase "colonial difference" can refer equally to a problem of epistemology. In fact, the dynamics of knowledge production within postcolonial studies have at times borne a striking resemblance to the deep structure of the most traditional colonial economic model. Whereas in the economic model, the colony is seen as a space for the mining of raw materials that are refined, manufactured, infused with surplus value, and then distributed in the metropolis, comparative literary studies in the United States often takes primary texts—novels, poems, plays, and films—from the Global South and then processes them via Western theoretical models, especially continental theory, albeit oftentimes elaborated in the form of its Anglo-American offshoots. Postcolonial theory in particular resorted to continental theory in the 1980s as a strategy to circumvent older, more oppressive models for analyzing the cultures of the Global South: commonwealth studies, Orientalism, and other various area-studies groupings. While it succeeded in discrediting these more ideologically conservative models, postcolonial theory never quite managed to move beyond the spatial imbalance represented by the old epistemological core/periphery divide, which retained Europe and Anglo-America's status as the exclusive domain of ideas and theory.

To put this point in terms of Edward Said's classic critique of Orientalism, postcolonial theory itself adopted a "textual attitude" toward the former colonies that subordinated their local histories, economics, and social structures to questions of representation, language, and the psychology of the colonizing subject.[6] In turn, this textual attitude meant that neither postcolonial theory nor postcolonial studies more generally ever really challenged the centuries-old claim that "the East proposes and the West disposes." By leaving this formulation unchallenged, the discipline has come to reinforce it in a subtle way.

Walter Mignolo seems to me to be making the same point in different terms when he claims that "knowledge production is not detached from the sensibilities of geohistorical location and that historical locations, in the modern colonial world, have been shaped by the coloniality of power. Scholarship, traveling theories, wandering and sedentary scholars, in the First or the Third World, cannot avoid the marks in their bodies imprinted by the coloniality of power, which, in the last analysis, orient their thinking" (186). Mignolo's phrasing of the problem is significant because it helps confront the issue of essentialism, which might be raised as an objection to this critique of postcolonialism. One need not insist that East/West, First World/Third World, and core/periphery are *essential* binaries in order to critique the Eurocentrism of comparative literary studies in the United States. Rather, the issue is simply the historicization of knowledge. Ideas are not transcendent but rather grow out of particular languages, institutions, and cultures. These contexts may empower or disempower particular concepts as they are disseminated. Thus, postcolonial studies must engage in critiquing the relative absence of the Global South's intellectual histories in its basic models.

Empirically, intellectual history from the Global South proves invaluable for my goal of understanding the workings of the colonial economy in Faulkner's fiction. I focus on a trajectory of thinkers that begins with Peruvian socialist José Carlos Mariátegui and includes the dependency theorists, Walter Rodney, Samir Amin, and Nestor García Canclini. Among these thinkers, whom I am grouping together under the phrase "the Mariátegui tradition," a materialist vision that views global culture and history in terms of spatial inequalities holds sway. I argue that this vision is particularly valuable for reading Faulkner's fiction. This dynamic within my analysis intentionally reverses the standard core/periphery division within much traditional postcolonial studies. I will not dwell on this actual reversal in the course of the study; it will remain a tacit backdrop until the conclusion. But I should make clear at this point not only that this aspect of my study is intentional but that I am fully aware of the potential problem of essentializing intellectual traditions and intend to write against this potentiality. Thus, preliminarily, I will simply clarify that it is not any *essential* difference of the less familiar intellectual traditions of the Global South that I wish to emphasize, but rather the extreme limitations of postcolonial theory's adherence to so geographically narrow a canon of theoretical discourse.

While the intellectual histories in question—those of Latin America, the Middle East, and the African and Asian subcontinents, in rough order of my emphasis—are not essentially different in their modern trajectories from the recent intellectual histories of Europe and Anglo-America, there must be important empirical distinctions between these "Third World" conceptions of colonialism and metropolitan conceptions in order for the reversal I have just mentioned to have any significance. At the most general level, this distinction resides in the relative weight attached to the colonial economy. For institutional postcolonial theory, little importance attaches to the political economy of historical colonialism. Rather, such material histories are replaced by analyses rooted in linguistics, poststructuralism, and psychoanalysis, including colonial discourse analyses, studies of the concept of diaspora and exile, and elaborations of hybridity.[7] Postcolonial studies, as a subset of literary studies, is certainly not unique in its tendency to eschew economics, although one might argue that more productive initiatives have emerged in this area in the more traditional literary disciplines.[8] But for postcolonial studies to have any relevance to the Global South, it cannot ignore the important role of unequal economic development in collecting together nation-states and cultural traditions that have little else in common. Furthermore, the distinctiveness of the various histories of colonialism causes the collecting of something called "the postcolonial world" to break down rapidly if one tries to exclude the colonial economy from the equation. Even without the problem of places like Thailand, Iran, and the Arabian Peninsula, which were never systematically colonized by Europe, the distinction mentioned earlier—between settler colonialism and colonialism administered from a distance—remains. What significance is there to the fact that Egypt was never declared a colony, even though it was run by a British governor, occupied by the British military, and controlled financially by British business interests? And what should one do with Canada and Australia, which were both once colonies, not to mention the ultimate anomaly of the United States, which began as colonies, then emerged as an independent nation-state that proceeded to employ a systematic and virulent expansionist settler colonialism before ultimately morphing into its current neocolonial dominance of the world? Many of these confusions may be greatly simplified by a direct focus on the structures and processes of the colonial economy. Iran, for example, entered the constellation of Western dominance through an exclusive economic relationship with England that rendered official, administrative colonialism unnecessary and greatly hindered Iran's ability to pursue its own economic destiny, especially after the United States helped Britain void a brief attempt on the part of the Mossadegh government to dismantle the special arrangement in 1953. The equitable and respectful bilateral trading relations set up between the European industrial powers and states like Canada and Australia cannot be compared to the typical economic pillaging of colonized countries by colonizers, like the notorious arrangement between France and colonial Haiti, which C. L. R. James designated "the exclusive."[9] Further, focusing on the colonial economy, as I have already suggested, allows a more appropriate understanding of the unique brand of coloniality that the United States engaged in after World War II, whereby countries fell under the influence of U.S. corporations and U.S.-based transnational corporations without ever seeing American governors arrive to run the country—the very recent (and anachronistic) example of L. Paul Bremer in Iraq notwithstanding.

In sum, using the Mariátegui tradition to read Faulkner's South through the Global South forces upon us both an important revision of our currently existing Faulkner and a more specific conceptualization of the very concept of coloniality. My study is motivated neither by Faulkner's pronounced and enduring influence among writers from Latin America, the Caribbean, and the Middle East—an influence far beyond that of any other North American writer—nor by the current trendiness of invoking postcolonialism in readings of Faulkner and U.S. Southern culture, although both of these realities are symptomatic of the situation I have set out to describe. Rather, my study asserts a connection between the colonial economy and the production of culture. Several important claims follow from this primary assertion. One is that the South of Faulkner's formative years at the beginning of the twentieth century manifested many of the characteristics of a colonial economy. As one of the first spaces to be subjected to the American version of colonial economic hegemony, the U.S. South can be seen as an important central text in a very contemporary reading of the literature of colonialism. Second, a distinct strain of verisimilitude inheres in Faulkner's fiction writing that Agrarian/New Critical aestheticism has blocked us from fully appreciating. The claim here is not that we have never read Faulkner accurately. Rather, the deep ambivalence of Faulkner's position in the global polysystem is still not fully appreciated. In his pathbreaking study of a decade ago, Afro-Caribbean poet and intellectual Edouard Glissant found himself alternating between passages in which he identifies with a fellow writer produced by plantation culture and others in which he sees a shadow of the Caribbean's White French colonial master underpinning Faulkner's socioeconomic position as a propertied White male. One element of Glissant's complex Janus-faced symbol needs further exploration. While brilliant work has been done connecting Faulkner to nearly every school of North American literary theory, as well as to writers of many regions colonized by Europe, the lens of coloniality requires an approach that has not been tried: namely, using ideas and thinkers from former colonies to radically reconceptualize Faulkner's project.

Just as the Mariátegui tradition forces us to see what Faulkner scholarship has traditionally deemphasized, this new Faulknerian reading forces upon us a reconsideration of the postcolonial. Although postcolonial studies has been evolving and changing with the rise of discourses of globalization and with changes in the actual postcolonial condition, the basic assumptions under which many postcolonial theorists still work are those shaped by the Anglo-French experience before World War II. Not only does invoking the Mariátegui tradition's reading of coloniality shift the focus to current circumstances, it does so with an unapologetic move toward a critical discourse of globalization that draws on global voices and eschews Eurocentrism.

∿

My first chapter is devoted to an elaboration of the distinction between economically inflected conceptions of colonialism in the Global South and the poststructuralist discourse of postcolonial theory. This comparative analysis of Latin American intellectual history—as represented in the Mariátegui tradition—and mainstream postcolonial theory—represented primarily in the work of Homi K. Bhabha but also in work by Robert Young, Bill Ashcroft, Sara Suleri, and others—emphasizes the notion of "hybridity," which operates as a transcendental signifier in Bhabha and is also manifested throughout Mariátegui-tradition writings, and simultaneously points to the prejudice favoring European ideas and thinkers in the U.S. Academy's canon of critical theory. The distinct alternative represented in the Mariátegui tradition includes not only Latin American thinkers from the 1920s to the present—Mariátegui, Fernando Ortiz, the dependency theorists, Angel Rama, and Nestor García Canclini—but also Arab intellectuals like Samir Amin and Mahdi 'Amal and African and Afro-Caribbean writers including Walter Rodney and Ngugi wa Thiong'o. This trajectory of Third World intellectuals emphasizes the concrete structures and material history of colonialism, in contrast with postcolonialism's overriding interest in identity, language/utterance, subjectivity, and representation. At the same time, the historical materialism of the Mariátegui tradition can be distinguished from Euro-American Marxism in its emphasis on space as a category for analyzing the political economy of exploitation in the modern world. Whereas Euro-American Marxism focuses on the tripartite division of socioeconomic classes (aristocracy, bourgeoisie, proletariat), which first appeared in Europe during the Industrial Revolution, the Mariátegui tradition reads class alongside *spatial* inequalities—core, semiperiphery, and periphery, for example. The overrun regions of the semiperiphery and periphery can be said to be "peripheralized" in the modern world system. Reading the Mariátegui tradition thus allows for a shift in understanding the operations of power and subjugation. Power is economic and political as much as it is discursive and cultural. It makes subordinate not only individual subjects, psyches, and consciousnesses but whole regions. The Other is not an individual, but a space: Other South.

Mariátegui-tradition writers tend to insist on reading culture, political economy, and history with an awareness of local problems and local dynamics.

One of the ways this manifests itself is in recognition of subtle but significant distinctions between socioeconomic class structures in postcolonial societies and Euro-American Marxism's traditional tripartite division. For example, peasantry may be emphasized in the Mariátegui tradition alongside the urban proletariat more central to Euro-American Marxist thinking. The nature of the bourgeois class is also distinctive in modern societies of the Global South, its members' "comprador" character leading them to see their interests lying in the stability of metropolitan socioeconomics. It is in the core—not in the local/national economy—that this group invests its allegiance. In this sense, the comprador class presents a substantial obstacle to full-blown economic development in the Global South. The comprador phenomenon forms the basis of chapter 2, which considers its historical role in the creation of a colonial economy in the U.S. South. The U.S.-based comprador phenomenon finds its most important literary manifestation in the novels of Faulkner's Snopes trilogy, which he began writing in the 1920s and returned to regularly until *The Mansion* was published in 1959. Flem Snopes represents the value system of the new colonial economy, his separateness from the community and from communal values and standards embodying the essence of compradorism.

The next two chapters turn more directly to the relationship between literary form—poetics—and the problem of political economy described by the Mariátegui tradition—peripheralization. Chapter 3 makes the claim that Mariátegui, the dependency theorists, and Samir Amin were also advancing a view of history when discussing the problem of economic dependency, their historical vision constituting an alternative to the equally historical but monolithic and Eurocentric perspective of classical development economists like W. W. Rostow. If Rostow saw history as unfolding in linear and causal stages that could be described by observing Europe's past, the Mariátegui tradition critiqued this Eurocentrism, viewing history instead as multiple, material, and not entirely linear. In the novel, this historiography expressed itself in a narrative structure that was multiperspectival, moving back and forth in time. While *David Copperfield* exemplifies the Eurocentric vision, many postcolonial novels use complications of time, space, and perspective to explicitly oppose a unified, linear, monolithic historiography. These novels challenge traditional historiography with a historiography that understands processes of peripheralization, their narrative art explicitly political, invested in a historical materialism that forcefully distinguishes the form of such works from the superficially similar structure of the modernist novel.

Although Faulkner has often been categorized as part of a very traditionally defined modernist canon, chapter 4 takes up the famously complicated structure of his masterwork, *Absalom, Absalom!*, as a test case for establishing his stronger relationship to the novelists of the Global South, who were producing their fiction against the background of unequal development. Modernist novels by authors such as D. H. Lawrence, Ford Madox Ford, T. E. Hulme, and their contemporaries sprang from a historiography that differed dramatically from the historical vision of novelists like Gabriel García Márquez, Ghassan Kanafani, and Arundhati Roy. Linearity in modernist works was often counterposed with a circular pattern invoking myth. In such cases, the attempt to transcend materiality through art is unmistakable. Although *Absalom, Absalom!* seems at first glance to create such a mythic and circular structure, its combined elements use the politics of space and time in a way that prefigures postcolonial narrative, rather than harkening back to a narrowly conceived high modernist moment. In its narrational complexity, characterized by constant shifts in point of view and backward and forward movement in time, similar to the workings of time in "A Rose for Emily," the novel reflects history's unwillingness to advance, evolve, or progress in a Hegelian sense. The analogy rests in a vision that does not start from the assumption that history has worked out nicely.

The easy equation of history and progress, critiqued by the Mariátegui tradition, has shown a frightening resilience through the twentieth century and into the present. In the mid-1990s, for example, Thomas Friedman expressed a Clintonian insistence that intellectuals and activists from the Global South, not to mention labor organizers and environmentalists everywhere, should acknowledge the inevitability of the G-8 countries' triumphal narrative of globalization. In many ways, the American invasion of Iraq in the spring of 2003, and the United States' subsequent occupation, were products of epistemological (not to mention other types of) colonialism, the war premised on the surety of America's "ability to reconstruct and reformulate the Orient, given the Orient's inability to do so for itself" (Said, *Orientalism*

282). Such recent developments build on a long tradition in Western thought of presuming that ideas are the sole purview of Euro-America. In its current manifestation, this presumption has led to an understanding of globalization as a univocal monologue directed at the Global South by the Western powers. But intellectual histories of the Global South suggest that, in fact, the counter-narrative, which is critical of the Clinton/Bush conception of globalization, grows out of a long and varied tradition of global dissent, a tradition that has on occasion even infiltrated the canon of Euro-American high modernism.

Chapter One

Comparative Southern Questions

The Unavoidable Significance of the Local

Space and the Myth of True Knowledge

In the early stages of writing this book, I was lucky enough to be invited to speak on topics growing out of my research by a graduate program in literary studies at a large public university in the Deep South. The invitation arose not from my fame (since I had none) but from a personal connection with an old friend, with whom I had taught on the East Coast while I was adjuncting and job hunting and he was between master's and Ph.D. programs. As we grew reacquainted, it became clear that undertaking doctoral work had crystallized many key intellectual issues for him; he was well on his way to excellent preparation for academic work. One of these key issues was the question of theory and its relationship to literary and cultural studies. He had become steeped in the major ideas of Lacan, Derrida, Foucault, Deleuze, and others, and this enhanced knowledge, which was being instilled so ably by his university, formed a powerful supplement to the training in more traditional literary criticisms that he had received at the master's level. Over the course of the three days he hosted me, I found myself regularly fielding questions from a whole group of graduate students about these canonical theorists that I could not answer, either because the questions were too subtle for my rusty memory of the central texts (although I was not nearly modest enough to admit this) or because they were far less subtle formulations of one question, which could basically be boiled down to: which one of the thinkers had written our theoretical Bible—which one was (in the graduate students' colloquial phrasing) "the man"? I returned home with two strong impressions: first, that I seemed to be growing more ignorant than I had been while undertaking my own graduate study; and second, that knowledge of Continental theory had become a kind of vocational training sometime around the late 1980s, as I began my doctoral work, and this status had only been reinforced in the intervening years. As a consequence, the theoretical canon had (both for better and for worse) become increasingly unproblematic, its ideas gradually further removed both from their origins and from many of their more controversial consequences.

In the third section of Said's introduction to *Orientalism*, the book that arguably started postcolonial studies in the United States, Said devotes several pages to critiquing "the distinction between pure and political knowledge," as it was understood at the time. "It is very easy to argue," he states, "that knowledge about Shakespeare or Wordsworth is not political whereas knowledge about contemporary China or the Soviet Union is" (9). As he develops this contrast, he plays out the examples of "an editor whose specialty is Keats" and a specialist in Soviet economics. (I often find myself reminding undergraduate students that in 1978, with the Cold War still going strong, the choice of the Soviet economist was by no means an arbitrary one.) What Said intends to demonstrate in this discussion is that "the general liberal consensus that 'true' knowledge is fundamentally non-political . . . obscures the highly if obscurely organized political circumstances obtaining when knowledge is produced" (10). Although not everyone agreed with Said's point at the time *Orientalism* was published, the claim that any literary work is part of a highly politicized discourse is far less controversial today.[1] Yet when it comes to histories of ideas, philosophical and critical texts, or "theory," a special place for the category of "true" knowledge persists. It may manifest itself in critical practice—for example, in scholarship that cites a barrage of theoretical authorities from various time periods and schools of thought (as though Kristeva, Barthes, Bakhtin, Heidegger, and Žižek regularly sat together in the same room playing cards) before launching into a reading of a cultural or literary text. Such a critical practice uses repetitive juxtaposition to extirpate the theoretician and her or his ideas from any historical, geographic, or even ideological context. The theorist floats above history, producing concepts whose universal applicability is unquestionable.

This transcendent place for theory is not simply a critical accident. When Homi K. Bhabha, a central voice in institutional postcolonial studies, insists on the "distinction to be made between the institutional history of critical theory and its conceptual potential for change and innovation" (31), he is setting aside just such a special place.[2] Bhabha's appeal reminds us that what he calls "the 'new' languages of theoretical critique," which became influential in literary studies and other disciplines in the United States in the 1970s and 1980s, provided a specialized language that allowed literary and cultural critics to create ideological solidarities and work across disciplinary boundaries more effectively. But eventually these new languages became a type of professional membership card. The professionalization of what used to be a new language has thus given the narrow theoretical canon of Continental thought a status comparable to that Said ascribes to Keats scholarship before the paradigm shift brought about by Continental thought's infiltration of the Anglo-American academy.

While much of cultural studies, and many other emergent historicist, materialist, and comparatist approaches, has made the uses of theory more complicated, the canon of Continental theory as a space for true knowledge has proved resilient, to say the least. This might be illustrated by a brief mention of John Beverley's *Subalternity and Representation*, a book from which I learned a great deal and which I will cite regularly as an authority over the coming pages. Particularly of value is the careful attention Beverley pays to Latin American intellectual histories and his comparative juxtaposition of key figures in this history with subaltern studies historiography on the Asian subcontinent. Still, amid all the insights in Beverley's work, one notes the blindness—an unspoken acceptance of canonical theory as true knowledge. In the case of Latin American intellectuals, their historical context is examined, their class standing foregrounded, and their commitment—or lack of commitment—to the cause of the subaltern critiqued, but for certain Continental theorists—Foucault and Benjamin, for example—such questions are never raised in spite of the thinkers' central place in Beverley's analysis.[3]

Here I will suggest several key concepts in an alternative theoretical canon. Granted, this is only one of many possible theoretical canons, but I have chosen it for its particular efficacy regarding reading Faulkner novels. Specifically, the elaboration of the colonial economy's structure as spatial politics—as a form of political and economic domination that inheres in regional relationships—elicits from Faulkner's fiction a social critique not heretofore emphasized in Faulkner studies. While there were several Latin American precursors to the intellectuals upon whom I focus, this alternative theoretical canon (more or less) begins with the Peruvian socialist José Carlos Mariátegui.

The Materialist Emphasis and the Cultural Turn

In contrast to the presumption that Continental theory represents true knowledge is Walter Mignolo's argument connecting "knowledge production" to "geohistorical location" and the latter to "the coloniality of power." Mignolo's position forms a counterpoint to prevalent theoretical practice separating ideas from their historical context. The correlation between the United States formally engaging for the first time in European-style colonial rule, in the aftermath of the war of 1898, and the 1900 publication of Uruguayan essayist José Enrique Rodó's early critique of U.S. hemispheric hegemony in *Ariel* clearly illustrates this direct link between "knowledge production" and "the coloniality of power." At one level, Rodó's essay is part of a long tradition of Latin American intellectuals attempting to define what was unique about their local reality. Indeed, this tradition, including Cuban José Martí (1853–95), Argentine Domingo Faustino Sarmiento (1811–88), and El Inca Garcilaso de la Vega (1539–1616), stretches back as far as the beginnings of European colonialism in the hemisphere. Rodó's essay adds the challenge to U.S. hegemony in the Americas as a distinct element of the attempt to define a Latin American reality in the aftermath of the United States' formally taking on colonial responsibilities outside the North American land mass. Thus, by emphasizing imperialism, *Ariel* helped set a new course for Latin American thought after the intellectual tradition had already distinguished itself as having a significant degree of autonomy from Europe in its concern with regional identities. Of course, the essay itself did not stop the United States from expanding its hegemony in the region. Consequently, as the historical dynamics of the coloniality of power in the Americas evolved, intellectual traditions in Latin America adapted critical discourses commensurate with the new realities. Among these new critical discourses were traditions of radical thought influenced by the various critiques of capitalism simultaneously emerging in Europe. These traditions built on the liberal, romantic Rodó's explication of the dangers of U.S. hegemony in the region but added the use of political economy to understand regional "identity" or "reality," which had long been a major subject for Latin American thinkers. Foundational to this intellectual history is the Peruvian José Carlos Mariátegui. But Mariátegui's ideas were subsequently taken in new directions by Fernando Ortiz, the dependency theorists, Angel Rama, Antonio Cornejo Polar, and a number of other intellectuals, who were also interested in analyses that consider the dynamic relationship among cultural production, social issues, and questions of political economy.

Of course, this strain of thought does not constitute *the* intellectual history of Latin America; rather, this is a history that I have chosen to emphasize for several reasons. First, this tradition understands itself as at some level separate and distinct from the North American and European intellectual traditions at which Eurocentric theoretical canons stop. The main component of this distinctiveness, I believe, is its situation across the colonial difference from Eurocentric theory, even in Eurocentrism's antifoundationalist strains. One of the results of this distinct location is a persistent emphasis on material history and political economy. For these Latin American intellectuals, a basic connection exists between the inequalities separating the metropolis from the periphery and the culture of the Global South. In light of this insistence, they emphasize the economic foundations of neocolonialism in Latin America; the operation of the colonial economy in the Global South—even in the absence of the actual concrete structures of colonialism, which had already been largely thrown off by the twentieth century; and the continued struggle with unequal development. Within this intellectual tradition, material conditions make a country postcolonial in the first instance because economics is foundational to colonialism's deep structure and is its most enduring legacy during the postcolonial stage.

In Europe and the United States, Marxist thought may be understood to have asserted a similar relationship between political economy and culture, but again, important distinctions must be made, in spite of the substantial influence of European Marxism among these Latin American intellectuals. First, this Latin American tradition reads political economy in spatial terms, whereas European Marxism usually reads the economic narrative in linear-temporal terms. Whereas a Hegelian Marxist view of historical evolution exerted a powerful force among Marxists in Europe and the United States, the notion that the world had one historical timeline, with Europe as its center, was persistently challenged among progressive thinkers in the Global South. The particular innovation of the Mariátegui/*dependentista* tradition was supplementing the old Marxian class structure—aristocracy, bourgeoisie, proletariat—with a spatial understanding of material inequalities.

Second, a culturalist fetish became suddenly manifest in much Eurocentric Marxism at the moment it turned to literature, cultural studies, and the historical phenomenon of colonialism. Michael Hardt and Antonio Negri, in their wide-ranging and highly influential study *Empire*, argue that in the age of globalization, there is no distinction between base and superstructure, that the economic and the cultural have become one.[4] While their claim is cogent, in practice, cultural studies—especially postcolonial studies—often uses such arguments to adopt a method that is purely cultural in its approach, even though the melding of economic and noneconomic realms would suggest that the critic should be forced to use various critical tools dealing with the cultural, the political, the social, *and* the economic.

In the area of postcolonial studies specifically, the culturalist fetish has meant that colonialism is typically seen as manifesting itself in hybrid subjects and identities, in cosmopolitan experiences of diaspora and exile, and in problems of representation as manifested in European and North American writing. The method by which these dynamics are examined emphasizes linguistics and psychoanalysis, drawing almost exclusively on the European bibliography of postmodernism. However, for the Latin American intellectual tradition I have designated—and indeed, for twentieth-century intellectuals throughout the Global South—the conjoined categories of colonialism and the neocolonial are viewed differently: it is axiomatic that colonialism's most enduring legacy is economic and that continuing regional struggles with unequal development are the contemporary manifestation of this reality. For most intellectuals within these traditions, speaking of colonialism without bringing up political economy is misguided at best. Furthermore, the notion that colonialism's legacy might be described adequately without taking into account the subject position of the Global South's intellectuals would be considered equally bankrupt. Not surprisingly, in the Global South, intellectual work is not produced as though ideas were the sole purview of the metropolis.

The contrast between these two approaches will be illustrated later through a comparison between Nestor García Canclini's use of the term *hybridity* and Homi K. Bhabha's. While both of these critics are now well known in the United States, García Canclini's impact remains primarily in the area of Latin American cultural studies, whereas Bhabha is now required reading for anyone aspiring to be current, theoretically speaking. The more important contrast, however, springs from Bhabha's commitment to Continental theory versus García Canclini's program of building on a Latin American intellectual tradition emphasizing the unavoidable significance of the local.

Mariátegui and the Roots of a Regional Intellectual Tradition

The specialist in Latin American intellectual writing might find it counterintuitive to trace García Canclini's conception of hybridity back to José Carlos Mariátegui, since discussions of *mestizaje,* a Spanish term comparable to *hybridity,* date all the way back to de la Vega, who had one Incan and one Spanish parent. By the nineteenth century, what was usually called *mestizaje* had become an even more prominent topic in the region's cultural criticism. Prior to Mariátegui, as I have mentioned, Latin American essayists demonstrated a critical attitude toward the United States as a destructive hegemon and a corollary insistence on the separateness of Latin American culture.[5] But Mariátegui distinguished himself by being the first such essayist to deploy political economy as part of his analysis of Latin American problems with such sharpness and depth. Thus, he pushed the suspicion Latin American intellectuals had long evinced toward the United States in a new direction, toward a global anticolonial critique.

The essence of earlier discussions of *mestizaje* was the relationship between indigenous communities and European settlers in the various regions of Latin America. By the 1920s, Mariátegui's Mexican contemporary José Vasconcelos was building a whole conception of the continent's future on the notion of *indigenismo,* but Vasconcelos's notion of a Latin American "cosmic race" was very distant from the Peruvian's analysis of the indigenous problem. Vasconcelos was unable to go beyond the conception of *indigenismo* as a strictly racial phenomenon, as his phrase "cosmic race" implies. What Vasconcelos shared with other Latin American writers was a clear conception of the United States as an imperialistic force that was distinct from, and must be resisted by, local cultures. Yet even within the context of discussions of *mestizaje,* he was extreme in his emphasis on the racial as the foundation for analyses of culture. A strong connection inheres between Vasconcelos's conception of the cosmic race—which has come to be erroneously understood, and even celebrated by the state, as pro-*indigena*—and his later slide toward fascism (Marentes 15–17).

If Vasconcelos represents a relatively isolated example of a Latin American conception of *mestizaje*/hybridity based on race, Mariátegui's distinction crystallizes the alternative analytical possibilities.[6] The influence of the Italian Marxist movement on Mariátegui instilled in him an ambition to view the situation of Peru's indigenous peoples in connection with the economic, social, political, and historical realities of that space at that time. This led him to conclude that "any treatment of the problem of the Indian—written or verbal—that fails or refuses to recognize it as a socio-economic problem is but a sterile, theoretical exercise destined to be completely discredited" (*Seven* 22). In the same essay, he adds (perhaps to make the contrast with Vasconcelos's racialism explicit): "To expect that the Indian will be emancipated through a steady crossing of the aboriginal race with White immigrants is an antisociological naiveté that could only occur to the primitive mentality of an importer of merino sheep" (25). This interest in the socioeconomic dimensions of Latin American problems was not limited in Mariátegui's thinking to the indigenous problem. Rather, it infused his method of reading culture, history, and society.

Several circumstances add to the originality and continued relevance of Mariátegui's analyses. First, his work represents the first major attempt from the region to apply Marxist analysis to Latin American problems. Second, a number of factors contributed to Mariátegui's insistence on a flexible application of Marxist principles that—while grounded in the socioeconomics of history and culture—refused to lapse into economic determinism. These factors included his originary position as a Latin American Marxist and his initial exposure to Marxist thought via the Italian group collected around *L'Ordine Nuovo,* the influential leftist Italian weekly.

Mariátegui's connection to Italian Marxism stems from the fact that he spent the years from 1919 to 1923 living in Italy in an unofficial exile imposed on him by Peru's Leguía dictatorship.[7] During this period, he wrote a series of "Cartas de Italia" for the Peruvian newspaper *El Tiempo;* he attended the famous Congress of Livorno in January 1921, which led to the founding of the Partito Comunista Italiano and *L'Ordine Nuovo;* he began incorporating questions of political economy into his readings of Peruvian and Latin American politics; and he met his wife, Ana Chiappe. The formative nature of this brush with Italy's emerging locally inflected Marxism, along with several biographical similarities, including comparably short lives plagued by poor health and long imprisonments, has led commentators to refer to Mariátegui as the Latin American Antonio Gramsci. In spite of being somewhat inaccurate, this comparison illuminates several important realities. While the presumption tends to be that Mariátegui borrowed Gramsci's ideas and then applied them to Peruvian and Latin American situations, the record disputes this. Mariátegui apparently met Gramsci only once in passing at Livorno. More important, he never cites Gramsci in his writings, while other Italians appear regularly, particularly Benedetto Croce and Piero Gobetti, with whom he became close friends during his time in Italy.

At one level, the imagined relationship between Mariátegui and Gramsci demonstrates the way global spatial inequalities reflect the reception and distribution of ideas and thinkers. Gramsci's primacy in the pairing—that is, his being made a central influence on the Peruvian—comes partially from the

Italian's greater propinquity to the core. Given the current emphasis in canons of theory, it would be ridiculous to call Gramsci "the Italian Mariátegui."

The comparison is also enlightening at the level of method. Both figures distinguish themselves from liberal thinkers through their insistence on political economy but also appear distinct from much orthodox Marxism in their emphatic rejection of economic determinisms that grow out of a rigid division between "base" and "superstructure." Both insist on the spatial dimension of political and economic hegemonies, but the extent and nature of their respective engagements with the politics of space are both distinctive and telling. Gramsci's relationship to the politics of space grows out of his early Sardinism, which Gramscians traditionally read as youthful indiscretion, corrected by a later, more mature understanding of Marxism.[8] Such commentators may show special interest in the concepts of hegemony and "civil society" in Gramsci's work, not to mention his distinction between the organic and the traditional intellectual. Increasingly, exceptions to this dismissive attitude toward his interest in the Italian South have emerged, particularly among those who study both Gramsci and the Global South, and who see parallels between his assessment of the problem of unequal development within Italy in the early twentieth century and global unequal development today. This latter group includes Said, literary critic Timothy Brennan, historian Peter Gran, and Egyptian intellectual Sami Khashabah. Their key text is the essay Gramsci had almost completed at the time of his arrest in late 1926, "Some Aspects of the Southern Question."

The essay begins with a special emphasis on the agency of the peasant class in southern Italy (442–43). This emphasis, which represents a break with the more traditional Marxist dismissal of the peasantry in favor of an emphasis on the urban proletariat as the vehicle for transformation of capitalist society, suggests a more subtle understanding of the problem of unequal development. Not only does Gramsci's respect for the peasant as an agent prefigure his development of the notion of an organic intellectual, but it also calls attention to the complex relationship among geography, power, and ideology. In this sense, the very concept of the organic intellectual, when understood with respect to Gramsci's early emphasis on the southern question, can be seen as an early argument for the necessity of a broad and representative theoretical canon.

Engagement with the politics of space also separates Gramsci from much Eurocentric Marxism of the time. He blames the Italian Socialist Party for a number of ahistorical prejudices about the South and Southerners (444), attempting to counter these by demonstrating that the "nexus of relations between North and South in the organization of the national economy and the State is such, that the birth of a broad middle class of an economic nature ... is made almost impossible" (458). For Said, the enduring significance of the essay rests in its giving a "paramount focus to the territorial, spatial, geographical foundations of social life" (*Culture and Imperialism* 49). Many Gramscians argue that this very emphasis on the spatial is what Gramsci outgrows in *The Prison Notebooks,* but whatever the proper understanding of Gramsci's future trajectory might be, a distinction must still be made between the politics of space in Gramsci's "Some Aspects of the Southern Question" and in Mariátegui's *Seven Interpretive Essays on Peruvian Reality* (1928). Both texts emphasize not merely the spatial and the geographic but the specific political and economic inequalities of space. In the case of Mariátegui, however, these spatial politics are read globally and as an outgrowth of colonialism. While Gramsci points to spatial inequalities, Mariátegui reads them historically as a product of colonialism and imperialism.

The first of Mariátegui's seven essays is entitled "Outline of the Economic Evolution," the topic itself reflecting Mariátegui's analytical priorities in its emphasis on political economy. And this emphasis is reinforced by the opening line: "The degree to which the history of Peru was severed by the conquest can be seen better on an economic than on any other level" (3). His reading of this economic evolution continually returns to spatial questions, however. For example, he notes that at the time of the Spanish conquest, Spaniards tended "to settle in the lowlands" because "they feared and distrusted the Andes, of which they never really felt themselves masters" (5). He comments that during the period of regional independence, trade—especially with England—was the most significant foundation of the region's economies, noting that "the countries on the Atlantic naturally benefited most from this trade because of their proximity to Europe" (8). In general, he remarks of this period that "because of geography, some countries would advance more rapidly than others" (9). In later passages, he develops more fully his analysis of the unequal development dividing coast and highlands within Peru.

The most important point of distinction between Mariátegui's spatial politics and Gramsci's, as expressed in "Some Aspects of the Southern Question," is that Mariátegui focuses primarily on the way English financial interests used the geopolitics of global capitalism to take gradual control of the Peruvian economy over the course of the nineteenth century and on the way the United States had recently substituted itself as economic hegemon. Without fully conceiving of a core-periphery economic structure, Mariátegui emphasizes the international nature of spatial inequalities and their historical link to colonialism. While Gramsci's central problem is the gap between the northern proletariat and the southern peasant as an obstacle to political action, Mariátegui only mentions the "proletariat" once in passing, as an important new phenomenon in Peruvian cities (14). This reference indicates his awareness of traditional European Marxist class analysis, but its passing nature suggests the distinctiveness of Mariátegui's focus.

One consequence of Mariátegui's reading Latin American history through the economics of spatial inequalities is the integration of the region—perhaps for the first time—into what could have been called the colonized world—what Mariátegui often simply refers to as "the East." While the majority of Latin American nation-states achieved their independence from Spain or France within fifty years of the United States' independence from England, Mariátegui's "Outline of the Economic Evolution" makes clear that for Latin America generally, and Peru in particular, national independence did nothing to liberate the region from a dire economic dependency that in turn fostered other dependencies. This dependency was instilled over the course of the nineteenth century by Anglo-American commercial and financial interests and by the legacy of the region's colonial economies.

In this socioeconomic sense, Peru and, by extension, the rest of Latin America were still colonized in very concrete and measurable ways. Mariátegui was thus able to describe and analyze the encroaching U.S. hegemony that other essayists had merely perceived as a vague menace. Thus, not surprisingly, Mariátegui's writing includes an underrecognized acknowledgment of solidarities between *politically* independent Latin America and those parts of "the East" continuing to languish under direct colonial administrative rule.[9] In fact, Mariátegui's sense of the importance of decolonization seems to have trumped even his strong commitment to the principles of socialism, if passages like the following are any indication: "Socialism was international in theory, but its internationalism ended at the borders of the West, at the boundaries of Western civilization. The socialist and syndicalist spoke of liberating human-ity, but in practice they were only interested in Western humanity" (*Heroic* 36). This sense of local solidarity with decolonization movements, expressed in Peru in the mid-1920s, is particularly interesting in light of Mary Louise Pratt's suggestion that (with the exception of certain Afro-Caribbean icons) main-stream postcolonial studies has had difficulty understanding Latin America's relationship to the overwhelmingly Anglophone canon of writing from Africa and the Indian subcontinent.[10] As Pratt explains: "When the Americas are brought into the mapping of the nineteenth century, alongside colonialism and imperialism, a third category of analysis surges into view: neocolonialism. For of course in the Americas, the nineteenth century begins not with colo-nialism but with independence, the breakup of the empires established dur-ing the first wave of European imperialism in the sixteenth century" (4). The introduction of the category of neocolonialism explains Mariátegui's strong sense of solidarity with parts of the world that were still officially colonized in the 1920s. Mariátegui saw a deep similarity between these regions and South America, whose predicament had resulted from postindependence economic colonization by British and North American finance.

While Mariátegui differed with orthodox Marxists regarding the impor-tance of decolonization movements, this was certainly not the only debate in which he took an independent stand. Some commentators describe his de-viations as evidence of the continuing influence of the intellectual hero of his youth, French philosopher Georges Sorel. But in fact, Mariátegui's relation-ship to Eurocentric Marxism is comparable to that of many Latin American intellectuals writing before and after him, particularly in his insistence on at least amending and at most radically revising Euro-American analytical meth-ods in order to account for crucial local differences. This revisionist tendency to emphasize the local (as manifested in essayists from Rodó to García Canclini) is a significant trait of Latin American intellectual history—a trait that Eurocentric postcolonialism might bypass.[11]

Mariátegui further distinguished himself from orthodox European Marxism in his conception of the movement of history, which orthodox Marxists insisted unfolded in a teleological materialist dialectic. While Mariátegui did apply a predominantly materialist conception of history, he was skeptical of easy teleologies. Jesús Chavarría, his biographer, paraphrases him as saying, "Human progress evolves in stages . . . stages that are not entirely linear" (86). This suggestion—that Mariátegui's conception of history included a subtle critique of linear, Hegelian historiography—has several significant consequences. It calls our attention to Hegelian historiography's emphasis on linearity and causality as a foundation stone for Eurocentric thinking.[12] It also suggests that the politics of space does not merely describe contemporary inequalities but may also complicate the presumption that history is solely a function of temporality. In other words, it enacts a revision of not only European Marxism's emphasis on socioeconomic class but also its notion of history itself, making it a function of both space and time. It further suggests one of Mariátegui's major contributions to the later work of the dependency theorists, who emerged after his death and eventually became broadly influential.[13]

Intermission: Faulkner and the Southern Intellectual

In constructing an intellectual context for Faulkner within the U.S. South, commentators have traditionally turned first to the Southern Agrarian movement, which began as a poetry circle at Vanderbilt University in the 1920s. This intellectual movement, which played a foundational role in both literary criticism and conservative thought in the United States throughout the Cold War period, argued against Northern caricatures of Southern backwardness (like H. L. Mencken's mocking depiction of the Scopes Monkey Trials, which he represented as a synecdoche for the intellectual vacuity of an entire region) and defended what it called agrarian values against Northern capitalist "industrialism," a culture that was—according to their argument—valueless in its crass materialism and its surrender to the forces of modernization.[14] While the Agrarians observed historical contradictions similar to the ones that played a role in shaping Faulkner's concerns, unmistakable and important distinctions separate their respective projects. The difficulty in recognizing these distinctions stems from several decades of mystification, whereby the Agrarians and their descendents, the New Critics, took upon themselves the primary role of interpreting Faulkner as something like the timeless South's poet laureate for life.

While both Faulkner and the Agrarians wrote with an odd double-voiced antagonism toward the Northern industrial metropolis, Faulkner was as averse to making stable proclamations regarding sociohistorical issues as the Agrarians were fond of good, loud polemics. Faulkner avoided academic discussions for most of his life; when he sought to make a home for himself late in life as a writer-in-residence at the University of Virginia, he found the environment did not suit him and ended up returning to Rowan Oak, his home on the outskirts of Oxford, Mississippi. Eventually, Faulkner's letters and speeches grew voluminous, but his greatest and most sustained energy over the course of his life was inarguably devoted to the creation of fictional narrative. The aesthetics of narrative—especially the elusive and baroque narrative that Faulkner deployed—were for him a more appropriate expression of his ambivalence, in contrast to the often crass political proclamations of the Agrarians, who subtitled the manuscript of *I'll Take My Stand,* their 1931 polemic in defense of Agrarianism, "An Anti-Communist Manifesto."

Rather than anticommunist, Faulkner's ideology might best be described as opposing traditional authority in almost all its manifestations; thus, he adopted an iconoclastic approach to both narrative art and social questions. However, his incongruous public statements, his impenetrable narrative art, and the Agrarians' distortion of his project all contribute to a critical heritage concerning his place as a Southern intellectual that is full of contradictions. The record left by Faulkner's voluminous and difficult writings is such that—taking two of the most prominent authors in contemporary Southern studies—Daniel Singal is able to tell us that "we must see Faulkner for what he was—an immensely gifted intellectual, living through an experience of intractable cultural change, a southerner just over the threshold of modernism" (156), while Michael Kreyling explains that even though "we invested

Faulkner with authority on many subjects: race relations, the history of the native people of the Old Southwest, the viability of the American Way versus totalitarian 'ideology,' the future of democracy and the human race under the cloud of the atomic bomb, the meaning of Christianity, the role of the artist in society … [he] had few or partially formed ideas and judgments on many of these issues, and he was normally reluctant to divulge, and never willing to debate, most of them" (130). Each of these two quotations has a distinct context: Singal is focusing on Faulkner's early writing and his prodigious output of the 1930s, whereas Kreyling is examining Faulkner's later career, his legacy among younger Southern writers, and his difficulty in dealing with the public celebrity that was so suddenly thrust upon him. Still, Kreyling's argument raises serious questions about the tendency to remove the Faulknerian text from the realm of the literary and read it for declarative insights regarding his positions as an intellectual. The larger goal of Kreyling's study is to expose the mystifying force of a certain idea of the U.S. South and Southern literature—an idea, he argues powerfully, that is an invention of the Agrarian ideology of the 1920s and 1930s. If the complexities of reading the modernist literary text as exposition are not daunting enough, the larger problem for readings of Faulknerian fiction is the obstacle created by the dense filter of the historically Southernist reception of Faulkner and the conservatism and ahistoricism it has imputed in our practice of reading the Faulkner novel.

Fortunately, Edouard Glissant's *Faulkner, Mississippi* offers an alternative approach. While Glissant does insist on marking the race and class privilege of Faulkner in his early comparison of him to Saint-John Perse (4), his interest proves ultimately to rest in the world Faulkner created—a postplantation, multiracial colonized region—and in the stylistics that underpin his vision. The implication of Glissant's text is that, unencumbered by an Agrarian/New Critical aestheticism, the reader can engage more fully with verisimilitude as a substantial component of the Faulknerian text. The urgent question for critics interested in acknowledging this aspect of Faulkner centers on what other intellectual contexts, besides the Agrarian one, might help describe the society that Faulknerian verisimilitude reflects. The ultimate goal of this study is to propose the Mariátegui tradition as such an alternative intellectual context, but if it is too early to do so convincingly at this point, it is worth devoting a few more sentences to a transitional intellectual who helps connect Faulkner to the Latin Americans with whom I am engaged here.

The phrase "colonial economy" was first applied to the U.S. South's post-Reconstruction years by historian C. Vann Woodward. Woodward made the case that economic development in the region had actually benefited Northern elites and their regional water carriers, while harming working- and peasant-class Southern Whites and Blacks. Woodward's goal in his fourth book, *Origins of the New South, 1877–1913*, which he began writing in the late 1930s and first published in 1951, was to show that a period that his predecessor historians had narrated as one of "restoration" of an "old order" actually featured a radical new program for holding down certain subaltern groups.

Years later, speaking of his influences, Woodward mentioned jazz and the Black Arts movement, labor unionists, communists, Chapel Hill liberals, and—importantly and somewhat surprisingly—writers of the Southern literary renaissance, whom he saw as innovative, provocative, and iconoclastic in a way that writers of Southern history were not (*Thinking* 10, 13, 18). Of the latter's conservative affiliation with Jim Crow rulers of the early twentieth-century South, Woodward wrote, "Rarely has history served a regime better by discrediting so thoroughly the old order [Reconstruction governments and populist movements] from which the new rulers seized power" (25). The germinal role of his having lived through the Great Depression at the outset of his training as a thinker and historian receives special emphasis, and Woodward also makes explicit mention of his differences with the Agrarians, noting that he once accompanied one of his mentors, W. T. Couch, on a trip from Chapel Hill to Nashville so that he could watch Couch take on a roomful of shouting, jeering opponents in a debate that ended with Allen Tate and several of his followers storming out of the hall in anger (18).

Three important strains in Woodward's self-description connect him to Mariátegui-tradition thinkers. First, his emphasis on local knowledge and contexts broadly reflects a Mariátegui-tradition perspective. Woodward speaks of a siege mentality among Southern intellectuals, who were constantly forced to confront Northern misrepresentations from the likes of Mencken. "The siege mentality resulted in part, at least, from being besieged," he states (16), before going on to describe the predicament facing a progressive revisionist in the U.S. South at the time. But Woodward's localism is not the same as the Agrarians', for by the time he published *Origins,* he was forcefully arguing for the existence of a disharmonious and discontiguous region, in sharp contrast with the conservatives' portrayal. Furthermore, Woodward was willing to think in terms of political economy: he was interested in wages, the cost of living, and investment patterns, not to mention segregation and disenfranchisement. Such concerns were part of dreaded material culture, as far as the Agrarians—who preferred to speak of spiritual values, religion, and myth—were concerned. Finally, Woodward's colonial-economy argument seems to share with Mariátegui's thought the belief that history unfolds in stages that are not entirely linear or orderly. In his account of his intellectual development, Woodward makes clear that he believes this notion constitutes his most decisive break with traditional Southern history. He characterizes his contemporary critics as thinking that *Origins'* "blasphemy included the replacement of continuity with discontinuity, unity with disunity, and harmony with conflict" (*Thinking* 63). Of the so-called Redeemers—the elite who came to power in the post-Reconstruction period, seen by traditional historians as leading the restoration of an old order—he wrote that their connection to the old planter regime was nominal at best, that they were of "middle class, industrial, capitalist outlook." The Redeemers, he concluded, "thus represented more innovation than restoration, more break than continuity with the past" (64).

Woodward's account of his intellectual milieu thus presents an alternative to the Agrarians in the attempt to shape an intellectual and cultural context for reading Faulknerian verisimilitude. The context Woodward provides should be incorporated into critical attempts to work out the puzzle of Faulkner's unusual resonance in certain cultural traditions of the Global South. At the same time, global intellectual engagement with coloniality and historiography demands even greater attention, as it is simultaneously the most fully developed consideration of the cultural ramifications of American-style hegemony and the most elusive to the North American Faulkner critic. Thus, I now return to my explication of this tradition.

Dependency Theory as an Outgrowth of Mariátegui's Thought

The strong connection between Mariátegui's writings and the later work of the Latin American dependency theorists illustrates the longevity of the Peruvian's influence on Latin American social thought. The dependency school is usually categorized as an outgrowth of work being done by the United Nations' Economic Commission on Latin America in the 1950s or as a reaction against the growing influence of the American W. W. Rostow's neoclassical theories of development. Discussions of the dependency school have taken place primarily among social scientists working in the areas of political economy, development theory, and economic history. Perhaps for this reason, Mariátegui's clear influence on the *dependentistas* has been largely ignored. For example, Jorgé Larrain's account of the school's rise and fall, which represents one of the most comprehensive narratives of the movement, never mentions Mariátegui. Marc Becker's account of Mariátegui's influence on leftist politics in Latin America focuses exclusively on revolutionary political movements without noting his currency among the region's intellectuals during the slow rise of the Latin American Left, which started around the time of Mariátegui and ended (approximately) with the defeat of the Sandinista government in the 1990 elections.[15]

But for those who read cultural production across disciplines and through time, the Peruvian's mark on the early formation of dependency thought is unmistakable. Several historians back up the notion, implicit in Becker's account, that Mariátegui's writings circulated widely in the region during the World War II period. Halperín Donghi states that the "impact of Mariátegui's thought was not felt until decades after his death" (169); Peter Flindell Klarén's history of Peru notes in passing, as it fills in the background of General Juan Velasco Alvarado, who took power in a 1968 military coup, that "like most educated Peruvians, he had read Mariátegui" (340). A very different source of testimony for Mariátegui's general currency during the 1950s and 1960s is Brazilian Walter Salles's cinematic account of the young Che Guevara coming to consciousness while reading Mariátegui in a climactic scene of the film *The Motorcycle Diaries.*

Such general accounts of the Peruvian's widespread currency during the rise of dependency theory make it unlikely that the first *dependentistas* could have been unaware of Mariátegui and the relevance of his work for their project. A clearer picture of the direct connection, however, is available through a focus on the Brazilian intellectual Theotonio Dos Santos, who was active in promoting dependency thought across the hemisphere. Dos Santos, along with Rui Mauro Marini and Vania Bambirra, was a founder in the 1960s of the Centro de Estudios Socioeconómicos de la Universidad de Chile (CESO), whose journal, *Movimiento Socialista,* reissued essays by Mariátegui, promoting his ideas across the continent.[16] Dos Santos's well-known essay "The Structure of Dependence" can be usefully compared to Mariátegui's "Outline of the Economic Evolution," the lead essay in *Seven Interpretive Essays on Peruvian Reality,* as a further indicator of the unmistakable influence of Mariáteguian historiography on Dos Santos's elaboration of discontiguous stages of unequal economic development in the region. Dos Santos virtually updates the Mariáteguian reading for his contemporary circumstances. Such direct connections are what lead contemporary Latin Americanists like Naomi Lindstrom to refer to Mariátegui's work as *"avant la lettre* dependency analysis" (118). From its (underrecognized) origins in Mariáteguian thought, the dependency school would eventually develop into the most widely influential worldview produced within the region over the course of several decades, beginning with the 1950s.

The dependency theorists included academics, economists, and intellectuals who primarily addressed issues of economic development but whose influence extended to Latin American intellectual, political, and cultural movements.[17] Dependency theory's initial stage sought to offer a comprehensive critique of the classical conception of economic development formulated most prominently by W. W. Rostow in the United States. The school emphasized the global nature of the capitalist system in the modern era, strongly rejecting the notion that national economic policy could lead to the growth and development of a national economy in the countries of the Third World, which *dependentistas* referred to as the "periphery" in juxtaposition to the industrialized Western powers, which they called the "core." For dependency theorists, the relationship between core and periphery was predetermined, riddled with structural prejudices that insured there would be no development allowing poorer countries to catch up with metropolitan ones. As in Mariátegui's work, the dependency theorists' reading of history understood Latin America's economic underdevelopment as a condition instilled by colonialism and imperialism, rather than a historical accident or the result of local policies or the laziness of the "natives."

The dependency theorists, like other Latin American intellectuals, can be understood as critics of Eurocentrism in the discourse of the United States and other Western powers. But they are also (along with Mariátegui) countering the *mestizaje* discourse of racialists following Vasconcelos. They approach the issue of Latin American reality from the perspective of political economy, specifically foregrounding the inequalities of global spatial politics. Postcolonialists encountering dependency theory for the first time are often put off by the oversimplification of dividing the world into "core and periphery," but if the core-periphery model lacks complexity, its emphasis on the spatial dimension of unequal development nevertheless deserves more attention.

The particular brand of Eurocentrism dependency theorists critiqued is its manifestation as economic development theory, its foundational figure Rostow, who believed in what was sometimes called a diffusionist view of economic history. In his *Stages of Economic Growth*, Rostow described five stages that all global economies anywhere might pass through in order to become developed. These stages were derived from a careful study of *European* history, the presumption being that history is linear and therefore best understood temporally. Methodologically, then, the core-periphery model was a simple attempt to make clear to Rostow's followers that the modern economy should be understood spatially rather than temporally. This shift led to the uncontroversial conclusion that (for example) modern Djibouti could not merely follow a template based on the past three centuries of growth in France and find itself developed.

By emphasizing the colonial economy and the politics of space, dependency theory fashioned a clear, Mariátegui-like sense of the region as neocolonial, sharing more in common with Africa and Asia than with Europe or the United States. Subsequently, dependency theory had a broad influence on other intellectual histories in the Global South that had their own distinctive traditions but also found themselves confronting challenges with respect to economic development. Two key figures in spreading the influence of the *dependentistas* throughout the Global South were historian Walter Rodney and economist Samir Amin.

Rodney, an Afro-Caribbean Guyanese national whose academic training and career as a teacher and activist spanned England, Jamaica, and Tanzania, was assassinated in Guyana in 1980. In 1972, he published his ambitious history *How Europe Underdeveloped Africa*, arguing that slavery, colonization, and neocolonialism had instilled a historical state of unequal development in the African subcontinent and that the West was therefore as complicit in the region's economic status as were local leaders and citizenry. Several years after this work's publication, Rodney paid homage to Latin American dependency theorists: "I see dependency theory as very much a profound nationalist response. It is very often Marxist but not necessarily so. Many of the liberal-progressive Latin Americans, who might describe themselves as structuralists or by some other description, believe in dependency theory and all that flows from it. They're coming to grips with the fact that they must have a set of ideas which will enable them to recover their national resources. This is what it boils down to" (*Speaks* 66). The reference to "structuralists" invokes the followers of Raul Prebisch, an Argentine economist who headed the United Nations Economic Commission for Latin America in the 1950s. Even before Rostow had published his theory of the five stages, Prebisch was working on a core-periphery model of global economics that laid the groundwork for later versions of dependency theory. The binary opposition between core and periphery was at the heart of the Prebisch school's "structuralism." Rodney's comment once again emphasizes a colonial difference, even within communities of politically committed intellectuals, separating Eurocentric Marxisms from the critique of global capitalism propounded by *dependentistas* and other Third World intellectuals.

Samir Amin and the Arab Dependentistas

The other key disseminator of dependency theory outside Latin America is Samir Amin. Born in Egypt, he has worked in both France and West Africa and has written in French extensively and in Arabic occasionally. His publishing career has now spanned six decades, and he recently played an important role in meetings of the World Social Forum, arguing for the protection of labor, environmental, and human rights in the face of challenges from corporate globalization policies. His connection to the dependency theory movement might be contrasted with Rodney's, since Rodney grew up in Latin America and remained connected to the region even as his study took him to England and Africa. In Amin's case, the ideas and methods of the dependency theorists, especially their relevance to the concrete situations he observed in the Arab Middle East and the African subcontinent, were decisive in his early application of the model.

The Arab world's modern intellectuals are often caricatured as holding views slavishly derivative of European thought and culture, but in fact, much in the intellectual history of Egypt and other Arab countries influenced innovations introduced at the beginning of the region's period of decolonization. As was the case in Latin America, local intellectuals under the mantle of European colonialism insisted that their intellectual perspective was distinct from the history of thought among colonizers (and this was true in spite of the fact that many of them had received at least some education in Europe). For example, Muhammad Husayn Haykal, whose best-known works include a widely read life of the Prophet and *Zainab* (1914), one of the first critically notable novels ever written by an Egyptian, complained in 1929 that "what was incorrectly presented as Egyptian history was nothing but the chronicle of the 'foreign' rulers, peoples, and cultures that had entered the Nile Valley from outside and dominated the people" (Gershoni and Jankowski 143). Haykal's vision of a new history that would take into account the perspective of Egyptians was distinguished in the first instance, according to historians Israel Gershoni and James Jankowski, by "a specific concept of time in which time was made an exclusive function of place" (145). Haykal's contemporary Tawfiq al-Hakim, playwright, novelist, and public intellectual, was the major figure offering such a concrete expression of this territorial conception of time: "It was Hakim's position that time and place together were the two forces that had shaped the Egyptian philosophical outlook" (Gershoni and Jankowski 145). The 1920s and 1930s were a period of rising anticolonial sentiment in Egypt, Palestine, and throughout the Middle East; thus, the dual concepts of a distinctive local worldview and of space as fundamentally politicized inhered even in the liberal bourgeois nationalist visions of thinkers like Haykal and al-Hakim.

The sense that local difference and spatial politics might be understood via political economy gathered momentum after World War II, around the time of the crisis in Palestine and the spread of regional decolonization, for it was only then that Arab Marxists became more creative in their application of Eurocentric ideologies to their local contexts. For much of the early twentieth century, Arab Marxists and socialists tended to try to translate an orthodox European model of Marxist thought directly into the local context. At the level of intellectual inquiry, this meant that figures like the Egyptian Salama Musa considered socialist ideas on an abstract plane as they related to society and the arts but showed relatively little interest in political economy (Hourani, *Thought* 339). With respect to political organizers and party politics, the earliest movements were plagued by an unwillingness to acknowledge the spatial distinctions so clear to al-Hakim and Haykal. One pair of historians of Egyptian communism explains: "The Egyptian movement failed to transcend its intellectual roots in seeking a communist praxis in the Egyptian milieu. A … significant indicator is the failure of the movement to make itself relevant to Egypt's peasant base" (Ismael and El-Sa'id 152). As in Sardinia and Peru, there was a distinct need to make a Marxist theory of urban proletarian uprising relevant to an economy that was still decidedly agrarian, with only a small cross-section of urban workers. Prior to the period of decolonization, with nationalism the primary focus of political and social thought, it was left to figures like Haykal and al-Hakim to define an early version of an Arab colonial difference.

Since World War II, Arab history has focused on a series of events that have caused intellectuals continually to reexamine their presumptions and reevaluate the received wisdom passed down from previous generations. For Arab society, and intellectual history generally, most prominent among these events is the series of defeats suffered by Arab armies at the hands of Israel and the Western powers. Robert Vitalis describes one result of these defeats when he claims that "by the early 1960s, during the era of Arab socialism if not before, concepts such as imperialism, feudalism, comprador and national bourgeoisie had become ruling ideas in governing and intellectual circles in Egypt" (8). Yet, for the intellectual Left, decolonization itself was often a similarly defamiliarizing event because the Arab regimes that paid lip service to socialism, including the Nasserist and Baathist governments, were almost always more hostile to Marxist intellectuals and movements than nonsocialist governments were. Still, the period of decolonization saw the emergence of new versions of Marxist-influenced thinking that gave primacy to local problems. In Iraq in the early 1960s, "an influential scholar was the economic historian Muhammad Salman Hasan, author of *Al-Tatawwur al-iqtisadi fi al-'Iraq…* (A Study of the Economic Development of Iraq from 1864 to 1958, with Emphasis on Foreign Trade) (1965)," which demonstrated "how Iraq's economy was caught in the world economy and how the development of capitalism changed the country" (Gran 79). In Lebanon, philosopher, teacher, activist, and Lebanese Communist Party member Mahdi 'Amal began working out a locally inflected concept of what he called the "colonial mode of production," describing his work, toward the end of his career, as the result of attempts "to think of the distinctions in the relationship between the formerly colonized societies and the Imperialist nations" (30). And in Tunis, even before independence from France had been achieved, the Neo-Dustour party had "succeeded in organizing the workers into trade unions and using them in the political struggle" (Hourani, *Thought* 365).

In newly independent Egypt, Gamal Abdel Nasser rode a wave of popularity to a startling increase of his own dictatorial powers. Meanwhile, the young Samir Amin was writing several case studies of economic unequal development as manifested in sub-Saharan Africa, culminating in a work greatly influenced by leftist dependency theory, aimed at a critique of the Nasser regime's bourgeois nationalist economic policies. Nasserism, at the same time that it argued for land reform, nationalization of industry, and pan-Arabism, also invested hope in an Economic Commission for Latin America— like road to development (i.e., import substitution) and criticized the class-based analyses of Marxists. Amin thus wrote *Unequal Development* (1973) as a direct challenge to what he saw as Nasser's contradictory vision.

He then undertook a series of theoretical discussions of more specific development situations and issues, including cultural and social problems.

The Arab Nation (1976) uses dependency categories to challenge the typical Europhile history of the Arab world, which associates the coming of Europe with cultural renaissance, subverting the traditional narrative by changing the methodological focus of the discussion. According to the traditional view, the Arab world "reawakened" when Napoleon invaded Egypt at the end of the eighteenth century, his forces bringing with them an Arabic printing press and distributing leaflets among the Egyptian populace, marking the first time Egyptians had seen their language printed by a machine. Printed Arabic—the story goes—eventually made possible the establishment of the region's first newspapers and magazines, which generated a local intelligentsia and raised the general intellectual level of the population. Many of these new intellectuals began to receive study missions, traveling to France, where they mastered French and translated examples from France's literary tradition into Arabic. From the French example, it is said, an indigenous Arabic novel was born.

Amin's counternarrative challenges this Eurocentric history by changing the categories of analysis, demonstrating how political economy works together with social advancement and cultural achievement. According to Amin, classical Arab society, which flourished economically as well as scientifically, was neither capitalist nor precapitalist—categories originally created to describe a different history. Amin begins his study by pointing to the economic dilemma engendered by the basic geography of the Arab world: predominantly desert-based and thus unable to sustain economic flourishing through agricultural production. Again, what Said calls the "territorial, spatial, geographic foundations of social life" are given special emphasis. Amin reads the region's economic success during the Abassid period (750–1258 A.D.) and later as partly a function of its strategic position in the middle of three resource-rich land masses (Africa, Asia, and Europe).

Amin's point is that surplus value was not extracted from laborers through the commodification of their labor—not, at least, until Europe industrialized after proletarianizing its own masses and then exported capitalism through colonial expansion. When this colonial expansion had covered the most heavily populated Arab regions, it incorporated them into global capitalism, proletarianized the Arab masses, and set up as its local agent a comprador class of former merchants who now extracted surplus value from the labors of the fellahin. In sum, according to Amin, the Arabs' main inheritance from the West was not civilization, culture, the printing press, or the potential to modernize or to generate Western-educated thinkers; rather, their main inheritance was capitalism, proletarianization of the populace, and aggravated class conflict. Juxtaposing Amin's narrative with the traditional Eurocentric narrative (of European invasion followed by the Arab Nahda, or renaissance) illuminates the stakes of what otherwise looks like a truncated economic history of the Arab world. Amin, like Mariátegui or Dos Santos in the Latin American context, is constructing a counternarrative that challenges histories unwilling to account for local circumstances.

While Amin's epistemological critique of the traditional Eurocentric narrative of the Arab Nahda remains implicit in *The Arab Nation,* it becomes increasingly more direct in later works, beginning with the publication in Arabic of *Azmat al-mujtama' al-'Arabi* (The Crisis of Arab Society [1985]). In a passage that centers on the eighteenth-century figure of Hassan al-'Atar, whom Amin reads as a critic of the (by that time moribund) Kalam school of thought, he compares al-'Atar's critique to the Protestant critique of Catholicism during the Reformation. Noting that al-'Atar was already a prominent figure at Al-Azhar University at the time of Napoleon's invasion, he argues: "We are definitely in need of a reevaluation of intellectuals of this period [the late eighteenth and nineteenth centuries], from Hassan al-'Atar to al-Jabarti and al-Tahtawi, for this group was the result neither of an accident nor of the mere influence of European ideas that entered the country with Bonaparte's invasion, as is claimed by many Orientalists and by many local historians following their lead" (*Azmat* 130).[18]

A few years later, writing in French, Amin further developed the cultural dimensions of his materialist argument in *Eurocentrism* (1988). This study crystallizes the emphases that emerge from the Mariátegui tradition in Latin American intellectual history: the colonial difference in intellectual production, the reevaluation of the dialogic relationship between political economy and culture (the base/superstructure question), and an emphasis on the political economy of spatial inequalities. Furthermore, Amin himself describes this text as the culmination of his work in political economy up until that point: "For thirty years, all of my efforts have been dedicated to seeking a way to strengthen the universalist dimension of historical materialism; my thesis concerning unequal development is an expression of the results of these efforts" (xiii).

The universalist dimension of historical materialism is by no means the predominant one; rather, "Eurocentric interpretation of Marxism, destroying its universalist scope, is not only a possibility: It exists, and is perhaps even the dominant interpretation" (*Eurocentrism* 120). For Amin, within Marxist thought, this colonial difference—between interpreting world history as a grand repetition of European events and taking into account what he calls universalism—is as definitive as Mariátegui's and the *dependentistas'* insistence on the distinct nature of Latin American social and cultural history. A universal historical materialism must take into account every variety of local circumstances, but the overwhelming power of a linear and monolithic view of history, reinforced by five centuries of Eurocentric thinking, makes it difficult for all manner of Eurocentric analyses to view distinct material histories simultaneously, without trying to dissolve them into one master narrative. The materialist underpinnings of Marxism should make it more open to this type of universalism, "but Marxism encounters limits that it always finds difficult to surmount: It inherits a certain evolutionist perspective that prevents it from tearing down the Eurocentric veil of the bourgeois evolutionism against which it revolts. This is the case because the real historical challenge confronting actually existing capitalism has proposed a homogenization of the world that it cannot achieve" (Amin, *Eurocentrism* 77).

In his emphasis on a materialist approach, Amin is not advocating a reductive economism; in fact, his understanding of the base/superstructure dynamic is perhaps most explicit in this particular text, where he argues that the base/superstructure binary only becomes an indispensable analytical tool in Europe after the emergence of capitalism, and elsewhere after capitalism has spread, primarily through colonialism and imperialism. One of capitalism's primary functions is to camouflage the bald economic exploitations at its roots; thus, the primary strategy for understanding these spaces after the emergence of capitalism is to read against this tendency and expose the interrelationship among material history, society, and culture.

With Amin, as with the other intellectual histories I have traced, the materialist approach emphasizes spatial inequalities over intersocietal class dynamics. Amin turns Marxism back into an argument about the politics of space: "The concept of international value explains the double polarization that characterizes capitalism, on the one hand in the unequal distribution of income on the world scale, and on the other by the growing inequality in the distribution of income within the peripheral societies" (*Eurocentrism* 122). Amin's view of the "unequal distribution of income on the world scale" makes global, spatial relations primary—especially in their inequalities. The unique inequalities of socioeconomic class in "peripheral societies" are largely a product of this hegemonic relationship between centers and peripheries.

The importance of Amin's work for the study of political economy in the Arab Middle East notwithstanding, the frequent references to Latin American dependency theorists in studies by Arab scholars working in the area of economic development probably owe as much to the highly comparable deep structures of the regions' colonial economies. Such references may be found in studies in both Arabic and English, including works by Yusuf Sayigh, Mahmoud 'Abdel-Fadhil, and Abbas Alnasrawi, dealing, respectively, with oil dependency, economic development theory, and the distinction between Ottoman and Euro-American colonial economies. As a group, these studies bear witness to the intellectual tradition's relevance and influence across the Global South.

Dependency Theory and Readings of Culture

Since most of the intellectuals within this tradition emphasize a complicated and ever-evolving relationship between socioeconomics and cultural production, it is not surprising that dependency theory in particular evolved into various theories of cultural studies and poetics, rather than limiting itself to questions of economic development.[19] However, in Latin America (in contrast to the Middle East and other areas within the Global South), the influence of *dependentista* thought was so pervasive for a time that it could not be avoided. The school's terms and methods were as familiar to local city council members as they were to intellectuals. André Gunder Frank reported that at a White House meeting in the early 1970s, "the assembled foreign ministers of Latin America . . . were able to reveal to President Nixon that foreign aid was flowing from Latin America to the United States" ("Dependence" 90). Ironically, this very pervasiveness at times made the *dependentistas'* influence invisible. Thus, when Angel Rama began explicating his version of the concept of transculturation, it seemed unnecessary to point out the influence of the *dependentistas* on his discourse, with the result that the connection later became invisible to many critics, who now read transculturation primarily as an anthropological concept.[20]

Rama borrowed the term *transculturation* from Cuban anthropologist, essayist, novelist, and public intellectual Fernando Ortiz, who invented it shortly after Mariátegui's death. In his *Cuban Counterpoint: Tobacco and Sugar* (1940), Ortiz coined the term to define a Cuban identity that he saw as too resilient in the face of absorbing external influences to be appropriately described as marking a culture of "assimilation," the popular descriptor in the functionalist anthropology of the day. Ortiz provides another example of a Latin American intellectual insistent upon distinguishing local ideas, languages, discourses, and cultures from the cultures of the United States and Europe. While his method in *Cuban Counterpoint* is primarily anthropological, a hint of proto–dependency economics may be found in its attempt "to integrate, through innovative methods of investigation and narration, the interplay of cultural forms and material conditions" (Coronil xiii). Although Ortiz was working on the other side of Latin America from Mariátegui, and engaging in an utterly distinctive discursive practice, critics have paired the two as participants in a unique Latin American intellectual trend. Román De la Campa, for example, states that the two were part of an "epistemological avant-garde that has been overshadowed by its literary counterpart" (*Latin* 79). Mignolo links the two as initiators of a new stage in the Latin American discussion of *mestizaje:* "Ortiz moved from race and culture toward the transculturation of objects and commodities [while] Mariátegui paid more attention to the economic arguments hidden under discourses" (169–70). But Beverley's contention that "there is a hidden agenda of class and racial anxiety in Ortiz's idea of transculturation" (45) returns our attention to the traces of Vasconcelos in Ortiz's work, which make him a moment in the Mariátegui tradition's trajectory that must be superseded by later developments.

When Rama adapted Ortiz's term, first in an essay that was published in Venezuela in 1974, then at more length in a book published in 1982, one year before his death, he shifted Ortiz's initial emphases to include narrative structure within the Latin American novel, and he added a more pronounced emphasis on the political economy of the process, incorporating his contemporary awareness of Mariátegui's work and the *dependentista* critique of development theory. This socioeconomic dimension of Rama's analysis is evident when he traces the genealogy of the regional narrative, taking it back to the *decada rosa* of the 1930s, the period when Marxist ideas began to circulate more widely in the region (Rama, "Processes" 155). Rama explains this point of origin as a "period of multiple cultural conflicts generated by the impact of modernization after the First World War, heralding progress and stimulating technology in cities and ports around the continent. [These conflicts] merely reiterated the impact of world economic expansion already registered in Latin America, although at a much higher level" (165). Later in this same passage, Rama discusses the impact of these global forces on intellectuals. He is particularly interested in the conflict between urban and rural intellectuals, a distinction that sounds quite Gramscian until one notes Rama's free use of the language of dependency theory in passages like the following: "When a better equipped intellectual sector [from rural spaces] has been generated, which is able to confront groups from the capital cities, the latter experience a rapid advance (within their own structures of dependency) due to the incorporation of Western technology which makes the relations more unequal and the demand for subordination to a norm more exigent" (165).

Rama, in his central emphasis on regionalism, shares with Mariátegui and the *dependentistas* a spatial conceptualization of the nature of the world economy's inequalities. In his model, the local dynamics—for example, within a nation-state—parallel global politics of space. In other words, he reads the core-periphery divide at both the regional and the international level, taking from Mariátegui his internationalization of the southern question without dismissing Gramsci's emphasis on the internal colony. The result is an argument that "the modernizing cities transfer to the interior of each nation a system of domination learned from their own dependence on international cultural systems" ("Processes" 157). When Mariátegui comes up, Rama discusses him explicitly as having translated orthodox Eurocentric Marxism's static socioeconomic class structure into a model of global spatial inequalities: "The region was a subjugated socio-cultural complex.... Regionalism would acquire vitality when it redefined itself as a social movement, interpreting the aspirations of a class" (166).

Antonio Cornejo Polar—another Peruvian and Rama's contemporary—places even more emphasis on internal differences within Latin America by deploying the term *heterogeniedad* (heterogeneity) as a complementary alternative to Rama's *transculturation*. For Cornejo Polar, he, along with Rama and García Canclini, is part of a distinct trend in Latin American cultural and literary history that reads through the plethora of "diferencias que separan y contraponen" [differences that distinguish and counterpose] inhering in all Latin American regionalisms (Cornejo Polar 12).[21] Within this diversity, difference from the metropolitan multiplicity of postmodernism is insisted upon. Cornejo Polar believes that critics to the North misread Latin America's heterogeneity because of a historical accident that makes the region look postmodern to outsiders—namely, "because paradoxically 'the postmodern condition,' the most advanced expression of capitalism, seems to have no better historical model than the crippled and deformed subcapitalism of the Third World" (15). Here the critic turns the question of the postmodern back into the question of unequal development. In doing so, he centers himself in the Mariátegui tradition.

Yet another important development in Cornejo Polar's conception of *heterogeneidad* also moves the Mariátegui tradition forward. Beverley says of Cornejo Polar's project that its "sense of resistance to forgetting, of negation and doubling is also, I would argue, a model for a new discourse of the national; but it is no longer a discourse of the national as the many becoming one; rather it is a discourse of the one becoming many" (64). Beverley intends here to use Cornejo Polar as an antidote to the "unacknowledged Hegelian basis" (45) that he sees underpinning the category of transculturation in Rama and Ortiz. In Cornejo Polar, a new emphasis presses against the "not entirely linear" nature of Mariátegui's stages of history.

Hybridity in the Mariátegui Tradition

After the Spanish-language publication in 1991 of García Canclini's *Culturas híbridas: Estrategias para entrar y salir de la modernidad* (*Hybrid Cultures: Strategies for Entering and Leaving Modernity*), Latin American intellectuals and North American postcolonialists began to experience an overlap in terminology. García Canclini, however, remains in conversation with the Mariátegui tradition, seeking to push it forward, even though he no longer uses the same term—*mestizaje*—employed by Vasconcelos, Martí, and others. García Canclini delineates his terminological preference in a note to the book's introduction: "Occasional mention will be made of the terms syncretism, mestizaje, and others used to designate processes of hybridization. I prefer this last term because it includes diverse intercultural mixtures—not only the racial ones to which mestizaje tends to be limited—and because it permits the inclusion of the modern forms of hybridization better than does 'syncretism,' a term that almost always refers to religious fusions or traditional symbolic movements" (*Hybrid* 11 n.1). For García Canclini, the poles being mixed, or hybridized, are not racial or even purely cultural. Diverse networks of hybridizations crisscross in his analyses, but primary among these intersections is the mixture of the traditional and the modern. Coming to García Canclini from the postcolonialist discourse of hybridity often leads readers to ask why he is even bothering with the loaded terms *traditional* and *modern,* why he cannot merely acknowledge, à la Bruno Latour, that Latin America, like everywhere else, was "never modern." It becomes clear, though, once he has been recontextualized as a thinker operating between the work of Bourdieu and the Mariátegui-tradition intellectuals, that García Canclini does not view the terms *traditional* and *modern* as evaluative, since he is operating within a semantic field that presumes a thoroughgoing suspicion of the benefits of modernization. Strictly speaking, these are not temporal categories, since the author argues for a continuation—even evolution—of the "traditional" alongside the emergence of the "modern."

These categories carry more economic resonance here than they might for García Canclini's fellow social theorists to the North, even though García

Canclini refuses to ignore complications glossed over by earlier and more monolithic theories coming from his region. In the following introductory passage, we see the full complexity of the dynamic that García Canclini sets out to examine, just as we see both his relationship to earlier discourses and the singularity of his own vision:

> Neither the "paradigm" of imitation, nor that of originality, nor the "theory" that attributes everything to dependency, nor the one that lazily wants to explain us by the "marvelously real" or a Latin American surrealism, are able to account for our hybrid cultures.
>
> It is a question of seeing how, within the crisis of Western modernity—of which Latin America is a part—the relations among tradition, cultural modernism, and socio-economic modernization are transformed. For that, it is necessary to go beyond the philosophical speculation and aesthetic intuitionism that dominate the postmodern bibliography. The scarcity of empirical studies on the place of culture in so-called postmodern processes has resulted in a relapse into distortions of premodern thought: constructing ideal positions without any real difference. (6)

García Canclini distances himself from the *dependentistas* of the 1970s in this passage, but it is not in their attention to the political economy of development that he finds fault. García Canclini instead objects to an overly theorized approach to Latin American problems that must efface contradictions in the matter it analyzes. Clearly, he believes that local intellectuals who translated the work of Mariátegui and dependency theory to the study of Latin American culture were overly facile in their approach: "The analysis presented in this book does not allow the establishment of mechanical relations between economic and cultural modernization. Nor does it allow this process to be read as one of simple backwardness—although it is, in part, with respect to the international conditions of development. This unsatisfactory modernization has to be interpreted in interaction with persistent tradition" (266).

If García Canclini's respect for dependency theory is qualified, his view of the usefulness of Euro-American cultural theory—of the discourse of postmodernism, the magically real, Latin American master narratives, and even certain discussions of hybridity itself—is equally qualified. Thus, he not only dismisses an overreliance on dependency as a foundation for explaining Latin American reality but also criticizes the "philosophical speculation and aesthetic intuitionism that dominate the postmodern bibliography" (6).[22] Both approaches suffer from an overtheorization of phenomena that do not often lend themselves to monolithic explanations.

García Canclini emerges from his study as a paradoxical figure: an empirical theoretician. The matter he analyzes, however, lends itself to this approach, since Latin American culture is neither completely dependent nor completely premodern. Rather it is unequally developed, containing elements both traditional (folklore, "crafts") and avant-garde or postmodern (the novels of Gabriel García Márquez and Carlos Fuentes). García Canclini's study seeks to take up these contradictions in all their complexity. High postmodernism, he points out, may overlap with popular culture—in North America, when *The Name of the Rose* becomes a best seller and lands Umberto Eco on the cover of *Newsweek,* or in Latin America, when poet and Nobel laureate Octavio Paz signs an exclusive deal with the Mexican television network Televisa. García Canclini builds on the work of his previous book *Transforming Modernity* by focusing on the Mexican "craft" industry, emphasizing market forces in the arts and critiquing definitional arguments (e.g., the distinction between "arts" and "crafts"), which no longer adequately explain cultural realities. Pottery, statuettes, and other traditional media may signify differently to different audiences at the same time, each group partially grasping different facets of the craftwork phenomenon. For the North American tourist or even the museum curator in the United States, the traditional form represents a reassuring image of Mexico's antiquity and backwardness, while the government of a Latin American country may unabashedly promote traditional forms as a gesture toward a monolithic, imaginary cultural nationalism. The North American interpretation may be critiqued by a *dependentista,* while the state promotion of the traditional would readily be deconstructed by a theoretician of the postmodern. For García Canclini, both groups are missing the point that these forms continue to evolve, have power, and do cultural work among large groups of Latin Americans generally ignored by theoreticians of whatever predilection or national origin.

García Canclini works out of a Latin American intellectual tradition that he would clearly like to make more flexible, more open to certain out-side influences. At the same time, his skepticism toward the "bibliography of postmodernism," and other attempts to create elegant contemporary essentialisms about Latin America, suggests that those commentators working in the field of Latin American cultural studies and its adjuncts who attempt to exaggerate the extent to which García Canclini has absorbed influences from Euro-American cultural theory have contextualized him incorrectly. In other words, the attempt to view García Canclini as a translator of Euro-American cultural theory into the Latin American context misses the extent to which he both builds on earlier Spanish-American discourses of dividedness and critiques the aery nature of the postmodern theory with which these commentators associate him.

The superficial equation of García Canclini with key figures in Euro-American postmodernism by his Latin American peers is often complicated by their association of his concept of hybridity with the theory of transculturation as elaborated by Rama.[23] The comparison to Rama, who was also an anthropologist from the Southern Cone, in fact suggests how unlikely it is that García Canclini is unaware of the roots of his ideas in Latin American intellectual discourse, as some critics have suggested. While Abril Trigo's overview of transculturation as a predecessor to hybridity in the Latin American context fills in a substantial amount of intellectual history, the essay still concludes with a brief conflation of the use of hybridity in the work of García Canclini and in the work of Homi Bhabha, even though the subject matter the former analyzes, along with his terminology, makes clear that his criticism bears the stamp of Latin American intellectual history, ranging far from the institutional postcolonialism of Bhabha.

The tendency to overstate the connection between García Canclini and postmodernism may stem to a large degree from his earliest writings' movement away from a more traditional Latin American leftist politics.[24] Out of this problem, of García Canclini's slide away from radicalism, grows a series of thorny questions that have been written about with intelligence and enthusiasm by scholars of Latin American studies. For example, Beverley takes a position influenced by Latin American subalternism, arguing that García

Canclini presents the category of the hybrid in overly celebratory discourse. Similarly, Misha Kokotovic laments that García Canclini's "concepto teórico principal ..., la hibridez cultural, oculta más que revela de la concentración de poder" [principal theoretical concept, cultural hybridity, obscures more than it clarifies about the concentration of power] (293). Generally, the major objections to García Canclini's project fall into several categories: what many find to be the antagonistic relationship between his project and radical popular political movements; the correlative but distinct issue of subalternism and its impossibility in García Canclini's model, since he reads hybridity across socioeconomic manifestations of cultural production; the proper place of tradition in contemporary Latin American culture; and the use of the traditional anthropological method (employed by García Canclini) in the aftermath of the postcolonial critique of anthropology as a contemporary genre of "colonial discourse."[25] The debates surrounding these questions are of marked urgency within the region, and it would be inconsistent with this book's general commitment to contemporary instantiations of politically committed regionalisms to dismiss them. While I acknowledge their significance, however, my goal is not to resolve such specific arguments. My central claim is, rather, that if García Canclini looks as though he has drifted away from the Latin American Left when compared directly to Marxists, subalternists, and dependency theorists, he has still not erased the marks that Mariátegui-tradition discourse has left on his project. Such marks emerge prominently when his "hybridity" is compared synchronically to the contemporary discourse of the hybrid within Euro-American postcolonialism.

In the final sentence of *Hybrid Cultures*, García Canclini sees the challenge of understanding modernity from an Americas-based perspective as a question of "how to be radical without being fundamentalist" (281). My understanding of this formulation is that being "radical" means foregrounding persistent inequalities in the tradition of Mariátegui, while being "fundamentalist" suggests an unwillingness to constantly revise and update the categories of spatial politics through which inequalities manifest themselves. A corollary to this question is the issue of how to be theoretical and still be empirical. While such binaries might suggest some distance between García Canclini and the more radical strain of Latin America's intellectual Left, his willingness to remain committed to both categories nevertheless distinguishes his work from the North American discourse of hybridity.

～

García Canclini's work first appeared in English in 1993, when his book *Transforming Modernity* appeared in translation, along with an essay entitled "Memory and Innovation in the Theory of Art." While this essay focuses more exclusively on high art, it otherwise summarizes the main arguments of *Hybrid Cultures*. It also—when compared to discussions of hybridity by Anglo-American postcolonialists—effectively delineates the difference between the use of the term *hybridity* in Latin American and in Euro-American theoretical discourses.

García Canclini begins the essay with a salvo toward the hegemonic critical discourse of postmodern theoreticians: "While, in the realms of economics and politics, the dominant nations pressure us to integrate modern development—in subordinate places, of course—into art and culture, they prefer our traditional countenance. In any case, they are fascinated by a certain way of combining the ancient with the modern that is almost always seen as our incapacity to stop being primitive"(424). García Canclini goes on to critique the idea (which, as he points out, is sometimes even propagated by Latin American voices of officialdom, as well as Eurocentric critics) that the "primitive" or "traditional" pole in Latin American art is a changeless realm that does not experience the dynamism of history. He wishes to propose a heightened occurrence of hybridity in Latin America due to its historical experience: "The multi-temporal heterogeneity present in Latin American culture is the consequence of a history in which modernization scarcely ever completely succeeded in substituting itself for the traditional and the ancient. There were ruptures provoked by industrial development and urbanization; although they occurred after similar ones occurred in Europe, these ruptures were more accelerated"(429). At the same time, García Canclini not only sees Latin American hybridity as a product of a particular cultural, political, and economic history but also sees the phenomenon as continuing to change, with history in both the traditional and the modern dimensions being hybridized.

Thus, he criticizes those commentators for whom traditional expressions are "in no sense ... seen as part of social organization much less as sources of new production" (428). With García Canclini working within the Latin American intellectual tradition, but aware of Euro-American discourse, his discussion of hybridity is more informed by development categories than by racial or semiotic/linguistic ones. While he never allows any of the terms that he puts into play to become static, neither does he celebrate fluidity for its own sake. Rather, he regularly reinvokes concrete issues relating to underdevelopment, traditionalism, and Eurocentrism.

Hybridity in Postcolonialism

While García Canclini's discussion of hybridity interfaces with the Latin American intellectual tradition I have delineated, much postcolonial theory has used the term *hybridity* as part of a discourse springing from a very different source—namely, the postmodern bibliography of semiotics, poststructuralism, and psychoanalysis.[26] For example, Robert Young's *Colonial Desire: Hybridity, Theory, Culture and Race* describes one of the term's origins, in its contemporary usage, by tracing a line back to the racial theories of Victorian England. While Young's analysis is intelligent and meticulous, its emphases locate the center of the colonial project in the mind of the colonizer, as does much postcolonial theory. Just such a centering is suggested by Young's opening, which uses a cultural text to illustrate the colonizer's psychological reaction to the specter of "mixed-race" procreation. The author, recalling being enraptured as a boy by the lush Orientalism of the film *South Pacific*, comments, "I had seen the film as a child but not understood its plot turned around the question of children" (xi). Young points out a doubling in the two romances that make up the story. At approximately the same moment in the film, each romance is threatened by an irrational fear of mixed-race children: first, when Ensign Nellie Forbush of Little Rock discovers to her horror the half-Polynesian children that the romantic Frenchman Emile de Becque has fathered; and later, when Bloody Mary, the mother of Lieutenant Joseph Cable's Polynesian sweetheart, speaks to Cable of a day in the future when he will father children by her daughter. Young's preface reads this dimension of the film as a portrait of the tension between desire for "exotic" sexual pleasure and antipathy for interracial procreation that plagues over a century of Euro-American colonial ambitions.

Young's reading not only provides insight into an enduringly popular—albeit Orientalizing—musical but also prepares the reader for his survey of the psychosexual underpinnings grounding the term "hybridity" as it emerges out of Victorian racialist and colonialist thought. Such a study is very much in the mainstream of the large British Empire studies wing of Anglo-American postcolonialism. As such, it manifests the basic prejudices of this critical school. *South Pacific*, in its very Orientalism, becomes a story of Westerners confronting their prejudices. The Polynesian islands (and their inhabitants) play the role of "an exotic locale in which [the Western subject's] own spiritual problems ... can be addressed and therapeutically treated," as Said famously described Camus's Algeria (*Culture* 183).

In addition to providing this prefatory reading of *South Pacific* and a more extensive analysis of Victorian race theory, Young also sheds light on the roots of *hybridity* in theories of language by briefly linking the concept to Bakhtin's notion of linguistic heterogeneity. He then brings the discourse up to the present day by describing Homi Bhabha's appropriation of Bakhtin for postcolonial discourse: "Homi K. Bhabha has shifted this subversion of authority through hybridization to the dialogical situation of colonialism, where it describes a process that 'reveals the ambivalence at the source of traditional discourses on authority.' For Bhabha, hybridity becomes the moment in which the discourse of colonial authority loses its univocal grip on meaning and finds itself open to trace complex movements of disarming alterity in the colonial text" (*Colonial* 22).

Bhabha begins his essay "The Commitment to Theory" by complaining that committed criticism is always forced into choosing between the binaries of politics and theory. Bhabha rejects this almost explicitly on the grounds that it is a binary: "Must we always polarize in order to polemicize?" (19). He refers in passing to the imperialist nature of contemporary global capitalism and to national struggles against histories of domination, but he expresses concern that black-and-white understandings of such problems have led to a prejudiced view of Western critical theory and its role in the global poly-system: "What does demand further discussion is whether the 'new' languages of theoretical critique (semiotic, poststructuralist, deconstructionist and the rest) simply reflect those geopolitical divisions and their spheres of influence. Are the interests of 'Western' theory necessarily collusive with the hegemonic role of the West as a power bloc?" (20).

On the contrary, Bhabha argues, deploying theory makes available many of the possibilities of resistance contained in nationalist struggles for independence. Through this essay's very title, he sets forth a challenge to the traditional binarism between action and reflection in discussions of activism and commitment. Theory is one of the most viable forms of commitment for Bhabha, because it is a commitment without the potentially totalizing nationalist consequences. "I want to take my stand," he declares, "on the shifting margins of cultural displacement—that confounds any profound or 'authentic' sense of a 'national' culture or an 'organic' intellectual—and ask what the function of a committed theoretical perspective might be, once the cultural and historical hybridity of the postcolonial world is taken as the paradigmatic place of departure" (21).

Bhabha makes two important moves as his argument continues to develop. First, he refers to John Stuart Mill, whose "On Liberty" he finds useful, primarily because it understands politics as rhetoric by defining "political judgement as the problem of finding a form of public rhetoric able to represent different and opposing political 'contents' not as a priori preconstituted principles but as a dialogical discursive exchange" (23). Thus, the disagreeable aspects of a less-theorized notion of politics (nationalism, perhaps even atavism) are subverted through an understanding of politics as discourse—contested and fluid. Theory, by deconstructing binarisms, allows a challenge to the representational truisms about the subaltern subject that create a particular type of domination.

At the same time, Bhabha acknowledges that challenging essentialist representations of the subaltern has not always been a priority in European theory. Rather, the prevalence of an Other as a point of departure ("Montesquieu's Turkish Despot, Barthes's Japan, Kristeva's China, Derrida's Nambikwara Indians, Lyotard's Cashinahua pagans" [31]) proves a commonplace among Bhabha's theoretical predecessors:

However impeccably the content of an "other" culture may be known, however anti-ethnocentrically it is represented, it is its location as the closure of grand theories, the demand that, in analytical terms, it be always the good object of knowledge, the docile body difference, that reproduces a relation of domination and is the most serious indictment of the institutional powers of critical theory.

There is, however, a distinction to be made between the institutional history of critical theory and its *conceptual* potential for change and innovation. (31, my emphasis)

It is this distinction that allows Bhabha to see theory as empowering. Only through theory and the politics of representation can we engage in the location of culture, rather than allowing ourselves passively to be presented with its location.

This essay demonstrates Robert Young's point that language theory is the primary semantic field in which Bhabha operates. Both his reference to Mill's equation of politics and discourse and his list of logocentric theoreticians who engage in the locating of cultures demonstrate as much. Culture is almost always discussed in this essay in terms of language, utterance, enunciation, and textuality. In other essays, Bhabha applies the general argument made here, about the proper understanding of theory, to the colonial context again and again, with the result that colonialism becomes a phenomenon whose primary existence is located in the linguistic and the textual. For example, in "Signs Taken for Wonders," he states: "The conflictual moment of colonialist intervention is turned into that constitutive discourse of exemplum and imitation, that Friedrich Nietzsche describes as the monumental history beloved of 'gifted egoists and visionary scoundrels.' For despite the accident of discovery, the repetition of the emergence of the book, represents important moments in the historical transformation and discursive transfiguration of the colonial text and context" (105).

Further, a particularly poststructuralist linguistic turn inspires Bhabha to display a relentless commitment to the breaking down of binaries. Finding and celebrating in-between, interstitial, hybrid spaces is the essence of cultural resistance here. The essay's concluding passage exemplifies these two characteristics: "A willingness to descend into that alien territory—where I have led you—may reveal that the theoretical recognition of the split-space of enunciation may open the way to conceptualizing an international culture, based not on the exoticism of multiculturalism or the diversity of cultures, but on the inscription and articulation of culture's hybridity. To that end we should remember that it is the 'inter'—the cutting edge of translation and negotiation, the in-between space—that carries the burden of the meaning of culture" (38). In his poststructuralist emphasis on in-between spaces, Bhabha's difference from García Canclini crystallizes. For Bhabha, not being fundamentalist is the same thing as being radical.

Anthony Easthope has challenged the philosophical viability of Bhabha's emphasis on hybridity, suggesting that Bhabha "treats hybridity as a transcendental signified," that Bhabha's emphasis on the term "remains an act of inversion rather than deconstruction" (345). But it is Easthope's critique of the political possibilities of Bhabha's theory that most illuminates the distinction between Bhabha's hybridity and the term (and its equivalents) as deployed in the Latin American context. Theory may feel empowering for some, but to Easthope, "no ultra-leftist 'politics of heterogeneity' based in a 'privileging of difference' can substitute for the possession of state power" (346).[27] Similarly useful is Easthope's questioning of Bhabha's unwillingness to limit the scope of hybridity's application: "By substituting 'hybridity' for 'difference' Bhabha makes us think we are solidly on the ground of race, ethnicity and colonial identity, but if the form of his argument is ubiquitous, what special purchase does it have on the particular content of colonialism? (On this, Bhabha is a long way from Said, whose analysis of colonialism at every point indicates a historically specific content)" (344). Not only does this universalization contrast with Said; it also presents a marked distinction from the insistence on local specificity (no matter how global the question) emphasized by Latin American intellectuals—from El Inca Garcilaso de la Vega all the way to García Canclini.

Elsewhere in *The Location of Culture,* Homi Bhabha himself compares the two semantic fields whose diverging uses of the term *hybridity* I have been contrasting. At one point in the essay "The Postcolonial and the Postmodern," he states that "the postcolonial perspective—as it is being developed by cultural historians and literary theorists—departs from the traditions of the sociology of underdevelopment or 'dependency' theory. As a mode of analysis, it attempts to revise those nationalist or 'nativist' pedagogies that set up the relation of Third World and First World in a binary structure of opposition. The postcolonial perspective resists the attempt at holistic forms of social explanation" (173). While Bhabha's critique of "holistic forms" and master narratives harmonizes with much critical and theoretical practice after structuralism, and clearly exemplifies his commitment to Derrida and French poststructuralism, it should be clear at this point that his reference to dependency theory acts as a straw man. Set aside for a moment Bhabha's circumvention of the fact that theories of "underdevelopment" and "dependency" were in the first instance *economic* theories. While the terms themselves may sound vaguely condescending, surely there is no advantage in pretending that economic inequalities do not exist. Even so, one would be hard pressed to find a thinker among these Latin American intellectuals who limits his or her analysis to asserting a straightforward binary opposition between the core and the periphery.

Certainly, a contemporary thinker like García Canclini, who has read dependency theory and has no compunction about deploying some of its terminology, is not restricting himself to global binarisms. Neither does he allow his sensitivity to interstices and fluidity to keep him from focusing on the unequal material circumstances of the postcolonial world. On the contrary, we find García Canclini making a statement about hybridity that we could never imagine Homi Bhabha accepting: "The hybrid is almost never something indeterminate because there are different historical forms of hybridization" ("Hybrid" 79). On the other hand, postcolonialism's commitment to the linguistic turn has allowed it to efface the role unequal development plays in the hybridization of postcolonial societies.

Both Easthope and Young describe Bhabha as deploying the linguistic theories of Mikhail Bakhtin in reading postcolonial culture, but the connection to Bakhtin does not seem to be based on textual reference.[28] In *The Location of Culture*, Bakhtin is referenced at the beginning of the eighth essay and at the end of the ninth, but if we take the example of the former, an essay entitled "Dissemination: Time, Narrative and the Margins of the Modern Nation," the brief references to Bakhtin are made in a seven-page section that refers with equal attentiveness to Jacques Derrida, John Berger, Fredric Jameson, Julia Kristeva, Eric Hobsbawm, Benedict Anderson, Edward Said, Partha Chatterjee, Ernest Gellner, Louis Althusser, John Barrell, Houston Baker, Michel Foucault, Freud, and Goethe. Obviously, Bhabha is not particularly interested in historicizing any one of these thinkers, nor is his goal to make fine distinctions among them. Rather, Bhabha sees himself entering into a conversation, participating in a sort of communal discussion of theory, a discussion in which Derrida, Kristeva, and Lacan play perhaps the most important parts, aside from Bhabha's own role as the shaper of the discussion he engenders. Bhabha's thought roots itself firmly in the dimension of discourse into which French poststructuralism virtually locks him. Is it not ironic that Bhabha's discussion of the hemispheric South is almost totally inscribed in theoretical categories derived from French poststructuralism, while Nestor García Canclini is seen by many of his Latin American critics as too Westernized, in spite of his clear affinities with aspects of Latin America's own intellectual history? The point is not that too many of Bhabha's citations are to Euro-Americans. Although he is often considered part of an exclusive group of founders of postcolonialism that also includes Said and Gayatri Spivak, he contrasts with Said, in his dismissal of Gramsci (see his previously quoted circumvention of the "organic intellectual"), and with Spivak, who regularly declares her (admittedly hybridized) commitment to Marxism.[29] Bhabha's primary commitment is not just to theory but to theory of language, which he seems to believe can do almost anything.

Comparative Hybridities

In a recent interview, García Canclini makes the following contrast between the disciplines of cultural studies in the United States and in Latin America: "Latin American work is more preoccupied with the social base of cultural processes, and of course, this has a lot to do with its emergence out of anthropology and sociology; whereas, in the United States and in other places … there is more of a connection to the humanities and so studies appear more concerned with texts than with social processes" (Murphy 81). In some ways, his remarks parallel the observations of a Chicana activist involved in attempting to bring together women's groups on opposite sides of the border: "Chicanas and Latinas in the United States have focused on questions of race and ethnicity while Mexicanas have focused on class issues and survival" (Carrillo 394). Both emphasize the spatial inequalities separating North Americans and Latin Americans working in Latin America, the latter insisting on methods that maintain a heightened awareness of material challenges. Bhabha's hybrid is certainly about much more than simply race and ethnicity, yet he conceives of the term *hybridity* as a method that can understand colonial discourse even as it deemphasizes colonialism's history, structures, and economics.

Yet another contrast to Bhabha's notion of hybridity might be made with Samir Amin's critique of what he calls "dualism" in contemporary Arab society. For Amin, dualism is essentially the result of the unwillingness of the region's early nineteenth-century leadership, particularly Egypt's Muhammad 'Ali, to extend its project of modernization to a critique of local elites. 'Ali strengthened these elites by modernizing Egypt's economy and military but opting at the level of ideology for a "'moderate conservative Islam,' more formalist than preoccupied with responding to new challenges. The cultural dualism that has characterized Egypt ever since (and whose analogues can be found in many regions of the contemporary Third World) has its roots in this choice" (Amin, *Eurocentrism* 129). An earlier version of this argument appears in Arabic, Amin using the term *izdowajīya* (ازدوجية) and even resorting to an Arabicized spelling of "schizophrenia" at one point (*Azmat*). His terminology implies a more decided separateness, to say the least, and often carries unmistakable pejorative connotations. If Amin is not talking about the same thing as Bhabha (and Bhabha in turn is not talking about the same thing as García Canclini), the point is that the sort of mixing and conflation that grew out of so many colonial histories did not always result in something to be celebrated. Middlemen, compradors, semiperipheries, and schizophrenics are also part of the history and culture of colonialism. *Hybridity* is essentially an empty term that must be historically located before it can retain any of its supposed power and meaning.

Easthope asks what special purchase the term has for the colonial context, but such a question can only be answered via an examination of the concrete histories of colonial contexts. Any resort to the realm of true knowledge will only reinforce a Eurocentrist history of ideas.

∽

I begin chapter 2 by briefly mentioning what could be called a worldly example of how the Eurocentric production of ideas directly harms the Global South, in the form of the "Washington consensus" that dominates global trade regulations. Although I emphasize the politicization of the regional in anti-Eurocentric thinking, this is not from a sense that class analysis plays no role in the Mariátegui tradition. Class analysis plays an important role for these thinkers, who are heavily influenced by the work of Marx, but it must be always geohistorically located. It must take into account the inevitable significance of the local. Specifically, the comprador class plays a dramatic role for many working out of the Mariátegui tradition. Such a locally sensitive class analysis moves the study back to Faulkner's South, for, as we will see, C. Vann Woodward builds his argument for the U.S. South's colonial economy on this very comprador category.

Chapter Two

Social Classes in the Southern Economy

Snopesism and the Emergence of a Comprador Elite

Globalization and Social Class

Recent discussions of globalization have frequently manifested a basic tension. On the one hand, in making the goal of liberalization policies the incorporation of a nation-state into the world economy, corporate globalization's cheerleaders insist that development fortunes are ultimately determined by the global marketplace. On the other hand, in forcing poorer countries to reorganize their local economies, they act as though such action at a national level can bring about dramatic change. Globalization as a political platform in the West has meant the international expansion of certain basic tenets of American capitalism. Particularly, it has meant a foreign policy focused on encouraging countries in the Global South to dismantle all barriers to foreign trade; to privatize government-owned service industries; and to reduce government spending as dramatically as possible, even if this means slashing funding for health care or primary education programs. Taking these steps will lead to economic development, according to institutions like the International Monetary Fund (IMF), which has had strong support in "encouraging" such globalization policies from successive American presidential administrations, whether Republican or Democratic. The basic theory fueling these policies seems to be the simple (or, perhaps more precisely, simplistic) notion that lowering trade barriers and opening up local industry to private ownership will help a poorer nation-state enter the global economy. These policies ask local governments to organize the economy of a nation-state with the expectation that its international status will be affected. Yet the trajectory of corporate globalization is toward a deterioration of the nation-state and its powers. Somehow or other, local policy is expected to bring about global results.[1]

Samir Amin speaks to this hypocritical tendency in *Eurocentrism*, insisting in his discussion of "the culture of capitalism" that "internal factors take on a decisive role in societal evolution only when a peripheralized society can free itself through delinking from the domination of international value. This implies the break-up of the transnational alliance through which the subordinated local comprador classes submit to the demands of international capital. As long as this delinking does not take place, it is futile to speak of the decisive role of internal factors, which is nothing more than a potential, and artificial to separate these factors from worldwide factors, which remain dominant" (111). In contrast to Amin's argument for the "universalist dimension of historical materialism," the self-contradictory narrative of corporate globalization dictates certain terms to nation-states that it pretends are internationalist policies. In fact, under present circumstances, Amin insists, such "internal factors" are not determinative.

Amin's critique of the inherent tensions in the discourse of globalization raises another issue of significance via his reference to "the transnational alliance through which the subordinated local comprador classes submit to the demands of international capital." The problem of local elites is part and parcel of the development quagmire, which pinpoints a crucial dimension of the dynamic that preserves the interests of the metropolis in the social formations of the periphery.

Thus far I have emphasized the notion of spatial inequalities as described by progressive intellectual traditions in the Global South. Furthermore, I have suggested that the emphasis on such disparities serves as an alternative, for many Third World intellectuals, to the static Marxist conception of socio-economic class that grows out of Eurocentric thinking. The introduction of the category of the comprador class raises an important point of clarification, however. The emphasis on the dynamic of spatial politics in thinkers like Mariátegui, Rodney, and Amin does not mean that class analysis plays no role in their critiques or is diminished as a method. Rather, such thinkers insist that class analysis be adaptable to the historical context in which it is deployed and are averse to reading the pronouncements on class division by Marx and Engels in a fundamentalist, Eurocentric way.[2] One example of an adaptation of class analysis to local contexts is in the emphasis observers of postcolonial societies place on the role of the comprador elites. This socioeconomic class owns the means of production in a peripheral economy or occupies a prime location in trade relations but almost inevitably does not see its fortunes as tied to its local context. Rather, it sides with the metropolis, which provides it with access to credit and to which it often returns to invest its profits. In its place in the international economy, then, this group is distinct from national bourgeoisies of metropolitan economies. In its local context, it represents a broad obstacle to economic development in peripheral economies, since in its traditional function it directs the largest concentrations of wealth away from internal development.

For this reason, the comprador class is the focus of both the analysis of economists and the critiques of writers and artists across the Global South. The comprador is an interstitial figure in the global economy that facilitates the disarticulation of development programs in the periphery. The comprador is a different type of hybrid, contrasting starkly with the figure idealized by Homi Bhabha, its cosmopolitan in-between status playing a direct role in supporting the economic hegemony of the core.

Part of the narrative of what intellectuals have called "the development of underdevelopment" in the Global South centers on the comprador elite's emergence in southern economies. This chapter later discusses the importance of the comprador phenomenon in the Southern United States in the period after Reconstruction. In fact, historians have argued that the U.S. South's "colonial economy" after Reconstruction was built primarily through links between Northern entrepreneurs and their Southern commercial agents.

The implementation of the colonial economy in the U.S. South is an example of what would become a global practice throughout the twentieth century, when U.S. hegemony spread first throughout the Americas and then, in the aftermath of World War II and the collapse of the British and French Empires, throughout the Global South.

Latin America's Comprador Class

At the beginning of the twentieth century, in Peru, Mariátegui complained that development of the agricultural economy (the dominant sector at the time) was hampered greatly by the monopoly of land ownership "by a class of *rentiers*." A large majority of agricultural production was undertaken by tenant farmers, who rented the land from an aristocratic class who had inherited it and—according to Mariátegui—showed no interest in agricultural development. Neither did the tenant farmer have any interest in development to increase productivity, since this would do nothing more than lead to increased rent on the land once its lease had expired. Mariátegui's analysis of this situation led him to the conclusion that "capitalist exploitation and industrialization of land cannot develop fully and freely unless all feudal privileges are abolished" (*Seven* 71).[3]

Simultaneously, the future of Peruvian agriculture (and Peruvian industry) was being forged by a group of protocompradors who were preparing to outpace decadent aristocratic landowners. This class was facilitating "the industrialization of agriculture in the coastal valleys under a capitalist system and technique . . . thanks mainly to British and American investment in our production of sugar and cotton" (Mariátegui, *Seven* 68). The choice of sugar and cotton was based on the fact that "these crops are important at present to English and American businessmen," the determinative group for obtaining credit in the absence of a national bank. If this new agriculture served these foreign businessmen, it could turn a profit locally and obtain more credit globally. Growing food, then, was left to old-style tenant farmers and a few farms near major urban centers. Thus, the new agribusiness class reoriented agriculture toward "these interests that do not take into account the special needs of the national economy" (68).

The regional relevance of Mariátegui's observations is confirmed by other historians. In Central America, Mexico, the Caribbean, and the countries of the Southern Cone, the external orientation of the business elite was equally problematic. For example, Central America specialists describe a "coffee elite" emerging at this time with a similar external orientation. In this region, "capital would be borrowed from Europe and North America for nine or ten months of the year, to be paid back at the end of the harvest season. Some of the native merchant men were native Central Americans who over the years proved their credit ratings with commercial houses in the industrializing countries, but many were immigrants who brought with them expertise, capital, and personal connections with coffee importers and manufacturers in Europe and North America" (Robert Williams 194). As a result, traders began to acquire plantations and develop small agricultural industry in the form of processing mills. They were able to protect themselves better against fluctuations in coffee prices by lowering the prices paid to growers during economic downturns. Most significantly for the development of the comprador class, the traders' external orientation was cemented through increased immigration from Europe and the United States as word spread of the successes of the Central American coffee sector. So, for example, "in Costa Rica, the orientation toward the British market led to a decided Anglophilia within the elite that was reoriented toward the United States when markets shifted to North America after World War I" (Robert Williams 194).

As I trace aspects of the history of Latin America's early comprador class, an important qualification should be kept in mind: my emphasis on the external orientation of this class is not intended as an argument for a closed-off nativism, either in economics or (especially) in cultural relations. An economist specializing in Latin America noted several years ago, largely with dependency theory in mind, that "external influences may do good as well as harm.... Individuals who listen only to themselves are unlikely to contribute positively to others, or to thrive themselves. And so with nations. Influences from outside may often be unambiguously negative, but they at times serve to enlarge understanding. The fact that they come from outside is not a sufficient basis to qualify them as undesirable" (Sheahan 175–76). The significance, then, of an externally oriented comprador class in the Global South has nothing to do with an aversion, on principle, to outside influence. The problem lies, rather, in the fact of the evolution of the unequally developed economies of Latin America and other regions. This is a problem of history, not philosophy, for historically, external influences from the United States and Britain were hegemonic financial—later political and military—interests that engaged with elites in Latin America from a position of power. The result was a region full of economies run by a class that was most often aligned with powerful foreign interests. The structure of Latin American economies, beginning in the liberal/neocolonial period of the late nineteenth century, was such that the elite class, in simply pursuing its own self-interest, operated against the interests of popular national constituencies.

André Gunder Frank refers to the comprador group as the "lumpenbourgeoisie," explaining: "I have been told that I ought never to use the word, 'bourgeoisie' because it denotes a social process which has never existed and will never exist in colonial and neo-colonial Latin America. But I have been unable to replace it with another term.... Thus, I have chosen to retain 'bourgeoisie' and to add 'lumpen' to it" (*Lumpenbourgeoisie* 9). The neologism comes from Marx's original classification of a "lumpenproletariat," a subgroup within the working class that is devoid of class consciousness and has given up on working within the structure of capitalist society and turned to crime. Frank's term suggests a merchant class that sees itself as outside the socioeconomic structure of the national economy, so that even when the lumpenbourgeoisie is not literally involved in white-collar crime, it is still pursuing its own enrichment without regard for the effect of its actions on the *local* socioeconomic system. (Frank's term is also interesting for the purposes of this study in the way it calls attention to the inadequacy of socioeconomic categories based on nineteenth-century Europe for describing societies of the Global South.) While Frank's *Lumpenbourgeoisie: Lumpendevelopment* (1972) traces the roots of Latin American class structure back to the colonial period, his main goal is to describe the way the colonial roots of the comprador class manifested themselves in the period of industrialization—that is, the period after Mariátegui's death. Frank's motivation for writing this study is relevant to my earlier argument. He begins the book by citing several reviewers of two of his earlier books, who have taken him to task because he "suggests a geographic or regional pattern of development" when, in fact, "it *is* more important to define and to understand *underdevelopment in terms of class*" (1, emphases in original). In spite of this opening statement of intent, however, a reading of the entire study proves it to be heavily invested in geographical, regional, and spatial questions of imperialism.

Frank cites historian James Cockroft's study of elite families in the Mexican state of San Luis Potosí during the nineteenth century as an example of the regional roots of the modern comprador. During this period (which Mariátegui characterizes as bringing Anglo-American economic hegemony to the region), a group of elite families emerged in San Luis Potosí who were involved in a network of powerful economic positions that included mining, banking, and ranching interests, encouraging foreign investment and developing close ties with both national politicians and "foreign businessmen." Such relationships usually resulted in personal enrichment for the local elite and the foreign investors, often at the expense of the public interest. For example, when local businessman Pedro Diez Gutiérrez became governor in the 1880s, he used old connections to gain a railroad concession from the federal government, then sold the concession to American investors at a handsome profit. The Americans in turn changed the original blueprint and, instead of building an extensive line that could transport passengers throughout Northern Mexico, opted for a shorter, cheaper line connecting their mines in the state to the north-south trunk line between Laredo, Texas, and Mexico City (Frank, *Lumpenbourgeoisie* 71–72). The profits of the comprador and the foreign companies thus took precedence over local public interests.

This pattern of comprador behavior continued to influence Latin American economic development during the period of industrialization between World War II and 1972, when Frank's study was published. Frank specifically cites the example of local industrial development in Brazil in the 1960s, when foreign firms found themselves able to buy into Brazilian industry without expending any of their own working capital, due to favorable conditions offered by local banks (98). He notes along the way that local industry and finance relied heavily on secondhand technology sloughed off by the metropolis, outdated but useful enough for local elites to make money (but not build infrastructure) in a dependent economy. It was not unusual for their profits to in turn be invested in foreign banks. He concludes his survey by stating "that the policy, pursued by Latin America's bourgeoisie and governments, of welcoming and collaborating with foreign interests that control internal as well as external borrowing and determine the products to be manufactured in each country, is a policy which serves only the class interests of the lumpen-bourgeoisie and promotes only lumpendevelopment for the peoples of Latin America. Foreign control is the cause, not the consequence, of the shortage of investment capital" (108).

Frank's study of Latin American elites appeared at a time when Mariátegui's influence—as translated through the dependency theorists— was at its apex. Inevitably, recent scholarship has revisited the critical position taken toward the Latin American bourgeoisie by the *dependentistas*. A good example of such constructively critical historical analysis can be found in the comprehensive history of Peru recently published by Peter Flindell Klarén. Following the Peruvian historian Alfonso Quiroz, Klarén makes several important qualifications to the *lumpenbourgeoisie* narrative. He argues that in Peru, where many *dependentistas* might have seen one of the more coherent and dominating oligarchies in Latin America, the group's influence was exaggerated by the dependency school, that it was, in fact, "more modern and entrepreneurial than has heretofore been represented" (216). In spite of his skepticism, however, Klarén also states, "There seems little doubt that an oligarchy, composed of exporters and Lima businessmen linked to the developing export economy, emerged in Peru at the end of the nineteenth century" (213). In later passages of his study, which traces Peruvian history from the Incas to Alberto Fujimori's 1995 reelection, Klarén shows that Peru's oligarchic class found it in their interest to turn away from building manufacturing during World War I; that the Velasco government of the late 1960s and early 1970s wrote up its five-year plan for 1971–75 with the specific assumption that "Peru had suffered since the early 1960s from the unwillingness of foreigners and the oligarchy to reinvest sufficiently in the economy" (341); and that President Alan García's provocative 1987 nationalization of Peruvian banks was carried out with the specific goal of challenging the persistent power of the financial oligarchy (394). Ultimately, Klarén's historiography calls for a reevaluation of the most critical and doctrinaire accounts of a unique regional social class, referred to variously in the literature as a comprador class, the elite, an oligarchy, the national bourgeoisie, and the lumpenbourgeoisie. The historical narrative, however, continues to be shaped to a large extent by the analysis fashioned originally by early stages of Mariátegui-tradition historiography. Certain facts about the operation of the comprador elite, and its relationship to the unequal development of national economies, have become part of the intellectual substratum within which the open-minded historian of Latin America operates, even if analysis of how the class affected regional economies is still evolving.

Strictly economic accounts of development in the region also reinforce a broad empirical foundation for the categories engendered by Mariátegui-tradition historiography. A reading of Joseph Stiglitz's recent critique of corporate globalization policies, for example, reinforces this view of the problematic role played by comprador elites in attempts at economic development in the region. Stiglitz is a former economic advisor in the Clinton administration, appointed during Clinton's second term as chief economist and senior vice president of the World Bank. Awarded the Nobel Prize in economics in 2001, in 2002 he published a book critical of the way the U.S. government and the IMF were implementing corporate globalization policies. Stiglitz, like Klarén and Quiroz, is no *dependentista;* he would probably have no enthusiasm for Amin's idea of "delinking" or for Frank's characterizations of "lumpendevelopment." Yet Stiglitz also criticizes the way in which the region's dealings with the global economy have benefited the metropolis and local elites. Stiglitz's criticism results from empirical observation, not from an ideological commitment to the Mariátegui tradition. Of the "Washington Consensus" and its implementation in Third World economies, he says, "In some cases it has not even resulted in growth, but when it has, it has not brought benefits to all; the net effect of the policies set by the Washington Consensus has all too often been to benefit the few at the expense of the many, the well-off at the expense of the poor" (20). Later he applies this generalization to Latin America: "In Latin America, growth has not been accompanied by a reduction in inequality, or even a reduction in poverty. In some cases poverty has actually increased. ... The IMF talks with pride about the progress Latin America has made in market reforms over the past decade ... but has said less about the numbers in poverty" (79).

Walter Rodney described the West Indian context for this problem in the early 1980s:

> After 1953, in Guyana, the curious thing is that although we hated the British, it was very clear from then right up until 1964 when we got independence, that the issue was no longer just Guyanese versus the British. It was one set of Guyanese against another set of Guyanese. Likewise, it was one set of Trinidadians against another set. And in Jamaica, before independence, it was already a question of the progressive elements as opposed to the more conservative elements in the society. Therefore, in a sense, when I was in Jamaica in 1960, I would say that already my consciousness of West Indian society was not that we needed to fight the British but that we needed to fight the British, the Americans and their indigenous lackeys. *That I see as an anti-neo-colonial consciousness as distinct from a purely anti-colonial consciousness.* (Rodney, *Speaks* 34, my emphasis)

Interestingly, Rodney describes his awareness to illustrate his mentality on moving to Africa in 1967; thus, this critique of local elites proves foundational to his understanding of a colonial nexus between the Caribbean and the African subcontinent. Although much of Africa had recently been decolonized when he arrived, "neo-colonialism had already overthrown Nkrumah" (Rodney, *Speaks* 34), and so he set out to examine the continent's socioeconomic dynamic from the point of view of this anti-neocolonial consciousness. Rodney worked primarily on the African subcontinent before returning to the Americas permanently in 1974, but he might have found that his consciousness of the role played by local elites in neocolonial societies would also have served him well in a critique of *North* African political economy.

The Comprador Elite in Egypt

Even though Mariátegui and the Latin American *dependentistas* were among the first to analyze and critique the problem of the comprador as an obstacle to development, the phenomenon was hardly limited to one region of the Global South. In Egypt, for example, the external orientation of the merchant class has historical roots distinct from those delineated by the development narrative of the Americas, yet the end results are highly comparable. The critical period for the emergence of a fully formed local comprador class was the Sadat era (1970–81), when Egypt's neocolonial status crystallized, but the history leading up to this era indicated the direction that this class would take.

Malak Zaalouk, an Egyptian economic historian, argues for a connection between "commercial agents" and foreign interests from the period of Muhammad 'Ali (1805–48) until well into the Nasser era. Thus, it should not be surprising that "during the inter-war period and into the early 1950s, commercial activity in foreign trade had been largely carried out by foreigners" (62) whose Egyptian clerks and junior partners took over their operations during the period of post-1952 Egyptianization. If the people undertaking import and export activity were often not Egyptian, this fact is less significant than the structural relationship between Egypt and its external trading partners. The West's leverage in the Egyptian economy was prominently marked by the presence of British administrators and military on Egyptian soil from the late nineteenth century until the Nasser era. As early as 1876, European powers had managed to force the debt-ridden ruler, Khedive Ismail (1863–79), into accepting the establishment of a "Caisse de la Dette Publique," consisting of members from England, France, Austria, and Italy, who would manage Egypt's finances and ensure the interests of its European creditors. England carried out an effortless military invasion of Egypt to put down the Orabi uprising and protect its commercial interests in 1882, resulting in an occupation that would last until the 1950s. In 1956, England again carried out a (militarily) successful invasion, with the forces of France and Israel fighting at its side. That the 1956 invasion was less successful politically had nothing to do with Egypt's economic liberation from the dominant role of the industrialized West, for it was only the opposition of the Eisenhower administration that forced the triumvirate to leave Egyptian land. Thus, Egypt—like other Arab countries in the mid-twentieth century—would substitute one Western master of its economy for another. Abdel Nasser was rewarded for standing up to what Egyptians call the "tripartite aggression" with an incipient American hegemony that would come to full flower after his death.

The Gamal Abdel Nasser era (1954–70), often seen as a period of nationalism, actually did not vary much from the long tradition of an externally oriented economy. While it was exceptional for Abdel Nasser's programs nationalizing commerce and industry, especially between the "victory" of 1956 and the crushing defeat of 1967, historians suggest that Abdel Nasser was as unsuccessful at economic development as he was militarily. First, Egyptian industry never took off in spite of public-sector investment during this period. One result was that no class of national industrialists emerged to counterbalance commercial agents. Second, Zaalouk's research finds that the class of commercial agents was already entrenched enough that many found ways to continue to make money during the period of nationalization. Ironically, Egypt's unfavorable climate, including a campaign against private-sector corruption in the early 1960s, seems to have reinforced the external orientation of the commercial agents, encouraging them to move their enterprises partly or wholly outside of Egypt, strengthening their contacts with external interests in the West and in the petrodollar states of the Persian Gulf. Third, Amin, Zaalouk, and other Left-oriented Egyptian historians point out that Abdel Nasser distrusted the working class and never allowed it to mobilize politically. The end result was that the collapse of the government's sponsorship of Nasserist ideology in the aftermath of the 1967 defeat left the country open to the triumphant return of the country's externally oriented commercial agents.

In many ways, the Sadat period in Egypt epitomizes the problems with the contemporary Eurocentric narrative of globalization. From an American point of view, Sadat's rule was characterized by moderation, especially in his 1977 visit to Jerusalem and his subsequent negotiation of the Camp David peace treaty with Israel. To this day, the notion that Sadat's assassination was the result of internal extremist opposition to the treaty is an oft-repeated truism in the U.S. media, bulldozing over the most obvious details of local history in order to make Egypt's relationships with Israel and the United States determinative.[4] From an Arab point of view, on the other hand, the Sadat period is overwhelmingly characterized by the rise of a new local comprador bourgeoisie. From the beginning of his tenure as president, Sadat set the country on a course to reverse Abdel Nasser's policies, at least when it came to resisting a local economy oriented toward the interests of the United States and Western Europe. He discontinued his predecessor's ties with the Soviet Union and sought a negotiated peace with Israel that might lead to closer ties with the United States. With respect to Israel, one historian sums up Sadat's thinking leading up to the 1973 War by saying, "When talk seemed to lead nowhere he determined to break the deadlock by a limited invasion of Sinai" (Al-Sayyid Marsot 132). Indeed, once Egypt had surprised Israel by managing to retake the Suez Canal area in 1973, the negotiations that eventually led to the Camp David agreements of 1978 began to progress.

But a different restructuring of Egyptian policy was going on at the same time, one that arguably had an even more dramatic effect on the internal dynamics of Egyptian society. Progress in developing local industry and protecting the livelihoods and basic rights of both rural and urban workers had been limited, at best, during the Abdel Nasser period. Still, Sadat also set out to reverse the few policies Abdel Nasser had pursued in these areas, seeking to ingratiate himself with the new compradors. He turned back the tide of Abdel Nasser's land reform and encouraged more foreign investment—as long as it was carried out in partnership with local commercial merchants. In 1976, Sadat set out to negotiate loans from the IMF to benefit his government and Egypt's local entrepreneurs. These talks led to the IMF convincing the government to dramatically reduce subsidies for basic staple foods, resulting in bread riots that began in Alexandria in January 1977 and spread throughout the country, nearly leading to the end of Sadat's government, with its *infitah*, or "open door," policy. But these bread riots did not cow the newly empowered compradors, who flexed their muscle only a few months later by proposing an ambitious new textile-production plant in Amereya, near Alexandria. This project, the largest of its kind ever proposed in Egypt, or anywhere in the world, primarily benefited, according to one account, "fractions of the modernizing bourgeoisie, composed of Bank Misr, foreign investors and commercial agents, all members of the new power structure and the newly formed alliances" (Zaalouk 10). While the Ministry of Industry and several investigative reporters examined the project and deemed it harmful to local industry, it went forward anyway—a clear mark of the power of the new elites, even when compared to certain government ministries.[5]

The effects on the Egyptian economy of this rise of the comprador class, emboldened and empowered by Sadat's policy, are anything but controversial among historians of the period. Irrespective of their ideological orientations, they view the new elites as a counterproductive force in development, with an extreme external orientation. For example, the ideologically liberal Afaf Lutfi Al-Sayyid Marsot describes the period thusly: "The bourgeoisie encouraged the growth of shops and restaurants which featured foreign goods and foods. For example, places selling fast food, of the type sold in the United States, but at exorbitant prices, blossomed, while local shops found little custom. It seemed that Westernization, interpreted as consumerism, was sweeping over the country with the blessing of the government and its president. Thus affluence existed side by side with abject poverty and there was a growing gap between the new rich, said to number 27,000 millionaires, and the poor" (137). Another liberal, Albert Hourani, defines *infitah* as "an opening to foreign, and specifically western, investment and enterprise," stating flatly that this aspect of Sadat's policy was not effective in facilitating long-term foreign investment, not only because Western investors were not eager to invest in so politically volatile a region but also because what Western money did come into the economy tended to go to "costly and over-ambitious schemes" (*History* 423). Meanwhile, Zaalouk, a dependency-influenced historian, pithily sums up the *lumpen* nature of the comprador group that emerged as a result of the *infitah:* "Through loans, the Western nations and America in particular have greatly encouraged and supported the creation of new classes in Egypt with whom they have close ties and shared interests. The new classes are highly parasitical. They serve foreign interests; they are largely unproductive; they indulge in lavish consumerism; they accumulate wealth that is easily transferable abroad; and they have no interest in the country's development—being in fact totally insensitive to its socio-economic problems" (6).

The Egypt described by these historians is particularly interesting in examining the role of comprador elites in Third World economies. The Sadat era was, of course, a time of unprecedented U.S. influence. American corporations and NGOs poured into the country after the Camp David agreements, and Egypt became the second-largest recipient of U.S. aid money in the world. The American embassy in Cairo—the largest foreign embassy in the world before the new U.S. embassy in Iraq opened in the summer of 2004—became the nerve center for the United States' policy making and military and intelligence apparatus in the Arab world. If the U.S. South provided the proving ground for the Northern colonial economy's effectiveness in spreading U.S. hegemony during the period of decolonization, Egypt arguably played the same role for the United States' post–Cold War ambitions in the Arab and Muslim worlds. The other notable characteristic of Egypt's *infitah* is the near-unanimous consensus among Arab historians about the parasitism of the externally oriented compradors the program spawned.[6]

The Comprador Elite in the U.S. South

Historians of the U.S. South have found it difficult to write about the period when Faulkner was born without some reference to the legacy of C. Vann Woodward's classic study *Origins of the New South: 1877–1913*. Woodward's argument takes the emergence of a comprador class after Reconstruction as its point of departure and foundation stone. Harold Woodman, a recent commentator on the study, sums up Woodward's contentions as follows: "The defeat of the Confederacy established the domination of business interests at the expense of the agrarians in the South. The victorious northern Radicals installed business-oriented Reconstruction governments; if the political affiliation of these postbellum state governments proved temporary, the class they represented did not" (791).

Of the group that emerged as the local elite in the 1870s and 1880s, Woodward remarks that "in the main, they were of middle class, industrialist, capitalist outlook, with little but a nominal connection with the old planter regime" (*Origins* 20). Their emergence did not simply lead the U.S. South toward an industrial economic formation and away from an agrarian one; it also shaped the character of Southern industrialization. The resulting dependent nature of Southern industrialization led to "changes of a profound and subtle character in the Southern ethos—in outlook, institutions, and particularly in leadership" (140). The South's new leaders "attached themselves to Yankee Carpetbaggers who came south for profits" (29), paralleling Egyptian, Peruvian, and other Global Southern compradors. This connection forms the basis of Woodward's famous historical argument for a "colonial economy" in the post-Reconstruction South.

The Southern socioeconomic system at the time resembled a colonial one in several ways. For one thing, widespread urbanization resulted when sharecroppers and subsistence farmers, unable to earn a living from the land in the aftermath of the sporadic depressions and crashes that accompanied the region's incorporation into the Northern economy, moved to towns and cities to look for work in mills and factories. Edward Ayers states that "the 1880s saw town and industrial growth in the South, but steady economic pressure on farmers" (7). Farmers with the economic resources to remain on the land found themselves pushed toward cotton, which guaranteed a payday even if its price fluctuated. The result was that the Southern United States developed a single-commodity economy, comparable to the economies of preindustrial Latin America. Furthermore, Southern industry, dependent on the North for technology, suffered from its derivative character and generally lagged behind its well-established "competition" to the North. Its second-class status was reinforced by a dizzying array of regional obstacles to growth, including "federal banking policy, railroad freight rates, absentee ownership, reliance on outside expertise, high interest rates, cautious state governments, [and] lack of industrial experience" (Ayers 104).

Greater than all these obstacles, however, was the unique alliance that formed between the Southern comprador and the Northern entrepreneur. Even as the South's new leaders claimed to be the "redeemers" of a prewar Southern prosperity, they in fact became willing accomplices in the region's refashioning as a colonial or dependent economy. In stating that "the vision that inspired the Southern businessman was that of a South modeled upon the industrial Northeast" (*Origins* 291), Woodward was also pointing out the Southern industrialist's lack of ingenuity and derivative status.[7] Woodward's most notable example of a Northern monopolist is J. P. Morgan, who in the aftermath of the panic of 1893 came to the region and "took over 4,500 miles of railroad and 150 miles of water line that had formerly been operated by thirty separate corporations" (292). The near-monopoly status that these acquisitions granted him was made palatable by his skillful use of the comprador system: "Morgan called his main road the Southern and named as its president a Southerner. Graduate of the University of Georgia and the University of Virginia and a Confederate veteran, President Spencer took personal charge of a large publicity organization that card-indexed newspaper editors according to their usefulness. Money, social pressure, sentiment, and tradition were brought to bear to protect Morgan's interest from legislative action" (296). While Morgan and Spencer may be somewhat extreme examples of their respective roles as colonizer and comprador, they were by no means anomalous.

Rereading Woodward today, one notes the close association he makes between the comprador class and a colonial economy. The comprador class within the U.S. South played a privileged historical role in what would become the full flowering of U.S. imperialism, first in the hemisphere and then throughout the Global South. Indeed, a new paradigm for hegemony was being forged in the post-Reconstruction South, one that relied on colonial economics and colonial class alliances instead of direct military and political assault, which had been only partially effective in integrating the South during the Civil War and Reconstruction. Britain was also perhaps learning this lesson around the same time in parts of Latin America and Eastern Europe, but its commitment to administrative and settler colonialisms was already too extensive to allow a change of course. As direct colonial rule broke down after World War II in Europe's global dominions, the United States was well placed to begin employing its new strategy in the postcolonial world.

Compradorism in Faulkner

Faulkner's *Snopes* trilogy depicts the emergence of a certain socioeconomic class in the first half of the twentieth century. Consequently, it serves to dramatize the historical changes delineated by Woodward in *Origins of the New South*. The first volume of the trilogy, *The Hamlet*, was published in 1940, while Woodward was still writing his history. The next two volumes, *The Town* and *The Mansion*, appeared in 1957 and 1959, respectively. As a group, the three volumes trace the processes of modernization in Yoknapatawpha County during the first half of the twentieth century. They do so primarily by focusing on the gradual rise of Flem Snopes, a nightmarish reversal of a Ragged Dick–type character from a Horatio Alger story. If Ragged Dick represents the promise and possibilities of American capitalism, Flem represents the perverse distortions of the Southern post-Reconstruction colonial economy; he is the most proximate, embodied form of the diffuse evil called modernization. Flem constitutes the U.S. South's equivalent of the Global South's comprador, not only in his obsession with material accumulation but more significantly in his separateness from the community in which he operates—that is, in his status as *lumpen*. At no time does he express any sense of philanthropy or interest in the community's development and well-being. If Yoknapatawpha were a nation, he would be the national bourgeois who makes a separate peace with the core at the expense of nationalism in the periphery.[8]

Flem, like the new elite described by Woodward, is of "middle class outlook," with "little but a nominal connection to the old planter regime," represented here by Will Varner, who shifts from Flem's landlord to his employer to his father-in-law, all in the first third of *The Hamlet*. Flem's poor White Snopes origins may not be typical of the South's new economy capitalists, but neither were such origins historically exceptional among this group. "William Henry Belk," for example, "founder of the South's largest department store chain, started as a clerk [at a country store] in a small town in North Carolina" (Ayers 94). While Flem cannot be compared to industrialists who were based in the North or were directly beholden to Northern interests, as described by Woodward, he succeeds through his willingness to exploit and deceive his fellow citizens and through his sensitivity to a new Southern order engendered by the colonial economy, which forms a backdrop to the trilogy's events.

In *The Hamlet*, the primary focus is the death of Yoknapatawpha's rural economy. Set almost exclusively in a small community called Frenchman's Bend, the story centers on a general store owned by Will Varner and run by his son, important because it extends credit to the community, made up of sharecroppers. Historically, the novel is set in a time when, Ayers reminds us, such general stores played a central role in small villages, not only extending much-needed credit but also providing a taste of the consumer culture that was leaving such spaces behind. "The presence of the new things," Ayers explains, "testified to the South's integration into the national economy, but the distant origins of those goods testified to the South's enduring provinciality" (81). The new consumerism centered around the stores made life better for the farmers who managed to keep up financially, but it also "pushed the harsher aspects of trade deep into rural life" (Ayers 93). This harsh quality of life for poor White farmers still trying to live off the land creates the conditions for the first stage in Flem Snopes's rise. While Flem—who eventually imposes a great deal of harshness on Frenchman's Bend, and later on Jefferson, the county seat—begins his career in *The Hamlet* via obtaining a clerk's position at Varner's store, "the peasants" suffer. Flem's cousin Mink, for example, kills a much wealthier farmer in cold blood after losing a lawsuit over money owed for the upkeep of a lost cow, while farmers spend money that they don't have on wild horses that Flem is suspected of having imported from Texas. A man named Henry Armstid buys a horse with three of his last five dollars and then injures himself trying unsuccessfully to take possession of it.

As at the opening to *As I Lay Dying,* Faulkner begins *The Hamlet* with an image symbolizing the collapse of the rural economy. In the former novel, the image is of a dilapidated cottonhouse that Darl describes as he and Jewel walk in from the field to the sounds of Cash constructing their mother's coffin: "The cottonhouse is of rough logs, from between which the chinking has long fallen. Square, with a broken roof set at a single pitch, it leans in empty and shimmering dilapidation in the sunlight, a single broad window in two opposite walls giving onto the approaches of the path" (4). This symbol of the destruction of the agricultural sector begins the novel by suggesting an alternative motive for the Bundrens' trip to Jefferson: flight from the impoverished countryside.

In *The Hamlet,* the narrator similarly describes the "Old Frenchman's place," an empty and decrepit antebellum mansion, sitting in a large expanse of uncultivated land. In Peter Alan Froelich's terms, the opening "identifies Frenchman's Bend as a geographical and cultural frontier where the progress of civilization has reversed" (226). The novel's first paragraph reads:

> Frenchman's Bend was a section of rich river-bottom country lying twenty
> miles southeast of Jefferson. Hill-cradled and remote, definite yet without
> boundaries, straddling into two counties and owning allegiance to neither, it
> had been the original grant and site of a tremendous pre–Civil War plantation,
> the ruins of which—the gutted shell of an enormous house with its fallen
> stables and slave quarters and overgrown gardens and brick terraces and
> promenades—were still known as the Old Frenchman's place, although the
> original boundaries now existed only on old faded records in the Chancery
> Clerk's office in the county courthouse in Jefferson, and even some of the

once-fertile fields had long since reverted to the cane-and-cypress jungle from which their first master had hewed them. (7)

This passage emphasizes the natural fertility of the land, contrasting it with the central image of the opening: the "gutted shell" of the house. While the Old Frenchman's place does not play a central role in the novel's various plotlines about the people of the hamlet until the last chapter, this description—like the description of the cottonhouse at the opening of *As I Lay Dying*—establishes a sociohistorical—indeed, an economic—foundation for the events that will play themselves out in the novel. The opening includes a subsequent reference to "the stubborn tale of the money he buried somewhere about the place when Grant overran the country on his way to Vicksburg" (8). This reference, which comes back into play at the end of the novel, serves as yet another reminder that the land that once bore riches is fertile no longer. Indeed, a culminating stage in Flem's rise, described in *The Hamlet,* is his unromantic view of the buried-treasure myth.[9] Just as Flem understands, before the village's other men, that there is no longer any benefit in farming, he also understands that the land will no longer magically produce wealth, as it once did. This separates him from representative figures in the community—an abjectly poor farmer, Henry Armstid; a comfortable and relatively shrewd salesman, V. K. Ratliff; and another poor White man, Odum Bookwright—whom he tricks into buying the Old Frenchman's place in the novel's last chapter.

The second and third volumes of the trilogy move into town, the natural destination of Flem's trajectory and Faulkner's narrative, *The Hamlet* ending with a vivid demonstration of the land's inability to yield the wealth that once sustained the agricultural sector. Thus, the countryside is left behind by both Flem and the trilogy, as both move to Jefferson. There, against a backdrop of modernizing urbanization, Flem's career plays out. The various narrators of these volumes describe in passing the changes in Jefferson. In the first chapter of *The Town,* Manfred de Spain is elected mayor on a modernizing platform of casting aside a recent law that declared no automobiles would be allowed on the streets of Jefferson. According to Charles Mallison, the character who narrates this development, this Luddite edict from an older generation presented "the opportunity that whole contemporary generation of young people had been waiting for, not just in Jefferson but everywhere, who had seen in that stinking noisy little home-made self-propelled buggy which Mr. Buffaloe (the electrician) had made out of odds and ends in his back yard in his spare time, not just a phenomenon but an augury, a promise of the destiny that would belong to the United States" (360). When de Spain wins the election, Charles declares: "The new age had entered Jefferson" (361). Just as *The Hamlet* opens with a scene depicting the effects of the colonial economy on the countryside, *The Town* also invokes economics in its opening. The election of Mayor de Spain inscribes modernization and mobility as the pretext for the novel's events. While Charles begins by celebrating the victory of the new age, however, over the course of the novel, the dissonance created by modernization's societal reordering will belie his optimism.

By the middle of *The Mansion,* Charles and Gavin Stevens, his uncle, are driving to the Memphis airport to pick up Linda Snopes upon her return from the Spanish Civil War. They are compelled to do so because the train—presented as the ultimate symbol of modernization's rapaciousness and Northern capitalism's demolition of the Southern pastoral in "The Bear" (see Willis 91–92)—no longer carries passengers to Jefferson; thus, a new stage in the Southern economy's integration into the national one has arrived.[10]

Like the first chapter of *The Town,* the last section of *The Mansion* emphasizes the restructuring of the Southern economy by presenting Flem's cousin Mink's release from jail after a thirty-eight-year incarceration. Mink's story is presented as a dark, poor-White version of the Rip Van Winkle narrative. Mink consistently and dramatically underestimates the cost of consumer goods, whether food, drink, or a gun with which to murder his cousin. Everything has changed dramatically, except wages paid to day laborers. When Mink arrives in Memphis, where he has gone to purchase the gun, he quickly realizes that "the Memphis he remembered from forty years back no longer existed" (932). Urbanization has spread the city out so drastically that even after he has traveled inside the city limits for over a mile, "he was apparently still as far from the goal he remembered and sought [a gun shop in central Memphis], as from Varner's store to Jefferson" (932). The sprawl of Memphis at the end of *The Mansion* contrasts with the deterioration of rural life in Frenchman's Bend at the beginning of *The Hamlet,* but it also contrasts with Jefferson, where so much of *The Town* and *The Mansion* takes place. Memphis is a third zone in the hierarchical plotting of spatial inequalities that the narrative establishes over the course of the trilogy. As in "A Rose for Emily," *As I Lay Dying,* and *Absalom, Absalom!* (see chapter 4), geography recapitulates socioeconomic hierarchy.

If the industrialized core of Northern capitalism has been moved to the periphery of the Faulkner text, as Susan Willis once suggested, the Snopes trilogy pushes the North even further from the scene of Southern history, transforming it into an almost absent presence. Indeed, in *The Hamlet,* before Flem moves into town, only fleeting reference is made to the Northern states, which only come up in the context of the Civil War or modern consumerism. Just a few more references arise in *The Town,* where, as in the earlier novel, they link history with a modern relationship based on political economy. So, for example, Charles notes that the town's oldest building, the Episcopal Church, "was built by slaves and called the best, the finest too, I mean by the Northern tourists who passed through Jefferson now with cameras, expecting—we don't know why since they themselves had burned it and blown it up with dynamite in 1863—to find Jefferson much older or anyway older looking than it is and faulting us a little—because it isn't" (614). However parenthetical, this reference emphasizes the two regions' contrasting economic fates during the early twentieth century and the subsequent cultural divide. If average Northerners are affluent enough to vacation in the South in search of a quaint antiquity that no longer exists, elite Southerners scrape together funds to go study for degrees in the North that may help them maintain their social status within their community. (In *The Mansion,* Charles leaves Jefferson to study at Harvard, following in the footsteps of not only his uncle Gavin but also Quentin Compson.) While Charles goes out of his way to point out the historical blindness of the tourists, who ignore Jefferson's Civil War destruction, he leaves without comment the economic ignorance that enables them to value old buildings without noting the slave system that produced them.

One scene in *The Town* is actually set in New York, in a neighborhood Ratliff calls "Grinnich Village" and Gavin Stevens characterizes as a "little place without physical boundaries . . . where young people of all ages below ninety go in search of dreams" (814). The two have traveled to New York for Linda Snopes's wedding to an artist, who will eventually convince her to follow him to Spain to fight with the Loyalists in the Spanish Civil War. Stevens has suggested the North to Linda as a place where a creative and talented Southerner can self-actualize, escaping the constraints of Southern society—in particular, the acquisitive, consumerist, dependent economics of the South, which Stevens and Ratliff call "Snopesism." The Snopes genealogy itself presents this consumerism through a variety of comical names: Wallstreet Panic Snopes, Montgomery Ward Snopes, Watkins Products Snopes.[11] Indeed, this particular trio of names not only emphasizes consumerism in the economy of the New South but also reinforces the geographic center of this system of unequal modernization: consumption belongs to the North, where each of the three entities from which the names derive is centered. Thus, the names of the Snopeses themselves constitute another of the text's peripheral references to the Northern role in the Southern process of modernization. Still, it is both important and useful to acknowledge the peripheralness of these references to Northern economic hegemony: the Snopes trilogy primarily concerns economic modernization's restructuring *within* Southern society. A major element of this restructuring in the work is dramatic changes in social relations and within the class system. For this reason, the Snopes trilogy, as the story of the career of Flem Snopes, is the appropriate Faulknerian text for examining the emergence of a comprador class in Yoknapatawpha.

Flem Snopes's Comprador Ethics

Amid the revolutionary changes brought about by Southern modernization, Flem pursues his goals until his murder at the end of *The Town*, serving as a constant reminder of the heartless single-mindedness that is most rewarded by the new system. From the first scenes in which he appears, Flem relentlessly follows money and power. He has a marked disregard for being well liked, for enjoying personal intimacy, or for being a part of a community of any kind. He is shocking—first to the hamlet of Frenchman's Bend, then to the town of Jefferson—not because he is unusually greedy but because he is so willing to disregard all of the rules that had held together a comparatively rigid

Southern social system in the past. He is absolutely forward-looking without being in any way progressive.

For example, at the beginning of *The Hamlet*, his first major advancement comes from the realization that his only hope to raise his class standing in the new South is to stop working the land and begin playing the colonial economy instead. Thus, he tells Will Varner's son, Jody, with typical bluntness that there "aint no benefit in farming. I figure on getting out of it soon as I can" (26). He then proceeds to negotiate an appointment as a clerk in Varner's store, which the younger Varner is willing to offer as insurance against the substantial Snopes reputation for barn burning. In this position, Flem discards an older system allowing customers to take whatever they want and pay whenever they feel like it. In Ayers's terms, he pushes "the harsher aspects of trade" out to Frenchman's Bend. So meticulous is he about accounts that he even makes his bosses, the Varners, pay for their own goods.

But it is not through a method or ethic that Flem establishes the power base that will eventually catapult him into the presidency of the town bank; rather, it is through associating himself with the central locus of village power, represented in the person of store owner Will Varner. When Flem has usurped Jody as the store's primary caretaker, the narrator describes the relationship among Flem, the elder Varner, and the community as a whole using a telling analogy to colonialism and the early formation of a class of comprador elites:

> In the tunnel-like room lined with canned food and cluttered with farming implements and now crowded with patient earth-reeking men waiting to accept almost without question whatever Varner should compute he owed them for their year's work, Varner and Snopes resembled the white trader and his native parrot-taught headman in an African outpost.
>
> That headman was acquiring the virtues of civilization fast. (61)

This metaphor is remarkable for several reasons. The final sentence quoted here is double-edged, a classic example of Bakhtin's concept of heteroglossia in novelistic language. The term *civilization* takes on a subtly pejorative connotation, as though the third-person narrator were actually a community member cynical about the new economy, like V. K. Ratliff. Also, there is a striking historical precision: the colonial project in Africa was indeed dependent upon the effective incorporation of "faithful" local servants into the colonial system. These locals would later become the African continent's compradors during decolonization.

Flem plays a more marginal role in the second and third sections of *The Hamlet*, but the fourth section begins with the auction of wild horses that he is suspected of having brought from Texas. Here, Flem most openly and directly exploits the poor of Frenchman's Bend for his own gain. By this point, his separateness from the community has already been established to such an extent that his first appearance after his return from Texas, accompanied by the horses and an auctioneer, seems so exotic that the poor farmers call the auction a circus (259). Ratliff warns them that Flem will sell the horses to them for his own enrichment, without regard for their well-being ("I'd just as soon buy a tiger or a rattlesnake" [266]), but several enter into the bidding in spite of this warning. An argument between one of the buyers and his wife makes it clear that these "peasants" are spending beyond their means to acquire horses they will never be able to take possession of ("'He aint no more despair than to buy one of them things,' she said. 'And us not but five dollars away from the poorhouse'" [277]). Flem's willingness here to directly visit economic exploitation on the poorest elements of the community is unusually blatant, compared with his more indirect compradorism in the rest of the trilogy. The result is that after the sale, as he watches Henry Armstid and his wife try to take possession of their wild horse, Flem finds himself "standing in his little island of isolation" (282).

The clear line of Flem's career as exploiter—from the African-outpost analogy to his circuslike return with the wild horses—is broken in the middle two sections of *The Hamlet*, where he plays a more marginal role, but even here the compradorist subtext of his trajectory as a character is reinforced. While the novel's second section, "Eula," focuses on Varner's daughter, leaving the story of Flem's rise until the very end, this culmination strengthens Flem's connection to Will Varner and his power within the community. Chapter 1 of "Eula" focuses on Labove, an Ole Miss student and football star whom Will Varner imports from a neighboring community to run the Frenchman's Bend schoolhouse. Labove becomes obsessed with Varner's daughter, a teenage student in his class. When his obsession leads him to sexually assault Eula, who rejects him, he disappears. The second half of this section focuses on Eula's sexual coming of age; her many suitors; and her eventual pregnancy out of wedlock, engendered by a young man named Hoake McCarron, whose intentions are strictly dishonorable. At the moment McCarron disappears, Flem, who has not been mentioned since the end of the first section, suddenly reappears in the narrative as Eula's fiancé. Flem's invisibility for so much of Eula's story emphasizes his opportunism in appearing as the provider of a deus ex machina solution to her problem.

The contrast between Flem's reaction to Eula's pregnancy and Jody Varner's further establishes Flem's comprador ethic of looking forward without either sentimentality or any interest in the advancement of the community as a whole. Jody treats Eula's pregnancy as a question of family honor, complaining to his unsympathetic father: "Maybe you dont give a damn about your name, but I do. I got to hold my head up before folks even if you aint" (138). This response, rooted in an antebellum social system centered on questions of honor, and highly reminiscent of the nostalgic position taken by Quentin Compson regarding his sister Caddy's romances in *The Sound and the Fury*, is cast aside in the commercially oriented and self-interested alliance between Flem Snopes and Will Varner.[12]

Thus, Flem's marriage to Eula constitutes the final step in his usurpation of Jody as Varner's heir apparent. Jody's position as Varner's successor is based on biology, patrilineality, and a social system that predates the emergence of the colonial economy. At a time when power—manifested as ownership of the means of production—ultimately rests outside the region, Flem finds himself able to advance his cause through an association with Will that disregards the traditionally unassailable bonds of, for example, biology. Flem's strategy of advancement by association is not lost on the community, even if Jody's nostalgia makes him unusually blind to it. Thus, in the first section of *The Hamlet*, the community realizes that Jody and Flem embody two different systems, that Flem represents a change when he takes over the responsibility of weighing the cotton brought in by sharecroppers at harvest time. Here is their communal response: "'That was when he passed Jody,' though it was Ratliff who amended it: 'You mean, that was when Jody begun to find it out'" (61). After Eula and Flem are married, the narrator comments on their unorthodox relationship: "She knew him well. She knew him so well that she never had to look at him anymore. She had known ever since her fourteenth summer, when the people said that he had 'passed' her brother" (141).

The marriage also establishes Flem's willingness to exploit his most personal relationship for individual advancement. Eula Varner may indeed have known Flem well at the time of their marriage, but she reveals near the end of *The Town*, just before she commits suicide, that she has never known him in the biblical sense, even after marriage. Flem's apparent impotence is yet another sign that the marriage is for him not so much one of convenience as of opportunity. When they move into the city in *The Town*, he allows Eula to carry on a fairly open affair with Mayor de Spain, whom Flem works under as bank vice president. Eventually, he uses the existence of the affair as leverage to usurp de Spain's position as bank president. When it seems likely that Eula will leave him, his only concern is for his own position and wealth; he thus temporarily ingratiates himself with his "daughter," Linda, just long enough for her to make him her sole beneficiary in her will. In sum, he only values his connections to Eula and Linda as a means to his own advancement. Flem's rise, then, is built on his relationships, not on hard work, like Horatio Alger's heroes'.

His unorthodox attitudes toward personal ties reflect Flem's comprador-like disinterest in any form of communal identity or national solidarity, especially if these stand in the way of personal enrichment. In a more traditional society, we might expect Flem's lack of a personal bond with either Eula or Linda to be a result of enduring allegiance to blood ties, over and above the ties of marriage. But Flem's relationship with the rest of the Snopeses reinforces the sense that he is motivated only by ambition. In fact, his lack of allegiance to his extensive clan of poor White relatives is a leitmotif that runs throughout the trilogy, leading to his eventual murder at the hands of his cousin Mink at the end of *The Mansion*, and reminding the reader along the way of his more general separateness from the community in which he moves.

The first emphatic statement of Flem's disregard for blood ties comes from Mink Snopes's wife in an early scene of *The Hamlet*. While Ratliff, who claims to have come to deliver a sewing machine that Flem has bought for them, looks on, she yells at her husband: "He'd let you rot and die right here and glad of it, and you know it! Your own kin you're so proud of because he works in a store and wears a necktie all day! Ask him to give you a sack of flour even and see what you get. Ask him. Maybe he'll give you one of his old neckties some day so you can dress like a Snopes too!" (74). Although Mink threatens his wife if she does not stop her anti-Flem diatribe, the scene ends with him asking Ratliff to pass a message on to Flem that reflects his wife's feelings: "Say 'From one cousin that's still scratching dirt to keep alive, to another cousin that's risen from scratching dirt to owning cattle and a hay barn. To owning cattle and a hay barn.' Just say that to him. Better keep on saying it over to yourself on the way down there so you will be sure not to forget it" (76). By the end of "The Long Summer," the third section of *The Hamlet,* Mink and Flem are in near-open conflict, the former hiding from the local authorities and the latter helping him elude them with the sole purpose of obtaining a share of the fifty dollars he believes Mink to have stolen off the murdered Jack Houston. When Mink is eventually arrested and tried, Flem arranges to be away while he is on trial. This act of disloyalty instills in Mink an old-fashioned desire to preserve Snopes family honor by murdering Flem. The urge is so strong it endures for nearly four decades of prison time. By the time Mink has been sent to jail, the community of Frenchman's Bend has marked Flem as a man with no sense of familial loyalty or solidarity. Thus, various community members comment incredulously in the last section of *The Hamlet,* "The Peasants," on Flem's behavior toward his relatives: "Flem would trim Eck or any other of his kin quick as he would us" (267); "Wouldn't no man ever give to his blood kin something he couldn't even catch" (296); "Aint no man, I dont care if his name is Snopes, going to let his own blood kin rot in jail" (305).

In *The Town* and *The Mansion,* Flem remains consistently isolated. He does nothing to help other Snopeses who move into town. Rather, he actively double-crosses them. For example, when Montgomery Ward is arrested for setting up a modest porn shop that projects images from French postcards onto a screen in a back room, Flem arranges for him to be framed for bootlegging, a federal offense. The bogus charge gets him out of a state prison and into a federal one, where Flem pressures him to trick Mink into trying to escape, an act that adds twenty years to Mink's sentence. Flem's disregard for familial solidarity provides a more extreme and obvious example of his general ethic of operating outside communal values or aspirations, manifested in his disregard for his wife's lack of marital fidelity; his willingness to exploit even the poor; and his dismissal of the entire legal system, refusing to allow himself to be served a subpoena when he is sued by farmers who have purchased the wild horses he is suspected of owning.

If no image of Flem better encapsulates his status as comprador figure than the description of him as a "native parrot-taught head man," no action better illustrates his comprador ethic than his decision to remove his money from the bank where he is an officer and invest it in the Bank of Jefferson. He is forward-looking enough to realize he cannot bury his wealth in his backyard but far enough removed from any sense of community membership to depend on a locally owned bank, even one he runs himself. In his disregard for the idea that he might act as steward of his own wealth, as well as that of the citizens of Jefferson, he is similar to the entrepreneur of the Global South, who ships the profits from his local enterprises out of the country to the secure investment vehicles of metropolitan economies.

Such passages raise Flem above the level of comical figure. Cleanth Brooks's influential early study of Faulkner's novels argued that *The Hamlet* is about the byplay between love and honor (174–85); Faulkner himself states in the preface to the trilogy's last volume that part of what had motivated his work over three and a half decades was the desire to explore the mysteries of the "human heart." Both of these accounts, however, are inadequate in that they presume that the text is only about characters other than the Snopeses. If the themes of love, honor, and the mysteries of the heart are played out in the relationships between the upper-middle-class White characters—Gavin, Eula, de Spain, Linda, and especially Charles—Flem's inverted Horatio Alger tale is the glue that holds together the wandering strands of the romantic narrative.

Flem and Point of View

Faulkner's formal presentation of Flem Snopes reinforces his extreme mental, imaginative, and vocational isolation, as dramatized in the trilogy's events. Two novella-length sections of the trilogy, book 1 of *The Hamlet* and the third and final section of *The Mansion*, are entitled "Flem," but—unlike chapters named after Charles, Gavin, and Ratliff, or sections named after Mink—the sections that bear Flem's name never present his point of view. Indeed, it is never presented at all. Rather, Flem remains a mysterious character from the trilogy's beginning to its end, always seen from the perspective of either single members of his community or the community as a whole.[13] When he is spoken to, Flem tends either not to answer or to say something completely incongruous. He responds to questions by changing the subject. As a character in a novel, Flem is marked by an inscrutable separateness that allows his identity to be filled in by the community observing him. As a figure representing a category in a complicated social system, Flem signifies interests incommensurate with the interests of the community. These two aspects work together in *The Hamlet*, for example, where the general sense of Flem as self-interested, exploitative, greedy, and cold emerges largely from the comments of the farmers who gather outside the general store and bemusedly observe his comings and goings.

In *The Town* and *The Mansion*, Faulkner uses narrative point of view much as he does in "A Rose for Emily." *The Town* is narrated in alternating chapters by Charles, Gavin Stevens, and Ratliff. On its face, this narrational structure seems reminiscent of Faulkner's approach in *As I Lay Dying*, but in *The Town*, the narrators form more of a consensus. They are fewer, of the same gender, and of the same social class. As a group, they come to represent the voice of the community, expressing shock, disgust, contempt, amusement, and approbation, as the occasion demands. Indeed, Charles implies this role on the novel's very first page when he explains, "When I say 'we' and 'we thought' what I mean is Jefferson and what Jefferson thought" (353). The main goal of constructing this communal perspective is to illustrate Flem's estrangement. Just as so many of his acquisitive and self-enriching actions are bewildering to those around him, so are his very processes of thought and feeling. One of the best illustrations of this is an early scene in *The Town* in which Flem stands calmly in a corner at the town's annual Cotillion Ball, while de Spain and Stevens fistfight in the alley behind the ballroom over Flem's wife. Joseph Reed offers a somewhat contrasting view of the narrative of *The Mansion*, arguing that the communal consciousness breaks down in the fragmented points of view of this final volume (248). In any case, the narration continues to stay outside the consciousness of Flem, which proves impenetrable throughout all the novels' various changes in voice, setting, and tone.

The last section of *The Mansion*, one of the two in the trilogy entitled "Flem," is mostly about Mink. It follows his release from prison and—as I have mentioned—his difficulties in trying to negotiate the changed environment of post–World War II Mississippi; make it to Memphis; buy the gun with which he hopes to kill Flem; and travel back to Jefferson, having spent the small amount of cash with which he left prison. The novel's final scenes are narrated from the perspective of the White middle-class men of Jefferson, who find Flem's thoughts and desires mysterious until the end. When Gavin warns Flem that Mink may be on his way to Jefferson to try to kill him, for example, he is surprised and confused by Flem's typically impenetrable reply: "much obliged" (1016).

Of all the trilogy's major characters, Flem is the most remarkable for his lack of interior consciousness. He never narrates, nor does a third-person narrator ever describe his internal desires or motivations. This formal strategy, of keeping Flem inscrutable to the very end, reinforces his radical disconnection from the community; this separateness, combined with his acquisitive materialism, marks him as a distinctive figure in the historical Southern economy, one that would be equally familiar to C. Vann Woodward, André Gunder Frank, or Samir Amin.

Postscript

Given the limited presentation of Flem's psyche, a sociohistorical interpretation is needed to analyze the possibilities of his role as a frame for the narrative. Here, as in all of Faulkner's work, the history and social thought of the hemispheric South add a layer of insight to the sociohistorical perspective. Ultimately, Flem's rise should be read as Ngugi wa Thiong'o proposes the comprador figure be read in African fiction.

This Kenyan novelist, playwright, and social critic suggests the comprador figure as key to understanding the work of Chinua Achebe, the Nigerian founder of the African Anglophone novel. Ngugi describes telling his students at an initial class meeting (for a course that his arrest would prevent him from teaching) that he plans to attempt to analyze socioeconomic class in Achebe's novels, starting with his first work, *Things Fall Apart,* and tracing the development of a modern African neocolonial class structure to *Girls at War,* the fourth of the Nigerian's novels. Ngugi's term for the comprador, in this particular essay, is the *messenger class.* In Achebe's novels, he sees the members of this class rising from "actual messengers, clerks, soldiers, policemen, catechists, and road foremen in colonialism as seen in *Things Fall Apart* and *Arrow of God,* to their position as the educated 'been-tos' in *No Longer at Ease;* to their assumption and exercise of power in *A Man of the People;* to their plunging the nation into intra-class civil war in *Girls at War*" (63). In his mere suggestion of the value of reading across Achebe's work with this goal, Ngugi brings to light the emergence of a social class whose existence also illustrates what a *dependentista* would call the development of underdevelopment.

Similarly, Flem Snopes represents a narrativization of the comprador class's emergence in the post-Reconstruction South. His representation is rooted in his unmitigated drive for acquisition and his isolation from his own community, emphasized by both the content and the form of the trilogy. Flem embodies a class standing made possible by unequal development. For this reason, his story "develops" over the course of the three novels in fits and starts, with regular detours. The next two chapters will look more directly at the close relationship between these two types of development, narrative and economic, in the writing of both Faulkner and novelists of the Global South.

Chapter Three

The Poetics of Peripheralization, Part 1

Historiography, Narrative, and Unequal Development

Genre and Geohistorical Location

Near the beginning of chapter 1, I referred to Walter Mignolo's argument connecting "knowledge production" to "geohistorical location," and the latter to "the coloniality of power," as a counterpoint to prevalent theoretical practice separating ideas from their historical context. In the next two chapters, I want to extend this connection between place and idea by demonstrating its relevance for literature. Both ideas and literary texts are part of cultural production, and both grow out of contexts. Just as place matters in the production and dissemination of ideas, place affects the nature of literary production, its genres, forms, and structures. Egyptian literary critic Sayyid al-Bahrawy expresses this same idea in slightly different terms when he states that literary "form bears ... within it a compendium of values and an ideology" (74). The problem, as García Canclini points out, is how to be radical without being fundamentalist. The connection between genre and geohistorical location must be acknowledged without being emphasized so much as to smother the literary signifier.

Faulkner's use of point of view in the Snopes trilogy is an example of the connection between literary form and geohistorical context. There are many possible explanations for Flem's lack of interior consciousness, for the constant presentation of him from some outside point of view. But when the representation of Flem is analyzed with the dialectical relationship between form and content in mind, this formal feature's roots in Faulkner's critique of Southern compradorism become manifest. I will expand this discussion of the dialectics between form and content and between genre and geohistorical location in what follows. This chapter considers the way the revisionist historiography of Mariátegui-tradition thought is reflected in the novels of postcolonial writers coming out of similar circumstances of spatial peripheralization. The next chapter returns to Faulkner, comparing the famous structure of *Absalom, Absalom!* to that utilized by these other novelists. The resulting comparison will form the crux of my argument for a remapping of Faulkner's geohistorical locale.

Even in the case of such masterpieces of the Western literary canon as the great nineteenth-century European novels of high realism, critics have uncovered enlightening connections between literary production and spatiotemporal context. For example, Franco Moretti understands the emphasis on youth at the outset of British novels like *David Copperfield* in terms of the "culture of stability and conformity" emphasized in England, where "the bourgeois revolution had taken place between 1640 and 1688," nearly half a century before the uprising of the merchant class on the Continent (181). Moretti views the European bildungsroman as the crystallization of a stage in European history, although he criticizes his own study for "never fully explaining why this form was so deeply entwined with one social class, *one region of the world*, one sex" (x, my emphasis). But Moretti's self-reproach perhaps discounts the value in merely claiming such an emphatic connection between literary genre and a particular place and time.

Moretti's self-criticism reflects the direction in literary and cultural studies provoked by Mignolo's connection between "knowledge production" and "geohistorical location." This relationship between literary genre (as a subset of knowledge production) and geohistorical location further extends the role of the politics of spatial inequalities. Literary genre's ethos, forms, and structures grow out of and are responsive to a place with a particular implication in global capitalism. Moretti's study of the European bildungsroman assumes such a connection as a point of departure. In this, he differs from the approach of mainstream postcolonial studies, which often substitutes abstract discourses of hybridity or exile for local material histories, generalizing broadly across regions and time periods of the Global South. For institutional postcolonial studies, the connection between region and genre proves elusive, since what Mignolo would call geohistorical location—that is, the context as a function of both local, regional history and geopolitical exigencies—is deemphasized from the start.

Fredric Jameson's essay "Third World Literature in the Era of Multinational Capitalism" is a well-known attempt to discuss fiction of the Global South via a methodology comparable to Moretti's treatment of the European novel, also presuming a connection between place and genre. Of course, its impact has been greatly undercut by the insightful criticisms of Aijaz Ahmad, among others. We learn from such responses that Jameson's essay takes a generalizing tone that groups together writers from various linguistic and literary traditions, from states with diverse experiences of colonialism, and from writers with disparate aesthetic agendas. Jameson's vision enacts an essentialism that his sympathetic and politically radical commitment to the work of the authors he discusses cannot completely overcome, in the view of these critics. They remind us that any attempt to generalize the politics of genre may be prone to a covertly essentializing logic and must therefore be understood as to some extent strategic and contingent. Nevertheless, this conclusion should not preempt attempts like Jameson's "Third World Literature," which do at least connect (however imperfectly) genre and geohistorical location in discussing postcolonial novels, especially politically committed ones. Drawing a connection between genre and place is critical to a comprehensive interpretation of such work.

By viewing all Third World literature as "national allegory," however, Jameson's argument goes to the politics of nationalism as the primary connector joining the states (and cultural traditions) of the Global South. Yet, as I argued in my introduction, what most strongly connects the unequally developed countries of the Global South is their common experience with the colonial economy. The Middle East in its diversity, for example, includes the heterogeneous histories of Turkey, Iran, the states of the Arabian Peninsula, the Levant, Egypt, Sudan, and the Maghreb, each with a unique historical experience of colonialism, each with a distinct history of state formation. Meanwhile, the problem of *economic* unequal development is more uniform across the region. Even the relative wealth of the region's petrodollar states does not exclude these countries from being understood in the context of unequal development, especially considering analyses of the problem of the region's "oil dependency" that have been produced by Arab-world economists including Abbas Alnasrawi and Yusuf Sayigh.[1]

Furthermore, not only does unequal development run through the nations of the Middle East, but such development also parallels regional experiences throughout the Global South.[2] (The cross-regional parallels might help deconstruct the mainstream media's exceptionalist treatment of the region as one dominated by Islamic fundamentalist forces, what Maxim Rodinson called "theologocentrism.") The political economy of underdevelopment finally leads the critic directly to the problem of history. Whereas the history of the Global South as seen through the lens of Jameson's national allegory appears to be smooth and abstract, the lens of unequal economic development allows a view of histories that appear comparable yet are locally distinct. The novelist, artist, poet, or intellectual of the Global South—based on an intimate regional experience with colonialism/imperialism—is positioned to view very critically indeed the Hegelian concept of history as a linear, causal, teleological affirmation of European supremacy and to search for an alternative structure as a vehicle for expression. This chapter examines the manifestation of this southern, critical, and anti-Eurocentric view of history in the vision of postcolonial novelists, considering the connection between geohistorical location and genre as it is revealed in novelistic structure.

History and the Global South

Toward this goal, it is helpful to consider various claims that have been made about a particular narrative structure that manifests itself broadly in the postcolonial novel. Its characteristics include complication of the temporal scheme in such a way that events are presented out of order and often from multiple perspectives. At times, this structure resembles the circular narrative of myth, as described by Northrop Frye. My interest, however, is in how this ostensibly ahistorical mythic structure is deployed in postcolonial narrative—particularly in certain anticolonial movements in the Latin American and Arabic novel—to express a very concrete, politically engaged, materialist critique of Western historiography.

The type of Western historiography that I have in mind manifests itself literarily in the nineteenth-century European bildungsroman, as it is understood by Moretti. The narrative structure of the bildungsroman is predominantly linear; *David Copperfield*, for example, begins at the beginning and moves forward in time toward a telos. This structure is characterized by causality and can, as Wallace Martin reminds us, be connected to a Eurocentric philosophy of history: "the varied meanings critics have attached to the concept of causality can be correlated with three conceptions of reality discussed by the German philosopher Hegel" (61). In Martin's discussion of "three ascending stages of realism" derived from Hegel, a teleological, stage-based narrative structure is shown to be characteristic of post-Enlightenment thought, whether manifested in a fictional work focused on an individual (as in a bildungsroman) or in nonfictional writing focused on the "Universe" (as in Hegel's historiography).

This classical realist conception of narrative structure—as organically linear, causal, and teleological—did not cease to exist with the end of the nineteenth century. While the structure of the Victorian novel is always complicated, of course, and while many counterexamples that do not display these classical characteristics might be cited, the trend traced by Martin eventually appears in a much cruder fashion in the twentieth century, underpinning various Eurocentric historiographies within both the humanities and the social sciences. Prominent among these twentieth-century manifestations is W. W. Rostow's ur-text of classical economic development theory, *The Stages of Economic Growth*, which so provoked the first dependency theorists, as we saw in chapter 1. First published in 1959, and still foundational to the basic vision of the World Bank, the International Monetary Fund, and the ideology of corporate globalization generally, Rostow's book argues that Third World countries should follow the pattern that the industrialized Western powers followed in the eighteenth and nineteenth centuries to develop their economies and achieve prosperity. Rostow delineates five specific stages that their economies should pass through, stating that development policy toward the countries of the Global South should be determined by which of the initial four stages preceding the final one, of high mass consumption, each is believed to be wallowing in. Rostow left little doubt about the comprehensiveness of his Eurocentric vision: "It is possible to identify all societies, in their economic dimensions, as lying within one of five categories: the traditional society, the pre-conditions for take-off, the take-off, the drive to maturity, and the age of high mass consumption" (4). Furthermore, Rostow not only considered his theory comprehensive but even suggested an almost spiritual transcendence to explain this comprehensiveness: "These stages are not merely descriptive. They are not merely a way of generalizing certain factual observations about the sequence of development of modern societies. They have an inner logic and continuity" (12–13).

Thinkers within the Mariátegui tradition, especially the Latin American dependency theorists, offered the most systematic and sustained critique of Rostow. They pointed out that globalization and colonialism had by then reached the point that national economies could not develop simply by re-organizing local policies. They argued that economic underdevelopment was actually a condition that had been imposed upon Third World countries by colonialism, rather than being the result of a historical lagging behind the developed nation-states.[3]

In narratological terms, the *dependentista* argument was that Rostow was stuck in the diachronic realm and that synchronic relationships with the rest of the global polysystem were most important for unequally developed economies. This was especially true in the case of relationships with the in-dustrialized Western powers. The metropolis had imposed unequal develop-ment on the South through the various operations of the colonial economy. *Dependentistas* saw this historical relationship as indicative of what synchronic economic relationships with the metropolis could (or could not) do for un-equally developed economies. They argued that investment from the indus-trialized West would lead to capital flight during economic downturns, when the comprador classes would take their leave, and that loans would merely further institutionalize economic dependency on the metropolis, recapitulating the exclusive economic relationships that colonizers had enjoyed during the era of formal colonial rule.

As I explained in chapter 1, dependency theory and other progressive narratives of unequal development were not limited to one region of the Global South. Rather, Latin American intellectuals, building on Mariátegui's work, provided the foundation for what would become, in fact, an emerging global intellectual tradition.[4] The shared history of struggle against the neocolonial forces of unequal development made the Latin American school seem relevant, for example, to the Arab Middle East. Thus, Egyptian Samir Amin and Lebanese Mahdi 'Amal emerged contemporaneously with the Latin American *dependentistas* to challenge the incipient bourgeois nationalism of postindependence Arab decolonization movements. Furthermore, the *dependentista* critique moved quickly from a debate about economics to a larger cultural vision that also considered literature, the arts, and cultural studies. This broadening demonstrated that the model was as much a challenge to Eurocentric historiography as it was a critique of classical development economics. Just as Rostow had argued for his model's "inner logic and continuity," his critics in the Global South understood that they were proposing not merely an alternative vision for economic policy formation but a theory of history with potentially powerful cultural applications.

The Novel and History in the Global South

In the area of literary narrative, for example, Angel Rama elaborated on the concept of transculturation to describe the way Latin American novelists used narrative as a response to North American hegemony and an expression of regional resistance. Rama placed special emphasis on what he called "regionalism" in Latin American fiction, insisting on its distinctiveness from the master narrative of the Euro-American novel, just as dependency theorists in the area of political economy insisted that Rostow's reliance on European history rendered his development plan unworkable in the Latin American context. Regarding the specific question of narrative structure, Rama made the following claim about the relationship between creation and the larger sociohistorical problem of dependency: "For a novelist these [narrative choices] represent purely aesthetic processes, but within them lies an implicit cultural programme resulting from the conflict which an entire population is experiencing" ("Processes" 158). This reading of transculturation as a manifestation of the regional novelist's political-economic unconscious claims for literature the same intimate connection between geographical space and literary production insisted upon in Moretti's analysis of the bildungsroman. Perhaps more significantly, it resonates with the basic thrust of the earlier-cited argument of Sayyid al-Bahrawy, who also searches for parallels between the historiography of socioeconomic underdevelopment in Egypt and the form of the Egyptian novel. Indeed, a longer quotation from al-Bahrawy makes this resonance between his work and Rama's explicit: "The form is not merely a collection of techniques or expressions of structure in the literary work, but rather it bears (as form per se and not in its content) within it a compendium of values and an ideology which grow out of society at the time form takes shape" (74).

Rama makes a broad connection between cultural production in general—narrative in particular—and political economy. But unlike al-Bahrawy and Doris Sommer, he does not put particular emphasis on the specific components of narrative *structure*. Sommer, on the other hand, making an aside during her reading of nationalism in Latin American romance, suggests a direct correlation between the structure of the novel composed during the Latin American boom and the structure of historiography in dependency theory: "In the 1960s a school of Latin American economists was consolidating some lessons of populism, without the lingering organicist developmentalism, and insisting that the problems of dependency could be solved only by clear breaks with the past, not by patience. At the same time narrators were breaking or bending the traditional straight line of history into vicious circles" (73).

Interestingly, Sommer's suggestive juxtaposition pinpoints linearity as the object of critique for both economists and novelists. In the case of Gabriel García Márquez, *Cien años de soledad* (*One Hundred Years of Solitude*) takes on the circular structure suggestive of myth that I mentioned earlier. The novel continually moves forward in time but then circles back at the end, when the linear history that has been presented collapses into a transcendent act of writing and reading. In light of the connections Sommer makes between narrative and *dependentista* historiography, we can understand this return not as a recourse to the level of the mythic, but as a subversion of the assertion that history equals progress—that is, as a subversion of Hegelian historiography, the bildungsroman, and W. W. Rostow's vision for Third World economic development. While *One Hundred Years of Solitude* is unmistakably a historical novel, and a novel about history, it rejects (in both form and content) the vision of history proffered by the historical novels of, say, Sir Walter Scott.

This type of postcolonial novelistic structure features an invocation of history combined with a jumbling of chronology and a rejection of teleology. Other Latin American examples include Juan Rulfo's *Pedro Páramo* and Mario Vargas Llosa's *The War of the End of the World.* While Rama would not place boom writers Julio Cortázar and Carlos Fuentes within his transculturation collective, because of their cosmopolitanism, Cortázar, in *Hopscotch,* and Fuentes, in *The Death of Artemio Cruz,* also rearrange time as an expression of the arbitrary, nonlinear nature of history. Indeed, the rejection of the historiography of the bildungsroman seems most pronounced in the Fuentes novel, as a comparison between its beginning and *David Copperfield*'s demonstrates.

Specifically, *David Copperfield,* a prototypical bildungsroman, begins as follows: "Whether I shall turn out to be the hero of my own life, or whether that station will be held by anyone else, these pages must show. To begin my life with the beginning of my life, I record that I was born (as I have been informed and believe) on a Friday, at twelve o'clock at night. It was remarked that the clock began to strike and I began to cry simultaneously" (3). These three sentences invoke the station of the protagonist, the beginning of his life, and time. The first sentence calls attention to literary genre by invoking the category of the hero. The narrator then moves immediately to the issue of origins—those of the character but also temporal origins generally. The word "begin" is repeated twice in the second sentence, and out of the continuum of time is carved a definite starting point: midnight. A novel could not announce its temporal point of departure more emphatically.

The opening pages of Fuentes's novel, on the other hand, are in direct contrast with Dickens's beginning. The title character here is an old man in this scene, barely clinging to life as he floats in and out of consciousness: "I wake … the touch of that cold object against my penis awakens me. I did not know that at times one can urinate without knowing it. I keep my eyes closed.

The nearest voices cannot be heard: if I opened my eyes, would I hear them?" (3). The paragraph continues with the narrator's vague consciousness of the medical instruments probing his body: "metal, everything is metal." He comments on his inability to control his own bodily functions and on the dullness of his senses. The first voices he hears confirm to the reader that the internal monologue of the first paragraph represents the consciousness of a dying man:

> "Look, Doctor, he's ..."
>
> "Señor Cruz..."
>
> "In the very hour of his death he had to trick us!" (4)

At the level of the individual, Fuentes's opening dismantles the autonomous subject embodied in David Copperfield. Cruz's body does not work; it has been reduced to an almost prepartum state. Simultaneously, at the level of narrative, this beginning willfully subverts the notion of history as ordered, linear, and causal, with definite starting and ending points.

In an early essay, written originally to introduce the English translation of Lebanese writer Halim Barakat's novel *Days of Dust* (and later collected in *Reflections on Exile*), Edward Said argues that the post-1948 Arab novel also uses structure to challenge the historiography inherent in the classical high-realist novel. For Said, the differences in the novelistic histories of Europe and the Arab world are rooted in the impact of the crushing 1948 and 1967 defeats of Arab armies and in the ongoing threat of U.S. imperialism, Israeli colonialism, and unequal development. He observes: "If the unit of composition [in the Arabic novel] is the scene, and not the period (prologue, middle, end in the Aristotelian sense), then the connection between scenes is tenuous. There is a tendency in fact to episodism, as if the rhythmic succession of scenes can become a substitute for quasi-organic unity" (49–50). Said's primary example is the Palestinian novel *Rijal fi-l-shams* (*Men in the Sun*), written by Ghassan Kanafani in 1956. This work relates a story of Palestinian refugees, scarred by their memories of displacement from their homeland, trying to make their way across the Iraq/Kuwait border. Its significance for my argument stems from the fact that it employs flashbacks in a way that makes the chronological sequence chaotic. The plot does not begin to move forward in time until the novel is almost half-finished. This jumbling of the temporal sequence makes the novel's individual scenes more autonomous, complicating their causal relationship with what comes before and after. In Said's words, Kanafani is trying to "make the present; unlike the Stendhalian or Dickensian case, the present is not an imaginative luxury but a literal existential necessity" (53).

The confidence reflected in Hegelian historiography is far removed from the feelings of pessimism, even of immanent extinction, that seem to be reinforced with every post–World War II historical development in the Arab world. For this reason, Said argues, the structure of the post-1948 Arabic novel asserts the total absence of an "Arab idea, identity, history, collectivity, destiny, drama, novel giving the diachrony of scene-events any synchronic intention, aim, structure, meaning. The present may after all be only that, perhaps not a consequence of the past and certainly not a basis for the future" (55). This characterization suggests a generic form simultaneously oppositional to the historiography underpinning the European bildungsroman and rooted in Arab geohistorical location—in the series of military defeats, in the disappointments of unequal development and failed decolonization programs, and in the cynicism regarding history and the future that the Arab politics of space instilled in the Arab artist.

Time in Arabic Novelistic Structure

The Arab defeats of 1948 and 1967 represent important historical markers for the cultural history of the region in the last century, but the general problem of unequal development, instilled by the project of European colonialism, has older roots. The region's colonial history—England using commercial interests to facilitate its colonization of Egypt, the United States and England extracting beneficial oil concessions in the region—is well-known. With respect to culture, Samir Amin has argued that the Arab Nahda itself included the roots of unequal development, in its fear of a true national popular social movement that would bring about local development independent of the European powers: "Mohammed Ali believed he could separate material modernization (undertaken by borrowing its technological elements) from calling ideology into question, which he judged to be dangerous, because it would have associated the Egyptian bourgeoisie with a power whose exclusive control he wanted to maintain. He thus opted for a 'moderate conservative Islam,' more formalist than preoccupied with responding to new challenges. The cultural dualism that has characterized Egypt ever since (and whose analogues can be found in many regions of the contemporary Third World) has its roots in this choice" (*Eurocentrism* 129). From the time of Napoleon's invasion of Egypt (1798–1801), and the first Egyptian experiments with modernization under Muhammad 'Ali, Egyptian and Arab history had not reflected the "culture of stability and conformity" that Moretti ascribes to England in the eighteenth and nineteenth centuries. Rather, modernization's incomplete regional character, together with the twin pressures of a rapacious European colonialism and opportunistic local elites, engendered a history of unequal development.

For this reason, strikingly few good examples of the bildungsroman exist among major Arabic novels and novel-like texts. Naguib Mahfouz's trilogy might provide one example, but only if one considers all three volumes as one novel, ignoring the fact that the character Kamal plays a relatively minor role in *Bayn al-Qasrayn* (*Palace Walk*) (1956). Most of the other fiction from Mahfouz's social-realist phase has little to do with linearity. Certain spatial markers, like the coffeehouse and the alley, play a more significant role in *Zuqaq al-Midaq* (*Midaq Alley*) (1947) than any timeline does, and it is not clear that any of the novel's major characters (Hamida? Abbas? Hussein?) achieve any sort of education, culminating in the novel's dark climax. The education of the bourgeois subject is a theme in modern Arabic narrative, but rather than conforming to the conventions of the bildungsroman, texts like Taha Husayn's autobiography *Al-Ayyam* (*The Days*) (1939) and Tawfiq al-Hakim's *Yamiyyat na'ib fil-aryaf* (*The Maze of Justice*) (1932) express through their loose, episodic structure something of the chaos surrounding both narrative formation and the formation of social classes in semicolonial Egypt. Gaber Asfour makes this point most clearly when he repositions the geohistorical location of the Arabic novel. Whereas the European novel has been called the expression of that culture's emergent bourgeoisie, Asfour sees the Arabic novel as the collective expression of an Arab middle class "in search of its own identity, within a society divided against itself" (31). The colonial legacy's lingering effects on Arab socioeconomic class formations have a direct consequence—in Asfour's authoritative critical account—for genre in Arabic literature.[5]

Time—specifically a disorderly temporal scheme—is the most obviously distinctive element when Husayn's and al-Hakim's novels are compared with the Anglo-European bildungsroman. The sense of causality and orderly progress that one detects in most of Dickens's novels is replaced here by the episodism, the emphasis on the scene as building block, that Said discusses. Clearly delineated beginnings and ends were frequently eschewed by Arabic narratives even before the defeats of 1948 and 1967, but after these setbacks the arbitrary nature of beginning and end became notably willful. An excellent example can be found in Tayyib Salih's *Mawsim al-hijrah ila-l- shamal* (*Season of Migration to the North*), first published in Beirut in 1969, a novel whose complicated temporal structure, built on extended flashbacks, repetitions, and parallels, seems almost circular.

Salih is clearly responding here to his predecessors, to the work of Husayn, al-Hakim, Yahya Haqqi, and others, whose novels of East/West conflict feature a bourgeois, male Arab subject who travels to the West and discovers a sexual freedom that forces him to rethink his cultural heritage.[6] In linking sexuality directly to colonialism and political resistance, and in invoking Freudian psychology as a characterological point of departure, Salih presents a serious challenge to earlier Arabic novels of East/West conflict; but it is only through the novel's complicated narrative structure that he manages virtually to explode everything that has come before.

The key to *Season of Migration*'s structure is the doubling of the narrator, whom the novel never names, and the central character, Mustafa Sa'eed. The novel's circularity consists partially in this doubling, throughout the book's midsection, and partially in the way the narrative begins and ends with a return to origins.[7] In the work's opening lines, the narrator describes his return from studying in Europe in terms much less ambiguous in their proclamation of African superiority than the novel's subsequent discourse: "The important thing is that I returned with a great yearning for my people in that small village at the bend of the Nile. For seven years I had longed for them, had dreamed of them, and it was an extraordinary moment when I at last found myself standing amongst them. They rejoiced at having me back and made a great fuss, and it was not long before I felt as though a piece of ice were melting inside of me, as though I were some frozen substance on which the sun had shone—that life warmth of the tribe which I had lost for a time in a land 'whose fishes die of the cold'" (1).

Between this point of departure and the novel's final scene, one dynamic that plays out is an almost systematic paralleling of the narrator and Mustafa Sa'eed. Both have lived extensively in Europe and have come to know it well, only to abandon it for the deep roots of their Sudanese home. Both are interested in literature and somewhat tortured by their bicultural history. In the end, the narrator becomes guardian of Mustafa Sa'eed's family. All of this culminates in the final scene, when the narrator attempts to follow Mustafa Sa'eed to a watery grave at the bottom of the Nile—the same Nile that the novel's first page demarcates as the narrator's point of origin.

Much critical debate revolves around whether the final scene affirms life or is merely resigned to it. For my purposes, however, the critical aspect of the scene rests in its completion of the cycle set in motion first by the narrative, then by Mustafa Sa'eed. The notion that the narrator is coming full circle, returning to his origins, is infused in the details here: he is "as naked as when my mother bore me," entering the water "as the first glimmerings of dawn made their appearance in the East"; the river is "reverberating with its old familiar voice" (166). On the last page of the novel, he sees a flock of birds flying northward: "In a state between life and death I saw formations of sand grouse heading northwards. Were we in winter or summer?" (168). By the end of the passage, life, death, the day, and the seasons—in short, all the major cycles designated by Northrop Frye as inhering in mythic structure, except for menstruation—have been invoked. Furthermore, the suggestion that the narrator is here returning to the womb evokes an interesting trajectory—from *David Copperfield*, where the protagonist confidently asserts his separation from the dependence of the womb by taking his place in a naturalized world; to *The Death of Artemio Cruz*, where the collapse of the protagonist's bodily functions becomes a point of departure for the fractured history of the narrative; and finally, to *Season of Migration*, where the narrator's futile attempt to return to a natural starting point serves as a resort to the biological in order to express

frustration with the social, political, and historical treadmill of the postindependence scene.

Season of Migration to the North engrosses us in the politics of the East/West
divide, which torments its main protagonists, so it only makes sense that the
politics of the text would be congruous with its narrative pattern. The rejection
of telos, which meant a turning away from the bildungsroman for European
and American high modernists, means something different for Salih, who has
no Arabic bildungsroman from which to turn away.[8] For the post-1967 Arab
intellectual, the rejection of telos is political and social.[9] Literary form here expresses a turning away from the notion that colonialism, by "civilizing" Africa,
would lead to progress or, for that matter, that independence from colonialism
would usher in a new era. In 1969, the idea that Arab history might enact an
orderly progression from A to Z seemed much less plausible than the proposi-
tion that Arab history kept ending up back at the beginning.

Saree Makdisi points out in his discussion of Salih's novel that Mustafa
Sa'eed is born "in 1898, the year of the bloody defeat of the Mahdist forces
by Kitchener's army in the battle of Omdurman, which signaled the final collapse of Sudanese resistance to British encroachment" (540); further, Sa'eed
"disappears at the age of fifty-eight, or in 1956, the year of Sudan's independence—that is, his life coincides with the period of direct British occupation
of the Sudan" (548 n.17). This suggests two important realities about the text.
First, not only does its *récit*, or discourse, form a cycle, but its *histoire*, or story,
does also, since Mustafa Sa'eed's life begins and ends with an independent
Sudan. Second, the legacy of colonialism is the real mystery at the heart of the
story of Mustafa Sa'eed.

Furthermore, the narrator's role as Mustafa Sa'eed's doppelganger not
only provides a premise for a structure that subverts progressivism but also
ties this anti-Hegelian African historiography to the question of European colonialism in Sudan. For if Mustafa Sa'eed's life is framed by the British colonial
project in his country, the narrator's life broadly reflects aspects of the period
of decolonization. Not only is very little mention made of the narrator's life
before his return from Europe in the opening scene, but he repeatedly represents a modern, postcolonial Sudan, often in conflict with the village setting
where much of the novel takes place.[10] He regularly finds himself traveling

between the village and the capital, where he sits in bureaucratic meetings while Mustafa Sa'eed temporarily disappears. He single-handedly opposes the traditionalist marriage between an elderly, exploitative, and misogynist village patriarch and Hosna Bint Mahmoud, the young widow of Mustafa Sa'eed, on the grounds that such a marriage would be backward. When his grandfather suggests to the narrator that he solve the widow's "problem" by marrying her, the narrator says, "I felt real anger, which astonished me for such things are commonly done in the village" (86). He complains that her suitor is forty years older than the widow, an objection brushed off by the grandfather, who insists the older man is "still sprightly."

If the narrator doubles the person of Mustafa Sa'eed, he also provides a contrast to his boyhood friend Mahjoub, who has lived his whole life in the village and now farms a plot of land in the new Sudan, which the narrator is helping to run as a civil servant. In an exchange between the two at the novel's midpoint, the narrator praises Mahjoub's chosen profession, saying, "People like you are the legal heirs of authority; you are the sinews of life, you're the salt of the earth" (99). But the farmer takes little interest in the narrator's panegyric to the pastoral. In his rejection of the narrator's praise, Mahjoub calls attention to the continuities between Sudan's colonial and neocolonial states: "'The world hasn't changed as much as you think,' said Mahjoub. 'Some things have changed—pumps instead of water-wheels, iron ploughs instead of wooden ones, sending our daughters to school, radios, cars, learning to drink whisky and beer instead of arak and millet wine—yet even so everything's as it was.' Mahjoub laughed as he said, 'The world will really have changed when the likes of me become ministers in the government. And naturally that,' he added still laughing, 'is an out-and-out impossibility'" (100).

Mahjoub's comments call attention to the continuation of colonial structures in the neocolonial period and implicate the narrator in this continuity. In Waïl Hassan's view, the narrator "notes the corruption and hypocrisy of the 'new rulers of Africa,' but he is powerless to do anything except participate in the system" (124). The many parallels that unite the narrator and Mustafa Sa'eed are also indicative of the lack of reform in the independent Sudan, as is the new beginning that is described at the novel's end. If Moretti's "culture of conformity" suggests that David Copperfield must begin with his birth, and if a history of unequal development has already reduced Artemio Cruz to his deathbed as his story opens, the Arab world's modern history of defeat and uncertainty sends the Arabic novel back to its beginning, to the opening of the "season," just when the narrative should be culminating.

Space in Arabic Novelistic Structure

If the unit of composition in Kanafani's *Men in the Sun* is the scene, as Said has suggested, a comparable—if more complicated—structure plays itself out in Kanafani's second novel, *Ma tabaqqa lakum* (*All That's Left to You*) (1964). Again the author takes the effects of defeat and displacement on ordinary Palestinians as his subject matter, and again he mixes up chronology in an expression of opposition to the monolithic historiography of the Eurocentric triumphalist. In *All That's Left to You*, however, the explicit connection between this jumbling of time, on the one hand, and questions of the spatial, territorial, and geographic, on the other, forms the work's point of departure. The author announces in a prefatory note that "Time and the Desert" are characters in the work, treated at the same level as the human characters: "As will be obvious from the outset, the five characters in this novel, Hamid, Maryam, Zakaria, Time and the Desert, do not move along parallel or conflicting lines" (xxi).

Like many of the critics cited earlier, Kanafani makes clear that his aesthetic choices regarding structure are also expressions of historical and political realities. After explaining his use of contrasting typefaces to indicate shifts in narrative point of view—"[the] difficulty implicit in making one's way through a world which is jumbled in this fashion is one that is freely acknowledged"—Kanafani admits that this strategy has a drawback: "it gives the impression of assigning a deliberate order to a world which actually has none" (xxi). The novel the author has constructed is indeed quite difficult to follow. It constantly jumps among three different narrators with no warning other than the change in typeface. Moreover, two of the three flash back repeatedly to the past, forcing the reader to orient to new settings rapidly. Kanafani's statement about this structure makes two things clear. First, such a strategy is the most appropriate for expressing the reality of defeated and occupied Palestinians. Second, an even more appropriate strategy in the Palestinian case would be still more confusing: the diverse typefaces in fact make the text too well ordered to fit the chaotic reality. Barbara Harlow succinctly sums up Kanafani's narrative aesthetics along these lines: "Kanafani's stories interact with historical time and plot, proposing alternative forms and outlining new narrative possibilities. They neither reproduce reality nor do they impose either the finality of an ending or the solutions of dogma" (54).

One of the consequences of the novel's subversion of linear time is the reinforcement of space as an alternative. This manifests itself in the personification of the land, as previously mentioned: the land becomes a character as an expression of post-1948 Palestinian reality. Kanafani's first novel, *Men in the Sun,* opens with a passage that makes this strategy explicit: "Abu Qais rested on the damp ground, and the earth began to throb under him with tired heartbeats, which trembled through the grains of sand and penetrated the cells of his body. Every time he threw himself down with his chest to the ground, he sensed that throbbing, as though the heart of the earth had been pushing its difficult way towards the light from the utmost depths of hell, ever since the first time he had lain there" (21). Similarly, *All That's Left to You* insists on an anthropomorphic land from its opening sentences:

> He could now stare directly at the sun's molten disc, and watch its crimson fireball hang on the rim of the horizon before disappearing into the sea. In a flash it was gone, and the last glowing rays that lit up the path of its descent were extinguished like embers against a grey wall that rose shimmering at first, then turned into a uniform coat of white paint.
>
> Suddenly the desert was there.
>
> For the first time in his life he saw it as a living creature, stretching away as far as the eye could see, mysterious, terrible and familiar all at the same time. (1)

This scene is narrated in the third person, but from the point of view of Hamid, one of the novel's main characters. Hamid's experience here of the desert as "an enormous body, audibly breathing," prepares the reader for even more emphatic personifications. The desert begins to narrate brief passages throughout the novel, commenting on Hamid's trek on foot from Gaza, seeking to cross over to Jordan, where he hopes to find his mother.

The passages narrated by the desert are shorter than those narrated by the other characters, and they exist only in the present, without the constant flashing back that characterizes the narratives of Hamid and his sister, Maryam. This may be because the desert's temporality is less complicated than that of the other characters because it is pure space, without time. The category of geohistorical location involves both spatial and temporal axes of historical development, both diachrony and synchrony, but in giving the desert a narrative voice—and in not giving one to time, which he also deems a "character"—Kanafani subordinates the temporal to the spatial, in direct contrast to the linear bildungsroman, whose structure prioritizes temporal order. This different structural reality reinforces itself in the narrative when Hamid discards his watch while making his way over the desert sands, having decided it is useless. The desert itself briefly voices the watch's demise, its observations culminating in: "It wasn't long before the watch went crazy. Abandoned in its exile, it went on ticking to itself, building up that impenetrable barrier that madmen erect between themselves and the world" (21). Time's mechanization, and its artificial structuring by the watch, provokes the desert to describe it as mad, cut off from spatial reality.

If the desert represents space, its politicization in the narrative dramatizes the separation and atomization of Palestinians, brought about by Israeli occupation. Roger Allen points out that in both this work and *Men in the Sun,* the desert is "a barrier," but whereas the earlier work focuses on internal disunity among different Arab communities, here Hamid's journey is determined by Israeli border patrols (109). Thus, Kanafani has invoked colonial occupation as part of the novel's politics of space.

The novel uses the breakup of a family based in Gaza to suggest the breakup of the Palestinian community. The story line offers history as rupture, presenting a historiography that is reinforced by the politics of space. Initially, the novel's main conflict is a dispute between Hamid and Maryam over her relationship with an older married man named Zakaria. It is Hamid's inability to accept Maryam's pregnancy and her planned marriage to Zakaria (as his second wife) that provokes him to embark on a quixotic attempt to traverse the desert and find their long-lost mother. Through flashbacks, the reader learns of their father's death in the Palestinian national struggle, of Zakaria as having betrayed that struggle, of rumors that the mother from whom they were separated in 1948 is living in Jordan, and of the subtly incestuous nature of the tensions between Hamid and Maryam. By the end of the novel, the narrative's complexities have been streamlined to the doubling of two plot strands: a hand-to hand struggle between Hamid and an Israeli soldier whom he has stumbled on in the desert, and a climactic conflict between Maryam and Zakaria over his insistence that she have an abortion rather than burden him with another child. If birth is effortless and natural, a mere prerequisite for life in *David Copperfield,* it is contested and difficult for Maryam.

The intersplicing of these two scenes is highly comparable to the doubling of the narrator and Mustafa Sa'eed in *Season of Migration,* putting into relief the parallel levels operating in the narrative. The nuclear family has broken up, as has the Palestinian community, a split represented in the separateness of Hamid's and Maryam's narratives. The twin causes of the defeat are an ossified patriarchy (represented here by the polygamous and dictatorial Zakaria) and colonial conquest (represented here by the Israeli checkpoints that invisibly menace the edges of the desert, as well as the soldier and his vast support network).[11] In her book-length study of Kanafani, literary critic Radwa 'Ashur remarks of the bifurcated final sequence that it does not constitute an ending but rather merely reiterates the extent to which *All That's Left to You* is really "a novel of beginnings" (82). As the doubling of patriarchy and colonialism re-presses both personal and national human aspirations in the Palestinian community, the narrative subverts linearity and progress through the doubling of narrative strands and through the emphasis on space and spatial politics.

The geohistorical location of the Arabic novel's structure evolved through historical stages that defined how an originally European literary genre would be translated into the Arabic context. These historical stages included the gradual displacement of Ottoman rule by European colonialism; the installation of a colonial economy in the relationship between the European powers and the region; the evolution of stark spatial inequalities between metropolis and periphery, which continued colonial dominance even after colonial governors left the region; and the post-1948 period, during which repeated defeats at the hands of Israeli and American armies reinforced the historical spatial politics of the region. Over time, in other words, a distinctive politics of space has emerged.

In Latin America, the dependency theorists described the way a highly comparable evolution of colonial economy had instilled a similar politics of space. With this critique in mind, Angel Rama elaborated on his notion that Latin American narrative was "transculturated," with a specific appeal to spatial politics, stating that "the region was a subjugated socio-cultural complex." Regionalism was thus for Rama not only a literary phenomenon but also "a social movement, interpreting the aspirations of a class" (166).

Delineating the context of the post-1948 Arabic novel requires a similar sensitivity to politicized space. The divides between country and city, embodied in tensions between the effendi narrator of *Season of Migration to the North* and his ancestral village, must be analyzed alongside the presentation of the desert as manmade obstacle in the work of Kanafani, and both should be understood in light of the structural subversion of linearity employed by these and other Arab novelists. The unity and naturalized biology suggested by the bildungsroman's embodiment of a monolithic Hegelian historiography in one central character are counteracted with a presentation of reality as multiperspectival and multivocal.

The larger divide in these schemes lies between the neocolonial metropolis and the unequally developed periphery. The action and structure of both novels acknowledge this larger backdrop of spatial inequalities, but without giving up the insistence on other spaces and other timelines, thus reiterating that history is local and cannot be reconfigured as a European monolith.

Space and Time in Another South

Arundhati Roy's *The God of Small Things*, set predominantly in her native Indian state of Kerala, includes a striking number of the characteristics found in the other postcolonial novels described here, even though its action takes place in a context distant from that of Latin American boom fiction or the post-1948 Arabic novel. Roy's narrative is arranged willfully to jumble chronology, forcing the reader to confront scenes as though they are detached from the events before and after them. It begins by invoking death rather than birth. Further, by focusing on twins, it also manifests a doubling motif, undercutting the suggestion—so prominent in the bildungsroman—of a complete and autonomous individual subject. Space and its relationship to the story's socioeconomic dynamic are emphasized. Finally, all of these characteristics are bound up with the novel's sense of the undeniable significance of the local. Corporate globalization is invoked in a way that pushes the World Bank agenda to the margins, while the center is occupied by a figure the narrator calls the God of Small Things. No final explanation preempts all other possibilities regarding the resemblance among Roy, Kanafani, and García Márquez. To presume otherwise would be to lapse into the generalizations of Jameson's controversial argument about the literatures of the Third World. Indeed, what makes *The God of Small Things* interesting is what it shares with other narratives—including commonalities of context, form, and content—*even though* it has many distinctive characteristics.

The novel is very much about Kerala, India's small southernmost state. While it would be going too far to suggest a direct parallel between Kerala's status as Southern in the Indian context, and the situations of Mississippi, Sardinia, Upper Egypt, and Chiapas, by the time *The God of Small Things* was published, Kerala was becoming increasingly comparable to these other Souths, with their colonial economies.[12] Indeed, when the novel appeared, Kerala was suffering from one of its worst economic depressions in recent memory, due to a set of familiar (to observers of Third World development obstacles) economic problems (Nair 373).

What makes Kerala anomalous among these other Souths, however, is what development economists call historically "high social indicators" compared to the rest of India, and indeed to the rest of the Third World. Kerala's health and education sectors have traditionally outperformed the rest of the country, and its coastal geography and history as a trade center have given the area a reputation for cosmopolitanism, even as the state has remained largely agricultural.[13] Economic statistics, however, do not indicate rates of growth or industrial expansion comparable to the rest of India since independence. What has historically been Kerala's main economic advantage—its openness to the outside world and the migratory nature of its inhabitants—has taken on a Janus-faced quality in the postcolonial period. Nearly half of the many Indians who work and live in the petrodollar countries of the Arabian Gulf are from Kerala, and a substantial proportion of the total earnings of all Keralites are collected in these foreign countries. Economic crises created by a break in the flow of these remunerations have occurred twice in the past two decades. Keralites lost millions when Iraq invaded Kuwait in August 1990 and they were forced to leave their jobs and money behind and return home. Again in the mid-1990s, around the time that Roy's novel appeared, a dip in oil prices caused a break in the flow of repatriated money, which in turn contributed to an economic collapse that was already imminent because of the loss of agricultural subsidies under the Indian federal government's structural adjustment program.

Kerala also manifests a southern character in its vulnerability to changes in federal law and in many cultural and social traits. The state's languages are Dravidian, incomprehensible to the citizenry of India's central and northern states. Increasingly, the federal government's decision making, centered in New Delhi, has adversely affected Kerala's economy, successive Indian governments pursuing policies of economic liberalization that disproportionately impact agriculture and trade (Veron 84; Nair 372). In sum, Kerala in the age of corporate globalization has seen its historically advanced status in the areas of *human* development suffer from various forms of what can only be called dependency.

This focus on Kerala's links to other Souths at the time of the novel's appearance might surprise readers of the novel who (correctly) observe its investment in issues related to gender, religion, and caste. My argument, however, is not that Kerala's economic dynamic *caused* Roy to adapt formal features comparable to those used by other southern novelists. Rather, the novel, rooted in a particular place, emerges as a text representing a particular spatial politics. In Rama's terms, the novelist engages in "purely aesthetic processes, but within them lies an implicit cultural programme resulting from the conflict which an entire population is experiencing" ("Processes" 158), with the population in question here being that of southern India. The novel's goal may be to achieve verisimilitude regarding a particular southern Indian experience, but the important point here is that this verisimilitude manifests itself in the novel's form, not just in its characters and plot.

Indeed, the novel's epigraph quotes John Berger: "Never again will a single story be told as though it's the only one," pithily summarizing the ideology of the novel's form. The Berger quotation suggests from the outset that the narrative stands in opposition to a monolithic historiography, warning the reader that it will be concerned with local questions and alternative histories. Thus, the novel fractures chronology in such a way that the reader cannot be fooled into thinking that the story it tells is a monolithic narrative.

Deaths are a prominent theme in Roy's novel, but while deaths would normally appear toward the end of a linear narrative, *The God of Small Things* spreads them throughout the text, beginning in the opening pages with a brief, decontextualized description of the death of Sophie Mol (6–7), which prefigures the event that will form the pivot of the novel, causing the collapse of the Ipse family line. The actual circumstances leading up to Sophie Mol's death, however, are not related until chapter 13, over two thirds of the way through the novel. Between these two chapters, the reader encounters small fragments of information: who Sophie Mol is, what she represents to the Ayemenem family, what sort of an interfamilial and intercultural dynamic she walks into, and how local conflicts play a role in her destruction. By beginning with a reference to death, the novel repeats the inversion found in Fuentes's *The Death of Artemio Cruz,* leaving little doubt that what follows will not be a story like *David Copperfield,* beginning with the hero's birth—such a linear narrative is the kind that can be told "as though it's the only one." Significantly, Sophie Mol's death, in spite of contextual factors, is a pure accident, even though it is the hinge upon which the narrative line turns. This accidental status further reinforces the novelistic structure's position against a linear, causal view of history, causality challenged by the circumstantial nature of the event that finally brings down the crumbling edifice of the family's social position.

Almost everything that will happen in *The God of Small Things* is referred to in its first thirty pages, but without elaboration of context or explanation. Typical of the novel's narrative strategy is the way it handles another death, that of Ammu. Although she is a main character, her death is mentioned as though it were an afterthought in the middle of the novel (154). Only later are the circumstances of her humiliation and exile described in more detail. The novel's last scenes take place while she is still alive, bidding her son Esthappen farewell for the last time in the penultimate chapter and then making secretive love with Velutha in the final pages. Again, this typifies the way time operates here, the narration hopping back and forth from the 1960s to the 1990s, following the characters from Kerala to Bengal to Oxford to the United States. Brief chapters commonly move among all of these spaces and times within just a few pages. As a result, the reader cannot escape the conclusion that the scene's events bear little or no causal relationship to what comes before or after them.

This same historiographical ideology inheres in the theme of the family's decline and disintegration, so prominent in the novel's events. A climactic scene toward the end of chapter 13—the chapter in which the novel's most important events unfold—illustrates this dynamic through the reaction of Mammachi, the matriarch, when she is confronted with the reality of her daughter's love affair with Velutha, a Marxist and a Paravan. When Velutha's father comes to Mammachi to tell her what is going on, she spends several moments vividly imagining their physical relationship, bringing herself to the verge of vomiting before her thoughts circle to the fate of the family line: "She [Ammu] had defiled generations of breeding (The Little Blessed One, blessed personally by the Patriarch of Antioch, an Imperial Entomologist, a Rhodes Scholar from Oxford) and brought the family to its knees. For generations to come, *forever* now people would point at them at weddings and funerals. At baptisms and birthday parties. They'd nudge and whisper. It was all finished now" (244, emphasis in original). Mammachi's innermost thoughts at this crucial moment turn instinctively to official occasions, like baptisms and weddings, when the family and its social position will be on display before the community. But in the aftermath of the revelation of Ammu's love affair with Velutha and the drowning of Sophie Mol, Mammachi's mental projections do not go far enough. Not only does the family lose its reputation; it breaks into pieces and is scattered around the globe. Esthappen is sent to live with his father, who eventually abandons him to immigrate to Australia. Rahel bounces from boarding school to boarding school, eventually marrying an American and living a brief, unhappy life in the United States before returning to Ayemenem. Chacko immigrates to Canada. Ammu dies. As in both *One Hundred Years of Solitude* and *All That's Left to You,* family history here stands in for larger questions of national and subnational autonomy and independence.

The patterns that the family's migrations and immigrations take also reinforce the theme of history as multiple, particular, and local, even as they establish spatial inequalities as foundational to the text's ideology of history. All of the characters mentioned in the previous paragraph try to escape their personal situation by going to the industrialized West, except for Ammu, who simply dies, and Esthappen, who stops talking. These personal conclusions reinforce the hierarchy of spaces present throughout the novel. Both Ammu and Chacko have already attempted to escape the confines of family life in Ayemenem through immigration and marriage, but both have ended up having to return after failed marriages. For both, an attempt at a personal separate peace falls short, as each tries to substitute exile through marriage for the familial and subnational narratives they want nothing to do with. The particulars of the novel's various spaces are given special attention by the narrative, emphasizing the politics of the synchronic in the face of the novel's diachronic disordering. History is not a straight line, because different spaces experience different realities; thus, the particulars of space hold a special significance for such a text. Indeed, spatial detail opens the novel, with a description of Ayemenem's summer that is in many ways reminiscent of Faulkner's scene setting at the beginning of *The Hamlet* or *As I Lay Dying*.

The theme of space as a sort of political foil to time is wonderfully illustrated in a brief passage at the beginning of the second chapter, which sets the scene for the family's road trip to Cochin. This eventful trip will lead to the family car being trapped at a Marxist labor rally; Esta being molested in a movie theater; the family walking out in the middle of *The Sound of Music* (before the ultimate Hollywood ending, which eludes the family from Kerala, with its misshapen line of history); and the reception of Chacko's English ex-wife and daughter at the airport. The chapter begins with the narrator telling us:

> … it was a skyblue day in December sixty-nine (the nineteen silent). It was the kind of time in the life of a family when something happens to nudge its hidden morality from its resting place and make it bubble to the surface and float for a while. In clear view. For everyone to see.
>
> A skyblue Plymouth, with the sun in its tailfins, sped past young rice fields and old rubber trees on its way to Cochin. Further east, in a small country with similar landscapes (jungles, rivers, rice fields, Communists), enough bombs

were being dropped to cover all of it in six inches of steel. Here however, it was peacetime and the family in the Plymouth traveled without fear or foreboding. (35, ellipsis in the original)

The reference to Vietnam seems a throwaway line at first glance, but when it is considered in the context of the novel's ideology of form, it takes on a greater significance. History is not a monolith, and no one story says everything. The political history of Vietnam is happening simultaneously with the personal history of the family from Ayemenem, and although all is peaceful in Kerala, the resemblances between the two spaces suggest that they share a lack of control over their future, given their position within the global polysystem. Here, as throughout the novel, the narrator uses such asides to establish impressionistically the geohistorical location of events in Kerala that might otherwise seem purely personal or familial. In the first chapter, for example, we are told that "Estha walked all over Ayemenem" after returning from his exile in Bengal. The narrator comments: "Some days he walked along the banks of the river that smelled of shit and pesticides bought with World Bank loans. Most of the fish had died. The ones that survived suffered from fin-rot and had broken out in boils" (14).

It is as typical of *The God of Small Things* as of the other novels examined in this chapter that the story's concern with seemingly personal issues (in this case gender, sexuality, love, and identity) are interwoven with national politics as a way of establishing the narrative's geohistorical ramifications. For example, Ammu gives birth to the twins during a decisive period in India's war with China in the early 1960s (40) and then leaves her husband to return to Kerala at the outbreak of war with Pakistan. The narrative also includes a straightforward description of the history of Keralite Marxism (64) and of the Naxalite revolt in Bengal and its reverberations in Southern India. Both histories form a backdrop to the transgressive affair between Ammu and Velutha, opening up possibilities for Mammachi's and Baby Kochamma's exploiting of fear of the authorities near the end of the novel.

The interplay between love relationships and geohistorical location has already by this point been established through the novel's descriptions of the relationships between Chacko and Margaret and between Rahel and

her American husband, Larry McCaslin.[14] The description of the latter relationship is particularly illustrative of the novel's interweaving of the political
and the personal. Few details of how the two fall in love are given. What is
presented about their interpersonal relationship seems to suggest that world
politics subverts any possibility of a healthy bond. McCaslin, for example, is
confused by the faraway look in Rahel's eyes when they make love: "He was
exasperated because he didn't know what that look *meant*. He put it somewhere between indifference and despair. He didn't know that in some places,
like the country that Rahel came from, various kinds of despair competed
for primacy. And that *personal* despair could never be desperate enough. That
something happened when personal turmoil dropped by at the vast, violent,
circling, driving ridiculous, insane, unfeasible public turmoil of a nation. That
Big God howled like a hot wind, and demanded obeisance" (20, emphases
in original). This passage argues that even the most personal relationships
are affected by national histories and spatial politics. It also establishes the
narrative weight invested in the text's multiple brief references to political history. Further, it makes clear that when the novel moves the "Big God" to the
margins in order to focus on the "Small God," this is meant to emphasize
that local histories are ongoing, that they won't disappear in the face of the
processes of globalization.

Postscript

The Small Things God of Roy's novel, read in the context of Mariátegui-
tradition writing, is the spirit of local, human development, as opposed to
World Spirit. A linear and causal history, told as though it were the only history, is broken up in this instance into fragments of time and units of space,
as is also the case in Kanafani's *All That's Left to You*. The individual subject,
autonomous and complete in the bildungsroman, is split into two, as it is
in Salih's *Season of Migration to the North*. What *Season* does through paralleling Mustafa Sa'eed and the narrator, *The God of Small Things* accomplishes by
centering the novel around twins. But the presence of these twins may be
read as equal parts reaction against the unified subject of nineteenth-century
European high realism and reaction against the twins of Salman Rushdie's
Midnight's Children, arguably the major text of postcolonial Indian writing in

English. Rushdie's novel offers a pair of twins who encompass all of the subcontinent and its modern history. They are born at the moment of independence/partition, just like the twin nation-states of India and Pakistan. Their allegorical invocation of the two nations makes clear that Rushdie's is a narrative of Big Things, reading all the major events of twentieth-century India and Pakistan through the lives of two individuals. But the large historical events that break in to occupy the center of Rushdie's text are moved to the periphery by Roy, even as they maintain their important role in the text's economy. Roy's very different pair of twins suggests a later moment in Indian history and a different political geography. The Indian South has experienced the "opening" of the Indian economy to world markets and has felt the effect of federal policy that poorly understands local socioeconomic dynamics. Roy herself, looking at India from the perspective of a Keralite rather than from Rushdie's position as a Londoner, presents a novelistic vision that openly confronts monolithic, universalizing historiography. The symptoms of this vision in Roy's political writings are what lead Rashmi Varna to conclude that Roy's "remains a resolutely political understanding of postcolonial development and its moorings in class exploitation" (228). Given Varna's observation, the manifest influence of development and its discontents on the ideology of form in *The God of Small Things* is not surprising.

Roy's novel describes the ideology of its own form—and (by extension of my argument) the ideology of the form of Mariátegui-tradition narrative generally—in a passage that describes the twins stopping at a temple to watch a kathakali performance: "The Great Stories are the ones you have heard and want to hear again. The ones you can enter anywhere and inhabit comfortably. They don't deceive you with thrills and trick endings. They don't surprise you with the unforeseen. They are as familiar as the house you live in. Or the smell of your lover's skin. You know how they end, yet you listen as though you don't. In the way that although you know you will die, you live as though you won't" (218). This unusually expository passage expresses quite clearly and poetically the claims inhering in narrative strategies that employ the poetics of peripheralization. As a manifesto, its claims would include the notions that stories are of value, that their local and regional character gives them their power, and that they are not linear or invested in monolithic lines of development. When read together with novels from Sudan and Palestine, or with criticism from Mariátegui-tradition writers, this passage makes clear that the poetics of peripheralization are about competing histories as much as they are about aesthetics.

Chapter Four

The Poetics of Peripheralization, Part 2

Absalom, Absalom! *as Revisionist Historiography*

Faulkner and Other Souths

William Faulkner's relationship to writers of the Global South has been the subject of a recent burst of innovative scrutiny. While Faulkner's inspiration of Latin American writers (Juan Carlos Onetti, Gabriel García Márquez, Carlos Fuentes, Mario Vargas Llosa, Edouard Glissant, Juan Rulfo, and José Revueltas, among many others) has been discussed and dissected by critics for decades, recent cutting-edge criticism has broken new ground, complicating the discourse of literary influence and turning the focus back onto Faulkner's work, in light of new developments in postcolonial theory and Latin American cultural studies.[1] A great deal of this new criticism has focused on Faulkner's magnum opus, *Absalom, Absalom!,* paying special attention to a scene in which the character Thomas Sutpen, around whom the novel revolves, travels to Haiti, makes money, puts down a revolt on a plantation, and starts a family that he eventually leaves behind under murky circumstances. Although this entire Haiti sequence is described quickly and extremely incompletely, its ramifications affect developments throughout the novel; its germinal role thus justifies the impressive body of recent criticism that has been reenvisioning Faulkner's place in the American literary landscape.

This trend in Faulkner studies and comparative literature has read the Mississippian as part of a larger hemispheric literature, in which similarities and transnational influences justify reading the works of the two Americas as though they belonged to one canon.[2] It would be petty indeed not to acknowledge the great contribution made by these new comparative, Caribbean-inflected readings of Faulkner, which have greatly informed my own work. At the same time, my problem with this scholarly discourse is that, by refusing to go beyond the Americas, it has insufficiently acknowledged what makes Faulkner a *Southern* writer in the global sense of the term.[3] By bringing other regions of the Global South into the discussion, comparative analyses of U.S. Southern culture must confront material questions relating to colonial economy and spatial/regional inequalities that determined so much of Faulkner's vision. These points of comparison connect Faulkner to the *Global* South, and without acknowledging them sufficiently, comparative criticism too easily lapses into readings that simply juxtapose Faulkner and a Latin American novelist. If such comparative study does not emphasize the two authors' historical contexts, the inadvertent result can be creating the impression that the United States, on the one hand, and Peru, Colombia, or Martinique, on the other, are equal worlds with equal socioeconomic realities. If strictly literary studies do not necessarily manufacture this false impression, they certainly do nothing to subvert it. Proactively circumventing such an erroneous impression seems important to me at this moment in cultural criticism. Thus, I would argue for emphases on the commonality of *Souths,* rather than on commonality within the Americas. Whereas the Americas emphasis highlights geography (in the traditional sense of the term), the Souths emphasis puts in relief the political economy of geography. To parallel Faulkner's South and the Other South, the critic must leave the Western hemisphere.

It is important, then, to acknowledge Faulkner's role in Arab writing, especially in the 1960s.[4] Not long before *All That's Left to You* appeared in Arabic, Kanafani's fellow Palestinian novelist Jabra Ibrahim Jabra published a celebrated translation of *The Sound and the Fury* into Arabic. As interest in Faulkner's project grew among Arab writers, Michael Millgate's classic study of Faulkner was translated by noted Jordanian author and critic Ghalab Halasa. In a sense, these developments represented the Arab Mashriq catching up with the Maghreb in Faulkner literacy, for the latter region had already witnessed the mature development of Algerian novelist, playwright, and critic Kateb Yacine, whose novels had earned him the nickname the "Arab Faulkner." In Kanafani's immediate milieu, however, the translations by Jabra and Halasa suggest that the period between Kanafani's publication of *Men in the Sun* and his second novel, *All That's Left to You,* was characterized by heightened awareness of Faulkner's work and increased access to writings by and about Faulkner in the Arabic-speaking world. In light of this history, it should have come as no surprise when literary critic Muhammad Siddiq discovered a remark Kanafani made in an interview the author gave shortly before *All That's Left to You* was published: "Last night I finished writing my new novel, and when I lay the pen down and got up to leave the room, something strange happened. Willy Faulkner was standing there shaking my hand in congratulation" (Siddiq 38).[5]

The mere fact of Kanafani's homage to Faulkner is not as interesting as how little his discovery of the Mississippian changed his aesthetic strategies. Indeed, his first novel, *Men in the Sun,* employs an ideology of form that is absolutely comparable to that of *All That's Left to You,* as Said's remarks, discussed in the previous chapter, make clear. Kanafani's discovery of Faulkner did not reveal new strategies to him, as much as it reinforced the aesthetic choices he had already been making, giving him a new and valuable perspective on what he was doing. At a level deeper than influence, similarities of socioeconomic context, as reflected in aesthetic choices, link the two writers. Indeed, this connection—between material culture and ideology of form—explains a phenomenon rarely commented upon in studies linking Faulkner with Latin American narrative: many Latin American writers' explicit denial of the Mississippian's influence.[6]

Indeed, Roy herself falls into the category of postcolonial novelists often linked to Faulkner who claim not to have read him. Comparisons between Faulkner's project and those of many earlier Indian writers in English offer a partial explanation for Roy's familiarity with certain narrative strategies and conceptual issues. The greatest novelist of the Indian South, R. K. Narayan, employs a politics of space comparable to Faulkner's in his creation of the fictional land of Malgudi, similar to Faulkner's Yowknapatawpha, rooted in the realities of his native Tamil Nadu and forming the setting for a series of novels published over his long career. Anita Desai seems to be rewriting *The Sound and the Fury* at times in her novel *Clear Light of Day*, whose ideology of form quite directly confronts Euro-American modernist values. Finally, Salman Rushdie, by translating Gabriel García Márquez's style into the South Asian context, also indirectly translates aspects of Faulkner. All of these writings are undoubtedly familiar to Roy, whether she has read Faulkner or not. In fact, her not having read Faulkner only reinforces the notion that critically perceived similarities in style arise from something other than direct influence.[7] Specifically, this "something else," I believe, is the connection both writers make between the ideology of their form and the material conditions of the spaces from which they write. Indeed, Roy has made a very similar claim herself, even while denying any direct knowledge of Faulkner's work: "Yes, I'm compared to Faulkner the most. But I've never read Faulkner before! So I can't say anything about him. I have, however, read some other writers from the American South—Mark Twain, Harper S. Lee—and I think that perhaps there's an infusion or intrusion of landscape in their literature that might be similar to mine. This comparison is not that lazy, because it's natural that writers from outside urban areas share an environment that is not man-made and is changed by winds and rivers and rain" (Jana). The two writers' styles are reminiscent of one another, in other words, because both are Southern. In Roy's reading of this term, its meaning is primarily geographical, but my interpretation adds to geography connotations of an experience with the colonial economy and unequal economic development.

By moving the comparative and postcolonial reading of Faulkner outside of the Americas and into other Souths, the relationship between the novels' forms and their material conditions comes into sharper focus, allowing for a more definitive challenge to the older notion that similarities in form are the result of writers from other Souths reading Faulkner and aping his formal strategies. This may indeed be the case for some writers; it is impossible for the literary critic to know. But even if a writer acknowledges directly borrowing a strategy from Faulkner, the critic must confront what it is about this borrowed strategy that speaks to the new local context into which it is being imported. In any case, whether the Faulknerlike writer has read Faulkner or not, the critic must look to the relationship between individual aesthetic choices and aspirations stemming from conflicts that an entire population is experiencing.

A reconsideration of the literature treating Faulkner's relationship with Latin American novelists confirms the importance of the ideology of form. For example, Gabriel García Márquez states: "I think it is the method. The Faulknerian method is very effective for telling about the Latin American reality. Unconsciously, this is what we discovered in Faulkner. That is to say, we were living this reality and we wanted to tell about it and we knew that the European method wouldn't work and neither would the traditional Spanish one and all of a sudden we found that the Faulknerian method is extremely well suited for telling this reality" (qtd. in Willis 100). Method, I believe, here relates to narrative structure. Specifically, a certain attitude toward narrative is shared by Faulkner, dependency theorists, Samir Amin, Kanafani, Salih, Roy, and the types of Latin American novelists García Márquez has in mind. Again, these writers' ideology of form rejects the notion of history as progress. While this often cited statement by García Márquez has sometimes been interpreted to refer to Faulkner's "modernist" style, the Colombian actually states that he is talking about a relationship between "method" and "this reality" that "we were living." In other words, he connects literary form and material conditions, arguing for a kind of experimental neorealism, for a literary phenomenon invested in verisimilitude, more than for a borrowing of modernism's fascination with the aesthetic realm. Borrowing this structure from Faulkner proves valuable for certain writers from the Global South because of parallels in their mutual experiences with colonial economies and unequal economic development, as these phenomena affect daily life, social conditions, political institutions, and personal relationships.

I have argued for broad similarities among the material conditions produced by the colonial economy and the postcolonial struggle with unequal economic development in various spaces throughout the Global South. That Faulkner's South participated in highly comparable material conditions during the time he was writing is another basic assertion of this book. Earlier, I argued that these material histories have played a role in many important postcolonial literary narratives of the Global South. Here I assert that these histories also play a role in *Faulkner's* fiction, taking the recently celebrated example of *Absalom, Absalom!* and its Caribbean connection as my prime example.

The Ideology of Faulkner's Form

José Carlos Mariátegui's description of the structure of history as encompassing "stages that are not entirely linear in their development" not only exemplifies the long trajectory of thinking in the Global South that challenges the Hegelian—and Eurocentric—association of history with linear, causal progress but might also be productively compared to William Faulkner's novelistic attacks on linearity. I noted in chapter 3 that thinkers like Mariátegui necessarily view the sweep of history with less optimism than Hegel (or, for that matter, Marx), optimism that resulted in the hyperemphasis on teleology present in Hegelian historiography. A Peruvian in the 1920s, rather, surveyed history from the subject position of an individual in a geohistorical context that had been branded by the era of Spanish colonization; by the undercutting of independence and nationalism by British and American commercial interests in the nineteenth century; and by the continuing struggle with economic, political, and social unequal development in the early twentieth century. I have distinguished between the Eurocentric historian—who might think of history as a linear series of stages, causally linked with one another, evolving gradually toward an apotheosis, with Europe's material preeminence serving as a sort of culmination—and an oppositional historian—who might start from a critical view of this European preeminence. History, in other words, might not be a straight line. Euro-American colonialism does not result from natural and organic laws of cause and effect or from the grand design of a powerful and knowing prime mover. Rather, historical trajectories are multiple and must be seen from multiple points of view.

As earlier examples suggest, the novel, like history, is inevitably built on a structure, and since post-Hegelian Europe in the nineteenth century marked the pinnacle of linearity in novelistic structures as much as it did in Eurocentric historiographies, the role that coloniality might play in structure also must be addressed, particularly in the case of novels that concern history in the broadest sense. In the previous chapter, I described the poetics of peripheralization as expressing a relationship between novelistic structure (poetics) and multivocal, anti-Eurocentric histories of coloniality (historiography of the periphery). These histories are deeply invested in a broadly shared experience across the Global South that consists of formal colonization followed by a protracted postcolonial history of economic dependency and unequal development. I have described examples of this historical narrative in Latin America, the Middle East, the African subcontinent, and South Asia. Political independence came to these areas at various times, and their cultural traditions were affected by the colonial experience in distinctive ways, but the deep structure of their experience with the colonial economy is broadly similar. My argument is that this comparable material experience amounts to the collective context of entire populations, often directly influencing the production of ideas, theory, and culture in such spaces.

This relationship is manifested in the structure of the novel. The resulting narrative is fragmented, jumbling time by presenting counterintuitive beginnings and endings and multiple flashbacks, flashforwards, and jump cuts. It uses multiple perspectives to emphasize the multiplicity of histories and realities and eschews the unified subject in favor of split narrative foci. Space is emphasized as another means of subverting the unity of a monolithic temporal line of history, and the geohistorical inequalities that determine the true nature of relationships between spaces play a heightened role. Political history and political economy infiltrate the narrative through glancing but repeated references that often play determinative roles at the margins. These characteristics mark Faulkner's major fiction along with many novels of the Global South. In García Márquez's terms, these characteristics are the "method" that best expresses the "reality" of unequal development. In Angel Rama's terms, the "purely aesthetic processes" manifested in Faulkner's narrative strategy express "the conflict which an entire population is experiencing," namely, the post-Reconstruction South's encounter with spatial inequalities.

When moving from the poetics of peripheralization in the Global South to the same phenomenon in Faulkner's South, an important complication arises as a result of Faulkner's traditional categorization as a member of the Euro-American modernist canon. Indeed, it might be argued that modernist narrative is itself characterized by many of the structures listed above and that Faulkner was instead working out of what he had learned from Joseph Conrad, Ford Madox Ford, Gertrude Stein, James Joyce, and other modernist novelists and poets. This reading turns the issue back to the influential status of the European artist, from whom all others derive their methods. To counter it, the critic must distinguish between the poetics of modernism and the poetics of peripheralization. While both ideologies of form produce certain comparable narrative characteristics, they diverge in their attitude toward historiography.

The modernist's disdain for politics, materialism, localism, and region-alism stands in sharp contrast to the views of proponents and propagators of the antievolutionist postcolonial narrative. If the modernists proposed a cyclic structure as an alternative to the linearity of nineteenth-century real-ism, their cycles represented a flight from the historical as much as a revision of it. Louise B. Williams, writing of modernist historiography, delineates the characteristics of the modernist embrace of cycles cum rejection of nineteenth-century linearity: "The following ideas, which are components of cyclic theories of history, have been taken into consideration as evidence of growing cyclic views: the sense that two distinct and constant traditions existed in the past; the idea that the universal order is essentially constant; the dislike of change and belief in, and preference for, a superior permanent and timeless reality; a sense that absolute time or accurate chronology is un-important or a belief that ages with similar values are equivalent regardless of the passage of time; and a sense that ideas or occurrences in equivalent ages can be compared without anachronism even though separated by a vast amount of time" (14). Whereas the postcolonial narrative reacts to the tyranny of linearity by proposing multiple historical materialisms, the work of high modernism seeks to transcend history through an aery aesthetics. The mythic realm is seen as far more real than the material realm, the European Middle Ages viewed as a golden age when idealism and transcendence were still pos-sible (Louise B. Williams 78–89). Little reference is made to the world outside Europe and the United States, except to hold up an exotic and timeless East as an antidote (and not an alternative) to European history.

Williams's account of modernist historiography is of particular value because it emphasizes the ideology of history in modernist thinking, even if it contains limitations in its characterization of the movement. Williams focuses on five modernists—Ford Madox Ford, T. E. Hulme, D. H. Lawrence, Ezra Pound, and W. B. Yeats—revealing a distinct bias toward an English, male, and pre–World War I version of the movement, which might be complicated by the incorporation of feminist, Jewish, North American, and late modernists. At the same time, a general consensus exists in much criticism focusing on the traditional modernist canon that the fixation on form in what David Hayman has called "texts that foreground tactics and sublimate narrative content" (4) was not merely a flight from content, but a flight from material, political-economic history toward a variety of other, more spiritual solutions. Thus, Ricardo Quinones, in an account that in no way limits itself to a particular modernist moment, emphasizes the movement away from historicism as an element running throughout what he sees as (temporally) diverse stages of modernist thought. Emphasizing the importance for literary modernism of Nietzsche's concepts of *unhistorich* and *uberhistorisch,* he argues that "the goal of modernism, for the sake of which the linear time complex had first to be disrupted, [was] mythopoetic art (which is, of course, the end Nietzsche had in mind for the art of the new era), and the recovery of some sense of the self in relation to the past and to the individual's own inner being" (11). Quinones's narrative is particularly interesting because—unlike Williams—he is interested in modernism's shifts and transitions across the first half of the twentieth century. Still, he too emphasizes the cyclical as an aversion to materialist historiography. It is this sort of broad consensus that leads Fredric Jameson to declare that modernism's "ideology can be easily recognized and identified: it is first and foremost that which posits the autonomy of the aesthetic, the supreme value without which, however committed the various critics and practitioners may be to art itself and its specificities and inassimilable experiences, such commitment cannot really be identified as the ideology of the modern" (*Singular* 161).

If a consensus exists among critics writing from various points of view, and out of various disciplinary backgrounds, that much mainstream modernism foregrounds the aesthetic and evidences a particular fixation with form, this position is certainly not unanimous. In fact, critical discourses of modernism are unmistakably trending toward reopening the definitional boundaries that have confined the movement as aestheticist and ahistorical, both revisiting the canon of modernism and reinterpreting the way the movement's key figures have traditionally been read.[8] Said's reading of Yeats as a "poet of decolonization," for example, provoked a series of revisionist readings by Yeats scholars interested in engaging postcolonial theory. But Said's treatment of Yeats shows a pronounced tension—even contradiction—regarding the issue of aesthetic form's centrality in modernist thought. In an early chapter of *Culture and Imperialism,* Said includes a "Note on Modernism" that lists Yeats alongside other canonical Anglo-European high modernists who evince "the extremes of self-consciousness, discontinuity, self-referentiality, and corrosive irony, whose formal patterns we have come to recognize as the hallmarks of modernist culture" (188). When, however, he engages directly with Yeats as a poet of decolonization in a later section of the same work, he operates from an engagement with the content of the poetry, drawing analogies to the work of other nationalist poets, including Aimé Césaire, Mahmoud Darwish, and Faiz Ahmad Faiz. The implication of this contrastive treatment is that Yeats's formal characteristics carry the marks of modernist ideology and that Said must read around them in order to discover the postcolonial Yeats.[9]

Writers on literary modernism who have taken up Faulkner as their focus inevitably see modernism's attitude toward historicism and aestheticism as anything but simple; this discursive trend grows out of Faulkner's imperfect fit with the European modernist novelists who were his predecessors and stylistic interlocutors. Patrick O'Donnell, for example, argues for gleaning insight into Faulkner through the lens of postmodernism, rather than viewing him as a mainstream modernist: "In essence, discussing Faulkner in postmodernist terms means accepting the assumption that what makes his fiction powerful and timely is its capacity to resist, disrupt, or exceed both Modernism (with a capital 'M') and Faulkner's own modernism—his intended response to the perceived literary, cultural, and historical contexts of his writing" (31). O'Donnell is operating here with a working definition of modernism that diverges only slightly from that of the other critics I have cited. There is slightly more ambivalence in his view of the relationship between historicism and aestheticism in literary modernism, perhaps because reading Faulkner requires the critic to think of modernism differently: "modernist works are bound over to a formulation that promotes and subverts the attempt to create a linguistic universe" (34).

The section devoted to Faulkner in Deborah Cohn and Jon Smith's collection of essays, *Look Away! The U.S. South in New World Studies,* takes O'Donnell's characterization of the nexus between historicism and modernism in Faulkner even further. Stephanie Merrim's contribution, dealing with *Absalom, Absalom!* and several works by Jorgé Luis Borges, remarks of Faulkner's most complex novel that "by its end, [it] has activated an Aristotelian sense of history versus poetry (that is, a fragmented, local sense of events versus a panoptic view that extracts general principles)" (313). Philip Weinstein's fine contribution repeatedly invokes Jameson's pithy summary of modernism's angst in the statement, "history is what hurts." Of course, history hurts more or less and in different ways for different peoples. The overall effect of such recent comparative readings is to bring the category of the postcolonial into the Faulknerian discussion in a way that shifts the emphasis toward the historical.[10]

My opinion is that Faulkner is more strongly connected to the ideology of structure found in the work of the Global Southern novelists discussed earlier than to that emerging from the work of these critics of modernism, but a both/and rather than an either/or conclusion might accommodate the argument I am making for Faulkner's unique place among other modernists, based on the attitude toward history reflected in his fiction. I have defined such an attitude toward history as central for the poetics of peripheralization, and I believe it to also be central for Faulkner.

Absalom, Absalom! *and Narration*

If a colonial economy evolved in the U.S. South after the collapse of Reconstruction, the critic should expect this context to play a role in the personal aesthetic choices of the Southern writer. In the case of Faulkner, as with many writers of the Global South, history is equated with continuing processes of peripheralization and disruption, which in turn are better expressed through a narrative that keeps ending up back at the beginning. For this reason, the workings of the colonial economy infuse both form and content in *Absalom, Absalom!* and must be accounted for alongside questions of race, culture, and American capitalism, the more traditional emphases of socially engaged criticism of Faulkner's work.[11] Earlier criticism has naturally focused on the novel's most signifying character, Thomas Sutpen, read (by Carolyn Porter, for example) as a figure comparable to Jay Gatsby in the way both embody and critique the "American dream." I, on the other hand, am interested in the seminal role played by the colonial economy in Sutpen's "design." Geohistorical location is as determinative in the development of Sutpen's story as it is in Mignolo's analyses of critical thinking. The colonial economy also helps define the relationship among the four spaces (northern New England, western Virginia, plantation states, and the West Indies) that provide the novel's settings. Geographical relationships are defined by economic inequalities, but these inequalities are better described as questions of spatial politics, rather than as straightforward issues of socioeconomic class, as it is traditionally understood by Eurocentric Marxisms (i.e., as the tripartite division of aristocracy, bourgeoisie, and proletariat). This key underpinning of the colonial economy in the Sutpen story, along with the novel's spatial movement, takes on the force of a dominant nodal system in the novel's structure. Generally, the colonial economy plays a determinative role in the form of the narrative (without, of course, preempting the text's inevitable multiple meanings). Indeed, Sutpen's story, pieced together retrospectively by characters living decades later, is as much about narration and narrators as it is about the material history of the antebellum and Civil War periods during which it is set; the reverberations of the colonial economy in the novel's settings and plot fragments would have blunted or insignificant effect if not presented through this particular formal structure. Indeed, *Absalom, Absalom!*'s famously complicated structure, which seems to subsume every other aspect of the novel, advances a powerful argument against the presumption of Western imperialism that history equals progress. This deep structure of dependent development underpins the postcolonial Faulkner manifest in the nonlinear narrational scheme of *Absalom, Absalom!*

Quentin Compson, the teenager leaving the faded glory of his landed-gentry family to study at Harvard in the early twentieth century, serves as the center of this narration, the novel beginning and ending with him speaking to another character. Why Quentin? The novel's opening pages direct us through Rosa Coldfield to the South's fractured history and resultant economic dependency for an answer: "'Because you are going away to attend the college at Harvard they tell me,' she said. 'So I dont imagine you will ever come back here and settle down as a country lawyer in a little town like Jefferson since Northern people have already seen to it that there is little left in the South for a young man. So maybe you will enter the literary profession as so many Southern gentlemen and gentlewomen too are doing now and maybe some day you will remember this and write about it'" (5). As a potential writer, then, Quentin may be able to record the myth/history of Thomas Sutpen. But it is also crucial here that the South's economic subservience is what makes Quentin a potential writer. Plantation owner, patrician farmer, cavalier lawyer, and gentleman of commerce are no longer reliable options for the elite Southern male.

This conversation between Quentin and Rosa is actually taking place in 1909, a full forty years after Sutpen's death. While little of this forty-year period is used as a setting for events in *Absalom, Absalom!,* we know from other sources, as I have previously suggested, that this time was marked by revolution in the South's economic structure and class relationships. In part, the Southern colonial economy was a product of the old elite being replaced by a new business class, but this new class served primarily as water carriers for the magnates of the already industrialized North, and "the economy over which they presided was increasingly coming to be one of branch plants, branch banks, captive mines and chain stores" (Woodward, *Origins* 292). Thus, Woodward bases his "colonial economy" argument on the emergence of a "comprador bourgeoisie," a group that saw its interests as lying with the outside colonial economic establishment.[12] The idea of such external orientation takes on cultural resonance in this early passage dealing with Quentin's exile to Harvard. Although *Absalom, Absalom!* does not mention this detail, *The Sound and the Fury* relates that the Compsons had to sell part of their land holdings in order to finance Quentin's enrollment. Again, an external orientation, in both the socioeconomic and the cultural spheres, determines the Compsons' life choices.

While Rosa's economic motive for implicating Quentin in the Sutpen story seems at first glance like an aside, significantly, Quentin's educational dependency on the East Coast establishment connects the *telling* of Sutpen's story to the colonial economy from the beginning of the narrative. The significance of Quentin's placement directs our attention to the novel's spatial politics as much as to the South's socioeconomic class structure. The power dynamic invoked by the novel's narrational grid is one of characters moving from the provinces toward the core, just as the main characters in Roy's novel move away from Kerala. Shreve McCannon, Quentin's Harvard roommate, is even further removed from Sutpen, but he too can be understood as a figure who reinforces the relationship between economic dependency and narration. A critical debate extending all the way back to Cleanth Brooks exists between scholars who read Shreve as an uncomprehending figure, on the basis that Sutpen's story is too uniquely Southern for him to grasp, and those who, without being able to explain why the story would so captivate the Canadian, acknowledge textual evidence suggesting a spiritual connection of some type between the two students. For example:

> The two of them not moving except to breathe, both young, both born within the same year: the one in Alberta, the other in Mississippi; born half a continent apart yet joined, connected after a fashion in a sort of geographical transubstantiation by that Continental Trough, that River which runs not only through the physical land of which it is the geological umbilical, not only runs through the spiritual lives of the beings within its scope, but is very Environment itself which laughs at degrees of latitude and temperature, though some of these beings, like Shreve, have never seen it—the two of them, who four months ago had never laid eyes on one another yet who since had slept in the same room and eaten side by side of the same food and used the same books from which to prepare to recite in the same freshman courses. (208)

I find Susan Willis, who first raised the issue of dependency theory's relationship to Faulkner, most convincing in her argument that Canada's peripheral status best explains Shreve's position in the novel. Both the Canadian and the Southerner have responded to their dependency situations by attending an elite Northern U.S. university (Willis 97). Both the post-Reconstruction South and Canada are nearer to the East Coast, geographically and in terms of economic development and industrialization, than are the poorer countries of the hemispheric South. In this sense, they can be seen as regions of what

Immanuel Wallerstein (in an amendment of dependency theory's binarism) calls the "semi-periphery." The novel leaves the reader in the dark as to why Shreve and Quentin are equally enthralled by Sutpen. While their connections to distinct spaces within the semiperiphery provides one explanation for why they find Sutpen's maniacal attack on peripheralization fascinating, in spite of their mutually exclusive regional backgrounds, in any case, Shreve's placement should call our attention back to narrative, since he serves mainly as a facilitator of the narration. The entire discussion of his relationship to Quentin only reinforces the politically charged nature of the process of narration in a situation where "telling about the South is, invariably, to tell against the North" (Romine 177).

The narrative structure of *Absalom, Absalom!* is made nonlinear through its several beginnings. The most literal one is Quentin's trip to Rosa Coldfield's, but there are also the several beginnings of Sutpen's story: the trip down from Appalachia; the affront at the door of the Tidewater Plantation; and, most significantly, the journey to Haiti. The repetition of beginnings is one of the ways that the novel's narrative structure undercuts linearity and progressivism. The reader never really advances to another stage, but rather always moves forward to yet another beginning. Similarly, the novel's endings do not offer any sort of culmination. The final exchange between Quentin and Shreve is potentially suggestive, but still ambiguous.

Shreve's thesis that people like Jim Bond, mixed-race Sutpens, will "conquer the western hemisphere" is prima facie a reference to Thomas Sutpen's obsession with patrilineality, which Sutpen himself desires to center in White privilege. But as Edouard Glissant astutely observes about the novel as a whole, "All this questioning about blood and race would be pointless if we did not think that Faulkner really meant something other than race, despite the overriding importance of race to … the South" (73). In my reading, the "something other than race" is the linear and monologic historiography undercut by the novel. Sutpen's obsession with his own bloodline invokes an obsession with linear progressivism, with a uniquely Southern "design." Shreve does not presume that history is linear or that such a Sutpenesque design is viable.

Quentin's last words, at the end of the novel, are even more ambiguous. As Richard Godden and others have pointed out, the very repetition of the claim

"I dont hate it!" has the effect of reversing its meaning. The only thing that is clear in the last sentence is that Quentin's words are being panted "in the cold air, the iron New England dark" (303). The suggestion here is that Quentin repeats "I dont hate it" almost as if to convince himself, the emphasis on setting taking us back to Rosa's remark that he might become a writer and write about Sutpen. But Rosa's suggestion directly connects becoming a writer with the economic colonization of the South. In this formulation, becoming a writer means becoming integrated into a modern, economically postcolonial system. The need to historicize in a linear, progressivist mode thus means, for Quentin, to "hate the South" at some level. For Quentin to insist "I dont" again and again is for him to resist becoming a Northern-based Sutpen chronicler, and the novel thus begins and ends by juxtaposing Quentin's spatial displacement to the North with his position as narrator.

Absalom, Absalom! *and History*

If the narrative structure exemplified in many postcolonial narratives, and in the historiography of Mariátegui-tradition thinkers, is reflected in Faulkner's vision of the post-Reconstruction South, one would expect those characteristics listed at the beginning of this chapter as inhering in the poetics of peripheralization to manifest in *Absalom, Absalom!* Thus far, I have emphasized the way the workings of narrative in the text undercut linearity, but this comprehensive textual attack on linearity also contains the other main narrative features of the poetics of peripheralization. The politics of space are narrated in the complex cartography of settings, which are described so as to emphasize spatioeconomic inequalities. The self-contained individual subject of Sutpen is systematically dismantled by the trajectory of the narrative. Finally, this all plays out against a backdrop that continually reminds the reader of the large wind of subnational politics, with its Big God narratives of colonialism, war, and economic development.

Primary among these interrelated features is the politics of space, never far from the center of the Faulkner text. In *Absalom, Absalom!* the narrative draws us back into a regional and material politics of space. I have stated that the colonial economy, for example, infuses the major aspects of *Absalom, Absalom!,* citing the nonlinear visions of dependency theorists, boom writers, and Ghassan Kanafani to explain its narrative arrangement. Furthermore, if Rosa Coldfield's opening charge to Quentin establishes the narration's Mariáteguian revisionism, Thomas Sutpen's murky primal experiences with colonial economies ground the plot in the same politics of space.

It is through spatial politics that *Absalom, Absalom!* can be understood as a narrative of peripheralization. Issues of peripheralization are seminal to the novel's story line, just as they are to the form its narrative takes. Sutpen's story begins with his primal awareness of the marginalization of the Appalachian region in which he has spent his childhood. His story begins with his first cognizance of Appalachia's status as periphery, thus marking dependent economic relationships as crucial, important (in narratological terms) for *histoire* as much as for *récit*. This awareness of unequal development comes to him when his family moves from the western hills to the flat plantation country of Virginia:

> The earth, the world, rising about them and flowing past as if the cart moved on a treadmill ... bringing into and then removing from their sober static country astonishment the strange faces and places, both faces and places—doggeries and taverns now become hamlets, hamlets now become villages, villages now towns and the country flattened out now with good roads and fields and niggers working in the fields while white men sat fine horses and watched them, and more fine horses and men in fine clothes, with a different look in the face from mountain men in the taverns where the old man was not even allowed to come in by the front door and from which his mountain drinking manners got him ejected before he would have time to get drunk good. (182–83)

Such a passage's heavy *geographic* emphasis on spatial and physical characteristics packs an *economic* thrust, for the young Thomas Sutpen learns about class difference and unequal development through what he sees in a new physical space. No distinction is made in this description between economic inequality and spatial dynamics. Rather, unequal development expresses itself in such a passage explicitly in terms of regional difference. For Sutpen, the progression from tavern to hamlet to village to town is experienced as a socioeconomic ascent, and he begins for the first time to realize that "there was a difference between white men and white men" (183). The unequal positions of Appalachia and the plantation South are made even more clear when Sutpen first sees the plantation owner, noting that "the man who owned all the land and the niggers and apparently the white men who superintended the work, lived in the biggest house he had ever seen and spent most of the afternoon … in a barrel stave hammock between two trees, with his shoes off and a nigger who wore every day better clothes than he or his father and sisters had ever owned and ever expected to, who did nothing else but fan him and bring him drinks" (184). This owner and his liveried slave will eventually be responsible for the affront at the door of the plantation house, which marks the culmination of the class consciousness growing in the young Sutpen. But it is important that the language in both these passages allows us to understand this new awareness explicitly in terms of spatial inequalities, as much as in those of class qua class. In the first passage, the change in physical geography connotes a change in level of economic comfort; in the second passage, Sutpen's inability to see the house slave as owned and subjugated creates the impression that this town-and-country divide is absolutely determinative. Sutpen is not merely poor; he is also displaced and coming from an economically unequally developed region. In short, this section of the novel, which leads directly to the Haiti sequence, portrays Appalachia as a periphery dependent on the flat plantation region around the Tidewater estate.

This use of geography can be productively contrasted with the geographical dimension of postcolonial readings of Yeats. Jahan Ramazani succinctly sums up this critical discussion: "Through acts of poetic imagination, Yeats seeks—as emphasized by Deane, Said, Kibberd, and George Bornstein—to reclaim a land violently possessed by the British" (41). But Faulkner's investment in territorial discourse seems less concerned with the romance of recapturing land, even if he adopts an approach in "The Bear" that is much more similar to what Ramazani describes, as Willis and others have shown. In passages like the one in which Sutpen describes his family's descent from the Appalachian hills, or the one marking Shreve and Quentin as connected through a "geographical transubstantiation," what is evoked is something closer to globalized geographies of power. The land has not been violently possessed by the metropolis in the instance of Faulkner's South. Rather, the region is caught in a network of colonialism without colonies, one that will continue to expand throughout the Cold War period. Thus, the emphasis on the landscape seems less about reclaiming (and in this we can distinguish Faulkner from the Agrarians) and more about acknowledging the marks on the land that implicate it in networks of coloniality.

When Sutpen is insulted at the door of the Tidewater plantation, he invents an elaborate plan (which he repeatedly refers to as his "design"), the first stage of which involves going to the West Indies and returning rich. This move, with its regularly repeated economic motive, creates yet another space to add to the novel's complex cartography.[13] The place he travels to is "the half-way point between what we call jungle and what we call civilization, halfway between the dark inscrutable continent from which the black blood, the black bones and flesh and thinking and remembering and hopes and desires, was ravished by violence, and the cold known land to which it was doomed" (203). The description of the West Indies and Sutpen's experience there, his success at gathering the riches he needs to execute the first part of his "design," marks it as a third space, semi-African in character and linked directly to the socio-economic system that Sutpen is fleeing.

Not only is the description of what happens in Haiti brief and vague, but the novel continually refers to its incompleteness.[14] Thus, Sutpen simply declares that he "went to the West Indies," leading to the following narrative editorializing (probably belonging to Grandfather Compson, but perhaps to Quentin): "Not how he managed to find where the West Indies were nor where ships departed from to go there, nor how he got to where the ships were and got in one nor how he liked the sea nor about the hardships of a sailor's life, and it must have been hardship indeed for him, a boy of fourteen or fifteen" (193). These few lines say much about the characteristics of the poetics of peripheralization and their role in the novel. Clearly, they concern the gaps in the linear, causal narrative of history. The space of the West Indies hovers above the reconstructed narrative, supplying a cohesion that temporality cannot. The details of the trip are missing because such concrete aspects of Sutpen's Haiti adventure are only important as he is having the experience itself. Before and after the trip, Sutpen and the narrators of his story work together to conceal the historical dynamics of the colonial economy that enriches him while he is in the West Indies.

Prior to the trip, the West Indies' existence for Sutpen is strictly textual: "I asked him if it were true, if what he had read us about the men who got rich in the West Indies were true. 'Why not?' he answered, starting back. 'Didn't you hear me read it from the book?'—'How do I know that what you read was in the book?' I said. I was that green, that countrified, you see" (196). Once Sutpen has returned to the U.S. plantation region, the West Indies again reverts to a cognitive construction; many facts about it do not add up (for example, Haitian independence, and the end of slavery, came two decades before Sutpen's trip), and many mysteries remain, principally the ethnicity of Sutpen's wife and the circumstances of his repudiation of her.

Still, enough exists in the text to classify the West Indies as another periphery. Sutpen gets rich there, as poor Whites from the metropolis inevitably did. The plantation system, sugarcane in particular, is the engine of the West Indies' colonial economy, and the slave population is seen as more repressed and more in touch with its African roots. For example, the slaves there practice tribal religion, leaving Voodoo artifacts scattered about before attacking the plantation owner. In its Africanness, its physical location, and most of all its enrichment of Sutpen, the West Indies plays the role of a second periphery—alongside Appalachia—compared to the U.S. plantation South. Kutzinski's reading of Sutpen's trip to Haiti claims at one point that "in the novel, the 'South' is part of the Caribbean, not vice versa" (61), but this formulation too easily dismisses the spatial inequalities upon which the novel insists. Even readings that focus on the critique of capitalism embodied by Sutpen's rise and fall fail to elaborate these spatial inequalities, rooted in colonialism's political economy and best understood via its elaboration by Arab and Latin American intellectuals.

Sutpen's end comes as a direct consequence of his obsessive White, male, linear patrilineality. From his viewpoint, the quest for a son, for the continuation of his line, is an extension of the rags-to-riches saga he envisions for himself. A son would mean that death cannot inhibit his continued progress.

The conflict between Henry and Bon seems to have left Sutpen without a son, and his quest for a new one leads to his death at the hands of Wash Jones after he impregnates Wash's granddaughter and then abandons their baby at birth when he discovers she is a girl.

All of these events play out against the background of the end of the Civil War and the subsequent economic ruin of Sutpen's Hundred. Along with references to colonial rule in Haiti and the collapse of the Southern economy during Quentin's time, this backdrop suggests the same investment in historical materialism and a subnational political narrative that is played out in *The God of Small Things.* In *Absalom, Absalom!* Sutpen's story comes to suggest to Quentin, Mr. Compson, Rosa, and Shreve that Sutpen's desire to become a self-made man and establish a patrilineal line was truly futile, even in its very conception of history as progress. A certain acceptance of the inevitability of Sutpen's destruction manifests itself, for example, in a lack of questioning of his patriarchal assumptions. (There is no reason, for example, why Rosa might not provide him with the son he wants simply because she had a daughter the first time she conceived.)

The narrators tempt the reader to view Sutpen's end at the hands of Wash Jones—a disenfranchised poor White whom Sutpen will not allow past the scuppernong arbor, just as the Tidewater plantation owner's house slave would not receive young Sutpen at the front door—as an almost mythic return to origins. Thus, the end of Sutpen's design reflects its beginnings; no "progress" has taken place. His murder is described with typical indirectness and uncertainty as Quentin reconstructs it for Shreve: "Sutpen... said, sudden and sharp: 'Stand back. Don't you touch me' only he... answered it: 'I'm going to tech you, Kernel' and Sutpen said 'Stand back, Wash' again before the old woman heard the whip. Only there were two blows with the whip; they found the two welts on Wash's face that night. Maybe the two blows even knocked him down; maybe it was while he was getting up that he put his hands on the scythe—" (231). In fact, Shreve—and presumably most readers—does not understand that Wash has actually killed Sutpen until the end of the chapter, when a posse of Jefferson's town leaders comes out to Wash's cabin to arrest him, and the poor White sharecropper is described as a veritable visual replica of the grim reaper: "Only he was running toward them all, de Spain said, running into the lanterns so that now they could see the scythe raised above his head; they could see his face, his eyes too, as he ran with the scythe above his head, straight into the lanterns and the gun barrels, making no sound, no outcry while de Spain ran backward before him, saying, 'Jones! Stop! Stop, or I'll kill you. Jones! Jones! JONES!'" (234). As much as Wash Jones seems in this passage like a character out of mythology, returning to punish Sutpen for committing against others the offenses that were once visited upon him, we are dealing with no myth here. Rather, the story of Sutpen's life ends as a narrative that challenges teleological history by reading history as dependent development. This is why the story of Sutpen's ascent begins with his benefiting from Haiti's colonial economy; for this reason, Quentin claims that his grandfather insisted that Sutpen himself, in narrating his story, "stop and back up and start over again with at least some regard for cause and effect even if none for logical sequence and continuity" (199).

In a pattern highly comparable to that of Salih's *Season of Migration to the North,* the circularity of Sutpen's story might suggest a mythic deep structure to a critic such as Northrop Frye, for whom the deep structure of myth is circularity, in contradistinction to the linear structure of history. One traditional view of Faulkner's narrative sees cycles like the Sutpen saga as enacting a connection with high modernism's interest in the classical or mythic realm as a counterpoint to the random incoherence of modern life, the opposition of transcendence to materiality. But André Bleikasten warns against such a reading of the novel: "Even *Absalom, Absalom!*, despite its ceaseless exposure and questioning of narrative practices, implies a realistic frame of reference, and its ultimate stake is nothing less than History" (85). More interesting to my mind than the possible link between repetition and modernist aestheticism is the way the repeated beginnings purposely suggest circularity in the plot as a structural critique of progressivism, reinforcing the novel's engagement with the political economies of space and colonialism. Here the parallel between Wash and young Sutpen reminds us that history has not progressed.

Both these components of *Absalom, Absalom!* can be related in turn to dependency theory's critique of the monolithic historiography of the industrialized core. This narrative subversion of telos is further reinforced by the plot's presentation of Sutpen as obsessed with, but ultimately frustrated by, his own patrilineal line. Subverting telos (or teleopoiesis, as Spivak and Derrida would call it) is part of the narrative's attack on linearity. Sutpen comes to an end in a scene that splits him in two by twinning him with Wash Jones, who experiences at Sutpen's hands the same insult that began Sutpen's career. Hereafter, the center of the narrative will not be Sutpen but Quentin, who splits the central character of the novel even as his own identity is split by Shreve, his conarrator. And at all times, indications of a political-economic unconscious—reminiscent of the political economy surrounding the narratives analyzed in chapter 3—lurk at the margins of what would otherwise seem a mythic story of a tragic individual.

Sutpen and C. L. R. James's Haiti

When C. L. R. James, a contemporary of both Faulkner and Mariátegui, wrote his classic history of the Toussaint L'Ouverture revolution in Haiti, he explicitly stated that his goal was to reenvision the Eurocentric histories that had existed up until that point. *The Black Jacobins* was first published only two years after *Absalom, Absalom!* When it was reissued in the 1960s, James noted, "Writers on the West Indies always relate them to their approximation to Britain, France, Spain and America, that is to say, to Western civilization, never in relation to their own history" (vii). Originally writing in the 1930s, James examined history as a contemporary of Mariátegui and Fernando Ortíz. In his later statement of his intentions as a historian, quoted above, his similarities with the ideological vision of the Mariátegui tradition manifest themselves. Like the Arielismo of Rodó, he sees the West Indies' "own history" as distinct from that of "Western civilization," and he believes this distinction to have direct significance for the purposes of intellectual production. But his analysis of Afro-Caribbean agency, which informs his reading of the Toussaint L'Ouverture revolution, shows him to be reading history with a vision that goes beyond Rodó to participate directly in Mariátegui-tradition historical materialist revisionism. Colonization for James was driven by the twin engines of capitalism and White supremacy, and part of the project of correcting the historical record for him was to expose this two-headed animal's role in the ravaging of West Indian society.

James's historiographic agenda is relevant to the discussions surrounding the Haiti episode in *Absalom, Absalom!* The most striking overlap between Faulkner's West Indies episode and James's history comes out of a passage in which James (surely without having Sutpen in mind) describes the Faulknerian protagonist:

> From the underworld of two continents they came, Frenchmen and Spaniards, Maltese, Italians, Portuguese and Americans. For whatever a man's origin, record or character here his white skin made him a person of quality and rejected or failure in their country flocked to San Domingo, where consideration flowed at so cheap a price, money flowed and opportunities of debauchery abounded.
>
> No small white was a servant; no white man did any work that he could get a Negro to do for him. (33)

The point of contact between James and Faulkner emerges ironically from *Absalom, Absalom!*'s most famous historical "mistake," sending Sutpen to Haiti after slavery had already been abolished there. While he may have been confused about the exact dates of the Haitian Revolution, however, it seems clear that Faulkner was in no way mistaken about the role White privilege played in the colonial economy, nor was he confused about the spatial trajectory that would have been necessary for Sutpen to go from subaltern to elite. If Sutpen repeats over and over again that he knows nothing of the West Indies except that people who go there become rich, his narrative emphasizes the simple yet crucial interplay between race and the colonial economy that was foundational to the regional history—and the spatial inequalities—that shapes this important first stage of his design.

In James's reading of prerevolutionary conditions on the island, race and the colonial economy go hand in hand, and any discussion of the former without mention of the latter is misdirected at best. His reading of racial identity is enabled, in other words, by his commitment to historical materialism. In this sense, he can be seen as a foundational figure in an Afro-Caribbean intellectual tradition that parallels and even directly participates in the Mariátegui tradition, with Walter Rodney particularly important here because he simultaneously acknowledges a debt to James, a commitment to historical materialism, and a commitment to the dependency model.[15]

Edouard Glissant, another important Afro-Caribbean intellectual, published a book-length essay on Faulkner, taking a particular interest in *Absalom, Absalom!*, that was one of the key factors in provoking a reassessment of Faulkner through a postcolonial lens. In some ways, Glissant must be separated out from the Mariátegui-tradition strain so prevalent in the work of James and Rodney. Indeed, Paget Henry's history of Afro-Caribbean thought categorizes Glissant as a member of the "poeticist" camp, as opposed to the more dominant "historicist" strain in Afro-Caribbean philosophy (6). Still, it is possible to exaggerate Glissant's investment in the poeticist/linguistic deconstructive turn, as J. Michael Dash does in a recent essay on Glissant and Faulkner that deemphasizes colonialism. While Dash's essay is accurate in its emphasis on Glissant's interest in *Absalom, Absalom!*'s obsession with origins and linearity, in spite of the impossibility of each, for Glissant, these are never merely questions of narration or style. From the opening images of *Faulkner, Mississippi* until its final lines, linearity, the baroque, and the originary are categories tied inextricably to colonialism, violence, slavery, and racism. Faulkner is repeatedly compared to two prominent French literary colonials: Saint-John Perse, the literary voice of French colonialism in the Caribbean, and Albert Camus, of French colonial Algeria. Each time the comparison is made, however, Glissant begins to parse his own analogy, finding in Faulkner a verisimilitude—tinged undoubtedly with colonialist racism—that surpasses the more predictable representations of the two French writers. Glissant's assessment of Faulkner's project has the value of emphasizing the chains of neocolonial hegemony that infused Faulkner's world by viewing the colonial economy primarily through the prism of racism. But the historicist tradition of James, Rodney, Eric Williams, and others might offer a more complete account of the source of Faulkner's heightened sensitivity to the colonial dynamic at work in all the social (and spatial) relations around him.

Faulkner's statements about racial politics in the U.S. South were scattered and wildly contradictory, ranging from progressive, in the context of his place and time, to reactionary, in his sporadic and usually tortuous attempts to defend "state's rights" as a legitimate context for solving the race problem. At various points in his career (and at various levels of sobriety), Faulkner was able both to insist on his willingness to take up arms to defend

Mississippi's right to solve the race problem on its own and to refuse W. E. B. Dubois's challenge that they debate the question publicly, on the basis that he and Dubois held the same position. Faulkner was widely regarded as a traitor to the Southern nationalist cause of White supremacy by many of his fellow Mississippians during his late career, but also as a reactionary by some national African American leaders. Both views may have been correct. Indeed, the extensive scholarship on Faulkner's engagement with the race question reflects his erratic thinking.[16] Reading Faulkner's fiction of the 1930s and early 1940s alongside James's *The Black Jacobins*, however, adds to this discussion a strategy the two shared, focused on reading hierarchies of power together with race by representing with greater complexity the continuum of racial categories (reduced in North American discourse of the color line to "black" and "white"), by understanding race in terms of the multiple shadings filled out as identities by the colonial economy and the politics of spatial inequalities.

James places emphasis on the "mulatto" community in San Domingo as a group that gained higher levels of trust, education, power, and wealth in the colonial hierarchy, thus providing a bridge for consciousness-raising among all peoples of African descent. James's emphasis on this group problematizes the ideology of White supremacy, which helped sustain the colonial power structure, because "mulattos" betray the very notion of radical separateness between the races. Their emergence proved that Caribbeans of African descent were subjected to an inferior existence because of the social conditions imposed on them by the slave system, not because of innate inferiority. White supremacy was an ideology, but it was also a socioeconomic system, and the Haitian revolt against it involved both consciousness-raising in local communities and armed resistance against structures of power.

Faulkner, writing from the subject position of a White Southerner, also represents a society in which the color line is totally fabricated, race a continuum of identities descending from a history of interwoven communities. A main plotline in the novel revolves around Charles Bon, Sutpen's son, whom he tried to abandon in the West Indies but who returns to court Sutpen's daughter before and during the Civil War. Ultimately, Bon's return causes the crumbling of the house of Sutpen and the subverting of Sutpen's design when Henry Sutpen kills Bon and abandons Sutpen's Hundred, leaving no one to inherit the estate. The conflict that brings about Bon's murder and causes Sutpen to live out his life in obsessive pursuit of a new heir centers around claims that Bon is mixed-race.[17] If the story of Charles Bon is the most widely discussed dimension of the novel that treats the issue of the U.S. South's racial continuum, the section dealing with Bon's son by an "octoroon mistress," Charles Etienne de Saint Valery Bon, also challenges the notion of a neat racial divide. The passage makes reference to the son's "sixteenth-part black blood" (158) as a source of confusion for the community. Descriptions of the events surrounding this son emphasize the tension surrounding various shades of color found in Mississippian reality and the community's insistence on trying to push these shades back into black and white. In the face of the community's regular questions about "whatever you are" (165), Bon the younger reacts by taking an unambiguously dark-skinned bride, further confusing those around him. His choice of wife and his resort to farming show his desire to create for himself a fixed place in the racial and socioeconomic hierarchy of the imagined Southern past that bears no relationship to present realities. In the end, his attempt is ironically foiled by a case of "yellow fever" (170), the very name of the disease emphasizing the ambiguity of his race identity until the end.

If Faulkner's attention to the problem of the color line continued in his fiction after *Absalom, Absalom!,* against the backdrop of changes in the U.S. South's race dynamic brought about by World War II and postwar calls for civil rights, this strategy—of representing a continuum in contrast to a clear black/white divide—continues. For example, Faulkner fills *Go Down, Moses* with racially mixed characters, including Tomey's Turl, Lucas Beauchamp, Nat Beauchamp, the Native American Sam Fathers, and the baby in "Delta Autumn." Criticism of this novel has at times focused on the positive representation of these characters as emblematic of the novel's racial ideology. Lyall Powers, for example, calls Lucas the novel's real hero because he possesses the three virtues of love, respect, and courage, whereas Ike McCaslin, the other logical candidate for a characterological center, lacks courage. Such a judgment, however, ignores the fact that Lucas disappears after the first story in the cycle, representing an attempt to impose a central focus where none exists. In fact, the notions of a textual center and of the attempt to present an exemplary racial type are both subverted by the third story, "Pantaloon in

Black," and its main character, Rider. Rider is a manual laborer whose lack of relation to any Beauchamp or McCaslin represents both a lack of participation in the racial hybridity that the other stories emphasize and a break from the novel's nodal system, which collects all its stories around the two interrelated family lines. Rider, who goes on a rampage out of grief after his young wife's death, is not integrated into Mississippian dependent capitalism like Lucas, who embraces land ownership, the accumulation of wealth, and integration into the New South. Read together—and alongside the other characters in the novel—these two represent not only the spectrum of racial identities in Mississippi but also the variety of responses to the realities of White supremacy and unequal development.

Such emphases on a race continuum work together with Faulkner's textual ideology reflecting the political economy of space, just as James's emphasis on the "mulatto" and the "small white" classes forms a component of his commitment to a Mariátegui-tradition historiography. Indeed, *Go Down, Moses* invokes a poetics of peripheralization almost as emphatically as *Absalom, Absalom!* The former's cycle-of-stories format makes it another prime example of Faulkner's episodic and nonlinear long narratives. More than perhaps any other of his novels, this work includes component parts that are unconnected, without even the thematic leitmotifs or nodal connections that hold *The Sound and the Fury* together. Over the course of the book, peripheral spaces—the hunting ground, the semiperipheries of Jefferson and Memphis, and the industrialized North (pushed to the extreme periphery of the text but nevertheless present in the appearance of the logging company, fleeting references to the Civil War, and mentions of the paternalistic Gavin Stevens's Harvard pedigree)—are carefully mapped according to their relative power relationships. Indeed, as Susan Willis has shown, this novel is one of Faulkner's most emphatic texts on the issue of the U. S. South's post-Reconstruction colonial economy.

Similarly, Sutpen's saga is about White privilege at the same time that it is about the accumulation of wealth and power against the backdrop of the colonial economy. Sutpen is so obsessed with a White male heir that he eventually gets himself killed, even though his "design" begins with using skin color to accrue wealth in a society where the black/white divide is collapsing.

His destruction at the hands of his own obsession with White patrilineality represents simultaneously the subversion of three powerful worldviews: linearity, the capitalist ideology of colonial economics, and the myth of pure whiteness.

Postscript

In chapter 1, I discussed Robert Young's preface to his study of the concept of hybridity in Europe in the nineteenth century, taking issue with the way his otherwise engaging discussion of the film *South Pacific* centers on the consciousness of the colonizer as the focus of the colonial project. The result is a reading of the film that sees an Anglo-European psycho-sexual obsession with race as foundational for not only the film's story line but, by extension, the colonial project.

One scene in *South Pacific* that goes unmentioned in Young's brief discussion suggests what is being repressed by the emphasis on certain types of postcolonialism. In it, three American soldiers corner the dashing Frenchman Emile de Becque and try to persuade him to change his mind about helping the United States on a dangerous spying mission. When they at first have no luck, a frustrated Joseph Cable resorts to impugning de Becque as selfish and irresponsible. The Frenchman's response is indignant: "I was exiled from my home and came to this island as a young man. Since that time I have asked for help from no one.... I have asked for help from no country." The Americans all nod in acceptance of his narrative of self-made manhood, as though French and other European colonies were places without systematic subjugation of the locals by the colonial economy, allowing even an exiled Frenchman a level of race privilege that guaranteed his economic success. Emile de Becque is in a position highly comparable to that of Thomas Sutpen. He is a refugee from a metropolitan social system, and he uses whiteness to enrich himself in the colonies. The difficulty in reading these texts stems from the problem of reading race without lapsing into racialism. This problem is compounded in Anglo-American criticism by a long-standing prejudice against historical materialism that turns Gramsci into an anti-Marxist proponent of cultural theory and Frantz Fanon into a proponent of racial uplift rather than Third World revolution.[18] In short, our cultural theory has an acute phobia regarding the economic. For this reason, among others, I have been arguing for an opening up of our theoretical canon to include Mariátegui-tradition thinkers from the Global South. But such an opening requires an assault on deeply entrenched truths embraced for centuries by Western metaphysics, truths that continue to play a dynamic role in the social thinking of the "world's only remaining superpower." What remains is for me to address directly the persistence of the traditions of Eurocentrism in the age of globalization.

The World, the Text, and
Eurocentric Intellectualism

The dependency theorists, who represent a significant moment in the Mariátegui tradition, looked at the economic history of colonialism and found that European colonizers had enriched their own national economies by appropriating the natural resources of the colonies and adding surplus value to them through manufacturing. Furthermore, this system of economic exploitation as understood by the *dependentistas* was left largely unchanged by neocolonial trade relations. The parallel structure in the realm of thought is pithily summed up in Edgar Quinet's formula: "The East proposes and the West disposes." The *matter* of production, history, politics, and even art may come from the Global South, but it must be refined, manufactured, processed, and theorized in the industrialized West.

This structural relationship between the "West" and the "East" is also an enduring trope in American culture and letters. Indeed, it has gone beyond trope to become an organizational force in the history of the United States as its imperial role has come to the fore. In the earliest providential historiography of English colonizers, the presumption was that White settlers in the

Americas think and have consciousness at a level not enjoyed by their adversaries. If *Moby Dick* can be taken as one beginning of the modern era in the United States, this novel's Ishmael significantly both describes and embodies this very structure for reading the world. He attempts to escape his malaise by setting sail aboard a ship owned exclusively by Anglo-American, Quaker residents of New England (86). Its crew consists of a group of captains and first, second, and third mates who are also Anglo-American. They form the management level of the *Pequod.*

The lower levels are filled by what contemporary terminology would call people of color. Ishmael makes note of this phenomenon while describing the makeup of the crew. Each mate has a harpooner for a right-hand man. The first mate's assistant is Queequeg, who also happens to be Ishmael's best friend. In an early passage of the novel, Ishmael observes his friend from the Pacific Islands in an odd ritual of getting dressed and comments that he "was a creature in a transition state, neither caterpillar nor butterfly. He was just enough civilized to show off his outlandishness in the strangest possible manner. His education was not yet completed. He was an undergraduate. If he had not been a small degree civilized, he very probably would not have troubled himself with boots at all; but then if he had not been still a savage, he never would have dreamt of getting under the bed to put them on" (46). In this passage, Ishmael associates civilization directly with knowledge, education, and thought. Thus, Queequeg's semicivilized state leads to Ishmael declaring him "an undergraduate." This metaphor suggests that civilizational and cultural differences are equivalent to levels of education—ranks on a hierarchy of knowledge and training. That Queequeg may—indeed, has—become more civilized is clear, but the passage suppresses the ultimate possibility of his becoming a fully civilized individual.

Once on board the *Pequod,* Queequeg takes up his natural position as a subject to his Anglo-American supervisor. The other two mates also have seconds from non-Anglo backgrounds. The second mate is assisted by "Tashtego, an unmixed Indian from Gay Head, the most westerly promontory of Martha's Vineyard, where there still exists the last remnant of a village of red men, which has long supplied the neighboring Island of Nantucket with many of her most daring harpooneers" (126). Rounding out the trio is Daggoo, the harpooner of the third mate, Flask. Daggoo is described by Ishmael as "a gigantic, coal-black negro-savage, with a lion-like tread" (127). Finally, Ishmael makes certain that his reader notes the racial character of the division of labor on deck by editorializing on this very phenomenon:

> As for the residue of the Pequod's company, be it said, that at the present day not one in two of the many thousand men before the mast employed in the American whale fishery, are Americans born, though pretty nearly all the officers are. Herein it is the same with the American whale fishery as with the American army and military and merchant navies, and the engineering forces employed in the construction of the American Canals and Railroads. The same, I say, because in all these cases the native American [Ishmael here means Anglo-American] liberally provides the brains, the rest of the world as generously supplying the muscles. No small number of these whaling seamen belong to the Azores, where the outward bound Nantucket whalers frequently touch to augment their crews from the hardy peasants of those rocky shores. (127)

In this account of the Pequod's division of labor, Ishmael expands the structure in place on the boat to American society, making it a cornerstone of the way the United States operates. Brains and muscles attach to the appropriate racial category of the particular human subject. In the end, the White man always disposes.

This passage appears in a chapter entitled "Knights and Squires," in which the knights are the Anglo-American captains and their mates, while the squires are their muscle-bound colored servants. By giving the chapter this title, Melville/Ishmael connects the division of labor on the Pequod with the master/servant trope embodied in the world's first novel, Don Quijote. Paralleling the relationship between the ship's management and its deckhands with the relationship between Quijote and Sancho Panza provides a foundation for reading the trope forward in time as well, across the many faithful, colored sidekicks that have populated the American popular imaginary, with one of the most prominent among them being the inarticulate Tonto, whose name means "silly" in Spanish and who somehow helped to facilitate the Lone Ranger's repeated successes in spite of his simple nature.

If the cultural dimension of the trope of Eurocentric intellectualism moves seamlessly from *Moby Dick* to the Lone Ranger, the historical-material manifestation of the trope has been no less persistent, albeit more obviously destructive. A fictional work could not invent a better illustration of the supremacy of the politically charged American imaginary than the historical statements made by American presidents at war in the years immediately before the dawn of the twentieth century and in those immediately after its end. *The Dogeaters*, Jessica Hagedorn's pastiche novel of Filipino postcoloniality, makes brilliant use of President William McKinley's actual pronouncement of the White man's burden in the Philippine Islands after the American victory in the War of 1898:

> And one night it came to me this way—I don't know how it was, but it came: one, that we could not give them back to Spain—that would be cowardly and dishonorable; two, that we could not turn them over to France or Germany—our commercial rivals in the Orient—that would be bad business and discreditable; *three, that we could not leave them to themselves—they were unfit for self-government—and they would soon have anarchy and misrule over there worse than Spain's was;* and four, that there was nothing left for us to do but to take them all, and to educate the Filipinos, and uplift and civilize and Christianize them, and by God's grace do the very best we could by them, as our fellow men for whom Christ also died. (71, my emphasis)

The portion of McKinley's statement I emphasize here shows clearly that, for him, the formal colonization of the Philippines was a civilizing mission targeting a people incapable of sorting out their own affairs or organizing their own lives. By definition, Filipinos needed the United States' superior brain power.

In the first decade after the twentieth century, American president George W. Bush was more careful than McKinley had been not to demean openly the natives who (according to his rhetoric) were depending on the United States for liberation. Still, the idea that democratization, civilization, and proper thinking were the property of the United States, and that it had shouldered a burden to spread these qualities to the Middle East, appeared in his every statement on America's campaign in Iraq, leading up to the March

2003 invasion and throughout the first years of occupation. In a November 6, 2003, speech before the National Endowment for Democracy, for example, President Bush made clear that the Iraq campaign was part of the historic civilizing mission that burdens the United States:

> This is a massive and difficult undertaking—it is worth our effort, it is worth our sacrifice, because we know the stakes. The failure of Iraqi democracy would embolden terrorists around the world, increase dangers to the American people, and extinguish the hopes of millions in the region. Iraqi democracy will succeed—and that success will send forth the news, from Damascus to Teheran—that freedom can be the future of every nation. The establishment of a free Iraq at the heart of the Middle East will be a watershed event in the global democratic revolution. Sixty years of Western nations excusing and accommodating the lack of freedom in the Middle East did nothing to make us safe—because in the long run, stability cannot be purchased at the expense of liberty. As long as the Middle East remains a place where freedom does not flourish, it will remain a place of stagnation, resentment, and violence ready for export. And with the spread of weapons that can bring catastrophic harm to our country and to our friends, it would be reckless to accept the status quo. Therefore, the United States has adopted a new policy, a forward strategy of freedom in the Middle East. This strategy requires the same persistence and energy and idealism we have shown before. And it will yield the same results. As in Europe, as in Asia, as in every region of the world, the advance of freedom leads to peace.

On the one hand, Bush makes clear that it is the American president who best understands the "hopes of millions" of Arabs living in the Middle East. Yet in this speech, as in most of Bush's statements regarding the Iraq campaign in the first year of occupation, he is careful to supplement the declaration of American indispensability with a reference to Iraqi partnership. Still, the trope of the colored native as squire or underling, rather than full partner, is so prominent in the American imaginary that this subtle shift in presidential rhetoric was often lost on lower-ranking spokespeople for the campaign. L. Paul Bremer III, America's governor of Iraq during the first year of occupation, for example, spoke to a *New York Times* reporter a few weeks after the capture of Saddam Hussein in terms that made it clear that Iraq needed to develop itself by imitating the United States. He called for "televised debates" and "town-hall meetings" that might infuse a sense of citizenship in the average Iraqi, explaining to the reporter: "You know, the kind of things that are sort of standard, and they're so much part of our culture it's difficult to distance yourself from it. It's the kind of things you do in high-school civics classes. It all needs to happen here. It's never happened here, and it needs to happen rather quickly" (Cohen). Later in the same article, an American sergeant puts it more bluntly: "We're just trying to get them to evolve, to open their eyes. That's the mission." These comments may be condescending, but they are generous compared to those of a captain quoted by the same paper two weeks earlier: "You have to understand the Arab mind. The only thing they understand is force—force, pride, and saving face" (Filkins).

What is striking about these early American statements, even in their more crafted, official versions, is the extent to which they reflect centuries-old categories for comprehending the relationships of Western imperial powers and their subjects. Edward W. Said's *Orientalism* is often viewed today as the text that created the field of postcolonial literary studies by exemplifying the way discourse analysis might be used to discuss the colonial project. But Said's analysis also includes several other important analytical strains that have not influenced postcolonial studies as much as they should have. Among these is a careful tracing through the book's second half of the emergence of Eurocentric intellectualism as a companion to the West's Orientalist/imperialist project in the Middle East and elsewhere.

Said's first sustained discussion of this connection occurs in a passage dealing with late eighteenth- and early nineteenth-century French Orientalist Francois René de Chateaubriand. Commenting on Chateaubriand's account of the Crusades as a pivotal moment in the global triumph of Western values, Said proclaims, "This is the first significant mention of an idea that will acquire almost unbearable, next to mindless authority in European writing: the theme of Europe teaching the Orient the meaning of liberty, which is an idea that Chateaubriand and everyone after him believed that Orientals, and especially Muslims, knew nothing about" (172). Compare this sentence to

Bremer's self-assured statement that practices of civil society, so common-place to every American, have "never happened here."

If nineteenth-century France provides the setting for Said's first observations concerning the presumption of Europe's superior knowledge, the twentieth century sees the same phenomenon exhibited prominently in England and the United States. In early twentieth-century British Orientalist H. A. R. Gibb's comments about the futility of the project of modernizing Islamic civilization internally, for example, Said sees "the now traditional Orientalist ability to reconstruct and reformulate the Orient, given the Orient's inability to do so for itself" (282). But Said's critique of Eurocentric intellectualism takes on special force in the final chapter of the book, when his critique shifts from a predominantly European emphasis to a focus on the United States. Indeed, Said finds in his survey of American experts in Middle Eastern studies statements far more blatant than those of Gibb, Chateaubriand, and their contemporaries, as for example in this discussion of a survey of American Middle Eastern studies authored by one Manfred Halpern: "We are reminded of the doubtless nonpolitical fact that Orientalists 'are largely responsible for having given Middle Easterners themselves an accurate appreciation of their past,' just in case we might forget that Orientalists know things by definition that Orientals cannot know on their own" (300).

The complex connection between the European Orientalism to which Said devotes much of his study and the United States' post–World War II imperial project has never been an important focus of the literary postcolonial studies that have grown out of Said's work. But the connection he draws between Eurocentric intellectualism and American Orientalism after World War II deserves further scrutiny, if for no other reason than to point out the prescience of the book's last section. Exactly a quarter of a century before the invasion of Iraq, Said wrote: "Without the usual euphemisms, the question most often being asked is why such people as the Arabs are entitled to keep the developed (free, democratic, moral) world threatened. From such questions comes the frequent suggestion that the Arab oil fields be invaded by the marines" (286).

Next to Said's prescient genealogy of the institution of Orientalism, which would eventually be transformed into the American institution of Arab studies, the most influential study for the formation of the field of postcolonial studies is Gayatri Chakravorty Spivak's "Can the Subaltern Speak?" Although I have referred much less often over the course of this study to Spivak's complicated and challenging project, I believe this essay to have special relevance for the problem of Eurocentric intellectualism. Spivak's main goal in this lengthy, rich, and multistranded study is to complicate what she saw in the late 1980s, when the essay appeared, as self-assurance in Euro-American cultural studies regarding *knowledge* of groups that were marginalized and othered. Because critical theory in Europe and America regarded the subaltern as transparent and knowable, the epistemologies of Foucauldian and Deleuzian discourse analysis were all that was really needed to create a solidarity between the Western academic/intellectual and those who were oppressed and silenced by the international division of labor. Spivak's problem with the self-assured international radicalism of Foucault and Deleuze is that "the two systematically ignore the question of ideology and their own implication in intellectual and economic history" (66). Following Spivak, I argue that postcolonial studies has increasingly granted itself the luxury of ignoring its own implication in intellectual and economic history as it has become more institutionalized and mainstream.

Indeed, much of the first section of Spivak's famous essay hammers at this problem of the production of theory. In a critique of Foucault's centering of the term *power,* Spivak uses language that seems to indicate that her problem is with how Foucaldian discourse analysis will be institutionalized, not simply with Foucault's own dependence on one term: "Such slips become the rule rather than the exception in less careful hands. And that radiating point, animating an effectively heliocentric discourse, fills the empty place of the agent with the historical sun of theory, the Subject of Europe" (69). Although Spivak focuses on a distinction between Foucauldian and Derridean discourse analysis, she makes it clear that the problem of "the historical sun of theory, the Subject of Europe," grows directly out of Europe's most powerful export to the world: capitalism.[1] Thus, she complains that "neither Deleuze nor Foucault seems aware that the intellectual within socialized capital, brandishing concrete experience, can help consolidate the international division of labor" (69). In a passage that might be fruitfully compared to Said's famous autobiographical "inventory" of his own personal investment in the study of Orientalism (*Orientalism* 25), Spivak criticizes Foucault's inability to "admit that a developed theory of ideology recognizes its own material production in institutionality" (68). Both Spivak and Said see the need for critics to begin any study touching on the geopolitical with a critical analysis of their own geohistorical location.

Yet I would certainly misrepresent Spivak's argument if I tried to suggest that this essay, not to mention her project in general, does not include serious disagreements with Said's analyses. Indeed, Spivak's extended emphasis on the distinction between two German terms that are both translated into English as "represent" (70–74) suggests that her real goal here may be as much a collegial challenge to Said's formulation of the problem of Orientalist discourse as it is a systematic critique of Foucault's and Deleuze's self-representations as political radicals. For in making this distinction, Spivak goes directly to the passage in Marx's *The Eighteenth Brumaire of Louis Bonaparte* from which Said chose his epigraph for *Orientalism:* "They cannot represent themselves; they must be represented."

Spivak's distinctions when compared to Said include a greater emphasis on political economy, which she is willing to discuss directly and at length, even though she is often represented as a critic who never breaks away from questions of textuality and discourse. For example, in the middle of "Can the Subaltern Speak?" we find the following passage, which exemplifies the type of attention to questions of political economy in which I am particularly interested:

> The contemporary international division of labor is a displacement of the divided field of nineteenth-century territorial imperialism. Put simply, a group of countries, generally first-world, are in a position of investing capital; another group, generally third-world, provide the field for investment, both through the comprador indigenous capitalists and through their ill-protected and shifting labor force. In the interest of maintaining the circulation and growth of industrial capital (and of the concomitant task of administration within nineteenth-century territorial imperialism), transportation, law and

standardized education systems were developed—even as local industries were destroyed, land distribution was rearranged and raw material was transferred to the colonizing country. With so-called decolonization, the growth of multinational capital, and the relief of the administrative charge, "development" does not involve wholesale legislation and establishing educational *systems* in a comparable way. This impedes the growth of consumerism in the comprador countries. (83, emphasis in original)

One might easily forget that "Can the Subaltern Speak?" includes such passages, given the way the essay and its author have been represented as uncomplicated defenders of Derrida's deconstructionist critique of Western metaphysics. Yet such a passage does distinguish Spivak from Said, who does not deny the role of political economy in imperialism but does make clear that he believes his own contribution to the study of imperialism lies in an analysis of the role of "culture" in its processes.[2]

Another important point that distinguishes Spivak's analysis from Said's is her controversial emphasis on the textual nature of postcolonial problems. She asserts this difference near the beginning of a long defense of deconstruction's potential for postcolonial criticism when she calls Said's statement expressing a preference for Foucault's method over Derrida's his "plangent aphorism, which betrays a profound misapprehension of the notion of textuality" (87).[3] The oppositional stance evident in Spivak's comprehensive definition of textuality is most directly stated in Masao Miyoshi's pithy claim that "there is always an outside to language" (55). Yet even on this point, Spivak's emphasis on textuality as a site of colonial and postcolonial dominance can be connected—with the help of an instructive recent essay by Elizabeth Jane Bellamy and Sandhya Shetty—to the same problem of Eurocentric epistemology that Said's work also exposes and that has influenced the methodology of this book.

Bellamy and Shetty argue that criticism of "Can the Subaltern Speak?" has so overemphasized the essay's final section, in which Spivak deals with colonial law regarding sati, or widow immolation, in Bengal, that the important role of antiquity as a text in colonial discourse, as exposed by Spivak in the third and fourth sections of the essay, has been lost. By effacing Spivak's emphasis on colonialism's insidious expunging of antiquity, commentators on "Can the Subaltern Speak?" have read around the political content of her emphasis on Derrida and textuality: "For Spivak, what gets effaced in Said's emphasis on the power/knowledge nexus within colonial modernity is the specificity of ancient Sanskrit texts not as 'discursive formations,' but as *language* available for—and vulnerable to—strategic (mis)interpretations dating back to antiquity" (Bellamy and Shetty 30, emphasis in original). It is in the "strategic" nature of the misinterpretation of the ancient that the politics of imperialism converge with textual analysis. Ancient texts must be manufactured, processed, and refined by colonial discourse. Spivak's emphasis on this point constitutes an argument against colonial epistemology and Eurocentric intellectualism. My claim is that even in this essay, arguing against many of Said's emphases in *Orientalism,* the two thinkers overlap in the link that they make between the West as the exclusive site of intellectual production and the project of colonialism.

⁓

In light of this neglected convergence between the groundbreaking early critiques of Said and Spivak, I return to my use of the Mariátegui tradition to read the novels of William Faulkner. Critical theory that relies exclusively on what Spivak and Derrida call Western metaphysics for its foundation is doomed to certain prejudices. The ones that I have particularly emphasized here include critical theory's "linguistic turn"—its aversion to materialist readings of culture and history in spite of Marx's strong influence in Europe's oppositional intellectual history. A belief in a monolithic linear progressivism is another basic tenet held by thinkers in the Western industrialized core. They work from a vantage point that invites the perspective that history has worked out nicely and that whatever problems exist in today's world, there is nothing that cannot be solved by some sort of universalization of Western values—although which Western values need to be universalized depends on the ideology of the thinker. Finally, thinkers outside the Global South commonly insist that there is no real difference to be found in the intellectual histories of the regions outside Europe and North America. It is this third strain in Eurocentric critical theory that struck Jorgé Larrain when he revisited dependency theory in 1989. He explained why he was turning back to a model whose zenith had passed: "The most articulate critics of dependency theory were European Marxists who rarely distinguished between its various strands and carried out their critique from a very orthodox and/or Althusserian position which I found profoundly mistaken. At the centre of their onslaught was a refusal to see anything specific in the situation of peripheral countries" (viii). At one level, Larrain was arguing that even historiography must be historicized and that historicizing involves positioning ideas, texts, and economies both temporally and spatially. Of course, there may be philosophers and intellectuals anywhere in the world who argue against the three prejudices I set forth, but in emphasizing the writers of the Mariátegui tradition, it has struck me that these three prejudices are deeply ingrained—especially the third, which speaks directly to the position of power occupied by the Western intellectual—in Anglo-American cultural criticism, even when it takes the Global South as its object.

I have not chosen to use the Mariátegui tradition to read Faulkner because I believe that Faulkner is actually an oppressed and colonized subaltern who cannot speak, and that generations of traditional Faulkner criticism have misrepresented him by not seeing this. Rather, I believe that the experience and dynamic of the colonial economy have a unique resonance in Faulkner's world, alongside the more traditionally emphasized aspects of his project. Faulkner is both a product *and* a debunker of the idea of American hegemony. His critique of American empire is not inherent in his work; rather, it emerges out of trying to understand his work in light of those who theorized colonialism more elaborately. If Faulkner was one of the first novelists to use both narration and story to challenge corporate globalization, this can be attributed to the fact that he lived in one of the first regions to experience the awesome potential of the United States in spreading global capitalism. To properly understand this dynamic in his fiction, however, it is imperative to read him through the work of those regional (in Rama's sense of the term) writers and intellectuals whose experience with U.S.-sponsored corporate globalization has been even longer and even more brutal. In this sense, a reading of Faulkner that resorts to the intellectual production of the Global South illustrates the potential of widening the canon of critical theory to include histories other than Europe's.

I have discussed political and economic institutions in passing here, focusing primarily on literary criticism to illustrate not only that Eurocentric intellectualism is all-pervasive in the industrialized corps but that it is in no way benign or harmless. As cultural theory goes through the process of renaming its emphasis on the "postcolonial" as an emphasis on "globalization," an opportunity presents itself. That the so-called era of globalization has not created vast and dramatic new opportunities for voices from the Global South to affect geopolitics, the march of transnational corporations, or international media's distribution of information is more than a mere irony. I would claim, rather, that it is an international crisis. Discussions of globalization have spread through a plethora of discursive registers over the past decade, but what should surprise us about most of these discourses is what a small cross-section of global interests constitutes what is called globalization. Indeed, what we now call "globalization" dawned simultaneously with the emergence of the "world's only remaining superpower." As a result, discourses of globalization have too often been surprisingly monologic. At the beginning of this study, I used as a point of departure the premise that the theorization of processes of globalization should be made more multivocal. I conclude by reaffirming that a literary practice that takes into account methods, ideas, and histories from across the globe would more appropriately fit the phrase "globalization studies."

Introduction: Faulkner's Spatial Politics

1. Criticism connecting Faulkner to Latin America and the Caribbean dates back to the 1950s. Recently, however, a group of scholars dealing with this nexus has brought forward readings that take into account questions of colonialism. The Faulkner portion of this study is in conversation with recent work on the global context of U.S. Southern literature by Deborah Cohn, George Handley, John T. Matthews, and Jon Smith, to name only a few. I discuss the most recent criticism dealing with Faulkner's relationship to Latin America and the Caribbean in more detail, distinguishing my own position, in chapter 4. While attention to postcolonial paradigms is most relevant to my own work, other recent breaks with the traditionalist bibliography of Faulkner criticism have also influenced my readings. These include Richard Godden's use of political economy to read the Faulknerian discourse of labor relations, Barbara Ladd's use of the discourse of nationalism, and Charles Hannon's account of culture in the Faulknerian text. References to such new trends in Faulkner criticism appear throughout chapters 2 and 4. I must also cite the earlier work of Susan Willis applying dependency theory to Faulkner, never fully developed. Readers familiar with her essays on "The Bear" and *As I Lay Dying* will see their obvious influence in my readings.

2. Unlike the work of his contemporaries in the field of literary studies, the historian Woodward's analysis of the U.S. South represented a strikingly

progressive approach rooted in social history. As a result, while the Southern Agrarian influence on literary studies has been almost erased, Woodward's name is still repeatedly invoked by historians as either an influence or a foil. Gavin Wright published a major economic history of the South in the 1980s that leaves Woodward's argument largely intact; more recently, Harold Woodman declared Woodward's colonial economy argument still valid in its basic outline. On the other hand, David L. Carlton, among others, has been critical of aspects of the "colonial economy" narrative set in motion by Woodward. One of the more influential recent historians of the region is Edward L. Ayers, whose *Promise of the New South: Life after Reconstruction* employs recent innovations in literary criticism to try to shift the subject away from the categories established by Woodward. Still, Woodward's influence over the field lingers to the extent that James C. Cobb invokes him at the start of both the introduction and the lead essay in his recent coedited collection of cutting-edge studies by Southern historians, *Globalization and the American South*. It was Woodward, according to Cobb, who opened up the possibility of reading the U.S. South globally through his assertion that its history "gave the South more in common with the rest of the world than with the rest of the United States" (Cobb and Stueck 1). In subsequent chapters, I discuss at more length Woodward's intellectual formation (chapter 1) and his use of categories of socioeconomic class in his conception of the colonial economy (chapter 2).

3. An amusing epilogue to this incident lies in the U.S. Postal Service's commemorative Faulkner stamp, issued in the mid-1980s. At the time, it was noted that the first commemorative stamp ever devoted to a former postmaster was dedicated to one of the worst in history.

4. See Matthews, *As I Lay* 71–75, for an enlightening discussion of the distinction between modernism and modernization in the context of Faulkner's novel *As I Lay Dying*.

5. For all references to "A Rose for Emily," see Faulkner's *Collected Stories*.

6. For an elaboration of the category "textual attitude," see Said, *Orientalism* esp. 92–96.

7. The postcolonialist conception of "hybridity" will be discussed in more detail at the end of chapter 1.

8. See, e.g., Kurt Heinzelman's *The Economics of Imagination* for a treatment of economic theory's significance for Romanticism; Ann Cvetkovich's *Mixed Feelings* for an analysis of Victorian England; Deirdre McCloskey's examination of rhetorical

theory and economics in *The Rhetoric of Economics;* and Marc Shell's *The Economy of Literature.*

9. See James, esp. chapter 2, "The Owners."

Chapter 1. Comparative Southern Questions

1. See, e.g., Fedwa Malti-Douglas's complaint at the time of *Orientalism's* publication that Said accounts insufficiently for the special status of *Bouvard et Pécuchet* as a work of fiction (729).

2. Similarly, Robert Young argues that with respect to postcolonial theorists and Third World intellectuals, "nowadays, no one really knows where an author 'is' when they read a book, apart from guarded information about institutional affiliations on the dust-jacket, and nor should it matter. The difference is less a matter of geography than where individuals locate themselves as speaking from, epistemologically, culturally and politically, who they are speaking to, and how they define their own enunciative space" (*Postcolonialism* 62). However, even if ideological allegiances are ultimately most important, the significance of institutional, cultural, linguistic, and even geographic affiliations cannot be so easily dismissed, since they form a substratum against which ideological claims are set in relief. Indeed, a great deal of colonial discourse analysis has been devoted to demonstrating that the writer cannot simply choose a position from which to speak, since such radical free will allows for the epistemic violence of speaking on behalf of the subaltern.

3. Uruguayan literary critic Angel Rama's concept of *la ciudad letrada*, e.g., is read by Beverley as "self-criticism framed by the incipient crisis of the project of the Latin American left in the 1980s"; this crisis was primarily a function of the limited results of regional movements like the revolutions in Cuba and Nicaragua in "breaking down previous cultural hierarchies" (48). I am in complete solidarity with putting a thinker like Rama in historical context, as Beverley does in this passage. My ambivalence stems from the double standard involved in historicizing the local intellectual while leaving intact the presentation of the Continental thinker as a producer of true knowledge, manifested here in repeated references to Walter Benjamin as a context-free authority: "Walter Benjamin reminded us" (24); "what Walter Benjamin called" (37, 44); "Walter Benjamin makes" (68), etc.

4. "In Empire and its reign of biopower, economic production and political constitution tend increasingly to coincide" (Hardt and Negri 41).

5. A generation before Mariátegui, José Martí of Cuba published a powerful argument tying *mestizaje* to the Americas. Also cf. the work of Vasconcelos and Rodó, discussed in this chapter.

6. A Vasconcelos-like racialist conception of Peruvian reality was being promoted at the time by Victor Raul Haya de la Torre (1895–1979), founder of the political party Alianza Popular Revolucionaria Americana (APRA). At the level of national politics, Mariátegui's debate was with Haya de la Torre, but at the level of theoretical discourse, his main interlocutor was the Mexican Vasconcelos.

7. For discussions of Italian Marxism's role as a catalyst in Mariátegui's thinking, see Melis; Chavarría 66–70; Quijano, *Introducción* 40–45.

8. See Davidson 71–72; Ransome 71.

9. Mariátegui's clearest statement on this point can be found at the opening of the essay "Anti-Imperialist Viewpoint" (*Heroic* 130).

10. On the question of postcolonial studies' relationship with Latin American studies, see also Mignolo (112–24) and Karem, although these treatments, unlike Pratt's, show little interest in the role of political economy.

11. As an excellent example, see the homage to—cum critique of—Bourdieu in García Canclini, *Transforming* 17–19.

12. I explore this claim at more length in chapters 3 and 4. It should be noted here, however, that the tradition of deconstructionist thought in Europe takes aim at this same philosophical prejudice.

13. Also cf. Kokotovic's statement about García Canclini's conception of the hybrid: "Su vision de la modernidad no cabe dentro de la lógica unilineal del desarrollismo, y la posmodernidad, según García Canclini, no es una etapa que sigue necessariamente a la modernidad" [His vision of modernity does not follow the unilinear logic of development, and postmodernism, according to García Canclini, is not a stage that follows necessarily from modernity] (292).

14. The critical bibliography dealing with the Agrarians is voluminous. Examples of the divergent characterizations of their project can be found in Kreyling 3–18; Singal 198–231; and Thomas Daniel Young 429–35.

15. The question of the Mariáteguian political legacy is complicated and deserving of the attention Becker gives it. Much more could be said about Mariátegui's place in contemporary Peruvian discourse. Mariátegui was an opposition figure in Peru, persecuted throughout his life but celebrated as a national hero

upon his death. Immediately after his funeral, his fiercest rivals replaced his closest followers at the head of the political party he had helped found, but he nevertheless remained a more influential and important figure than these party leaders over the course of Peruvian history. Mariátegui's name was also appropriated by the Maoist Sendero Luminoso group of armed revolutionaries in the 1980s and 1990s. Today, one finds his image featured prominently, alongside those of Marilyn Monroe and Batman, above the entrance to a comic-book store in the upscale Miraflores neighborhood of Lima.

16. Thanks are owed to Theotonio Dos Santos, for calling my attention to this publication history, and to Gabriela Maya, for putting me in touch with him.

17. For overviews and general discussions of the movement, see Chilcote; Dos Santos, *La teoría*; Larrain; Lindstrom; Palma.

18. All translations from Amin's *Azmat al-mujtama' al-'Arabi* are my own.

19. See, e.g., Dorfman and Mattelart; Quijano, *Dominacion*. For a critique of "the cultural dependency thesis," see Tomlinson.

20. For exceptions, see Lindstrom; Beverley; and Trigo, each of whom connects Rama and the *dependentistas*.

21. All translations from Cornejo Polar's work are my own.

22. García Canclini comments on the distinction between his approach and the North American postmodernist method in an interview with Patrick Murphy (Murphy 86–87). In the comment quoted there, one particularly sees his emphasis on the distinctness of Latin America's local situation.

23. Neither de Grandis nor Trigo, in articles comparing García Canclini to European and American postmodern critics, including Bhabha, finds significant distinctions. Beverley also emphasizes the similarities between Bhabha and García Canclini (123, 125, 126).

24. See O'Connor for a typical overview of García Canclini's career that interprets him as a lapsed leftist.

25. See Yudice, who, in introducing his translation of García Canclini's most recent work to be published in English, reviews the debates around each of these issues.

26. For hybridity's centrality as a concept in mainstream postcolonial studies, see Beverley 86; Ashcroft, Griffiths, and Tiffin 183–84.

27. A similar argument is offered by Yudice in his useful critique of Bhabha:

"Whether or not hybridity can discursively subvert Western reason is less important than its usefulness in pointing to practices that help democratize hierarchical and authoritarian societies both culturally and economically" (xiii).

28. Compare Rita de Grandis's tracing of García Canclini's use of the term "hybridity" back to Bakhtin, which is consistent with the Latin Americanist association of García Canclini and Euro-American postmodernism discussed earlier. As in Young's and Easthope's readings of Bhabha, de Grandis admits that her reading is not based on any direct reference to Bakhtin by García Canclini (46).

29. A potential qualification to this distinction might be found in Bhabha's regular discussions of Frantz Fanon, but this exception actually proves the rule when we consider Bhabha's hyperemphasis on Fanon as a theorist of the psychoanalytics of race and his systematic neglect of him as an advocate of Marxist Third World liberation movements (see Moore-Gilbert 144–48; Lazarus 40–43).

Chapter 2. Social Classes in the Southern Economy

1. Cf. this conceptual contradiction with contradictions in the way corporate globalization is implemented—e.g., as "free trade" without limits for poorer countries but with excessive farm subsidies for European and American agribusinesses, or as the free movement of *commodities* across the U.S./Mexico border, while *human* movement across the same border is curtailed.

2. Another example of distinctions in class analysis being made according to the specificity of historical context might be the role of the peasantry in Marxian analyses, which I discussed briefly in the Mariátegui section of chapter 1. Marx expressed (in *The Eighteenth Brumaire of Louis Bonaparte* and elsewhere) the belief that history would render the problem of the peasantry irrelevant and that the futures of both capitalism and communism lay in the urban proletariat. Both Gramsci and Mariátegui found this conclusion to be inconsistent with what they observed in their local circumstances decades after Marx's death.

3. I am reading this quotation, of course, against Mariátegui's stance that "history unfolds in stages, stages that are not entirely linear" (Chavarría 86). If feudal privilege were abolished, it is not clear what subsequent modernization would or would not accomplish. If Mariátegui never completely fleshed out such an anti-Hegelian stance, his initial steps in this direction were later actualized within the Mariátegui tradition, as I will demonstrate in chapter 3.

4. The passing of the "notorious 'law of shame,'" e.g., and the subsequent arrest and detention of fifteen hundred government critics in 1981, is described by al-Sayyid Marsot (138). Some in the United States may be familiar with this action as having led to the arrest of prominent feminist Nawal El-Saadawi, who had served in Sadat's Ministry of Public Health in the 1970s and who later published a memoir about her experiences in Sadat's women's prison. It is important to note, though, that almost every ideological flavor of Egyptian civil society was targeted during this moment of dictatorial insanity. The list of those arrested includes Muhammad Hasanain Haikal, Abdel Nasser's biographer, information minister, and the most prominent journalist in Egypt to this day; Gaber Asfour, a university professor and literary critic who would become the second-most powerful figure in Mubarak's Ministry of Culture; relatives of the Islamists who eventually planned and executed Sadat's assassination; and communists and other leftists. For an encore, Sadat went on national television and said that he had a list of fifteen thousand more people whom he was prepared to send to prison for criticizing his government.

5. For a contemporary account of the experience of workers in this factory, see Shehata.

6. Although Robert Vitalis's study systematically critiques the category of the comprador in reading Egyptian economic history, it ends with the 1952 free officers' revolt, never venturing into the excessive business climate of the 1970s and 1980s. Vitalis's work represents a significant challenge to the suggestion of historians like Zaalouk that Egypt's bourgeoisie was always already comprador, but the economic history of the Sadat and Mubarak eras must be taken into account before the relevance for Egypt of the category of the comprador can be dismissed.

7. The Arabic term for dependency theory is *al nazhariya al tab'aiya*, coined from a root verb meaning "to follow."

8. For helpful recent criticism dealing with questions of class in *The Hamlet*, see Skinfill; Lutz. Skinfill sees the novel as a marker of Faulkner's renewed interest in the class structure of Southern society, reading the representation of classes in the novel as markedly static: "Flem's career doesn't exemplify the accomplishment of an American rags to riches narrative: it represents a pure will to economic power born of the death of democratic idealism" (167). Lutz uses the Marx of *Capital* and *The Communist Manifesto* to read the role of commodity fetishism in the novel, focusing primarily on the auction of the spotted horses in its last section. He also observes that Ratliff and other narrators see Flem as representing an "external" force, but he

reads Flem's separateness as external characters' misrecognition of the South's new capitalism, rather than as a properly recognized compradorism embodied in Flem.

9. A dubious legend of buried treasure also plays a key role in "The Fire and the Hearth," a novella within the larger work *Go Down, Moses*, published a year and a half after *The Hamlet*.

10. In a recent study of *The Mansion*, John T. Matthews ties the novelistic discourse to the Cold War's discursive binary between American "freedom" and Soviet "equality." This last volume in the trilogy is heavily implicated in geopolitics, according to this reading: "*The Mansion* addresses numerous contemporary issues: U.S. Communist Party activities, red-baiting, Greenwich Village bohemianism, artistic avant-gardism, European fascism. The result is the most topical of all Faulkner's novels" ("Many Mansions" 7).

11. Of course, this is not to mention Montgomery Ward's father, I. O. Snopes. I.O.'s name functions differently than those of the younger generation, which are so firmly rooted in Northern capitalism, but it also points to the problem of economic dependency. Ownby puts it cogently: "Debt was the primary economic reality for poor Southerners. For a Snopes to be saddled with the name I.O. suggests that his entire identity is wrapped up in the poor man's condition and in the consequent need to economize" (116).

12. See Wyatt-Brown for a comprehensive scholarly discussion of the antebellum social system.

13. Several perceptive critics have pointed out this odd aspect of Flem's presentation. Nichol, e.g., argues that readings of Flem are often misdirected by the fact that "Faulkner scholarship traditionally follows Gavin Stevens and V. K. Ratliff, two narrator characters, in depicting Flem Snopes" (494). Froelich makes the point that "Flem's economic life seems disproportionate only because the rest of his character is flat. The narrative never reveals the interior of Flem's consciousness" (234). Both, however, go too far in attempting to recuperate Flem on the basis of this important aspect of his formal presentation, Froelich even calling him "not an economic monster but a frontier hero" (236). The flatness of Flem's character, as presented by the various narrators' points of view in the trilogy, only demonstrates that the others find him indecipherable; it does not provide a foundation for any renewed vision of him as a character that the reader could valorize.

For a more comprehensive recent overview of narrative patterns in the *Snopes Trilogy*, see Robinson, who uses the reader-response approaches of Iser and Fish to trace the construction of a community of readers over the course of the novels. My own account diverges from Robinson's in a small but significant detail and in a point of general emphasis. First, Robinson ignores the category of free indirect discourse in claiming that Mink Snopes has no point of view or consciousness. Second, the general direction of Robinson's analysis is toward the lack of authority of all individual narrators, resulting in instability within the trilogy's overall narrative epistemology. The prime example of an unknowable subject is, of course, Flem. My own emphasis on compradorism grows from an interest in the ways the reader's lack of knowledge signifies within the text.

Chapter 3. The Poetics of Peripheralization, Part 1

1. Studies by these and other Arab economists published in the late 1980s and early 1990s are greatly influenced by the work done on unequal economic development in Latin America in the 1960s and 1970s. The names of Latin American economists proliferate in the bibliographies of such studies, connecting them to the larger Mariátegui tradition discussed at length in chapter 1.

2. I have been trying to demonstrate throughout that across regions, the structure of unequal economic development is far more consistent than are literary, linguistic, or cultural traditions. Even the politics of colonialism vary greatly from one region to another in a way that the colonial economy does not. Latin America, e.g., was for the most part nominally independent from Europe—and had been for nearly one hundred years—by the time the African subcontinent was beginning to be colonized by Europe. Yet Latin American intellectuals like Mariátegui, Rodney, and C. L. R. James viewed the two regions as having virtually the same relationship to European colonialism and neocolonialism. The argument for an economic turn in cultural criticism treating the Global South has been made by thinkers including Brennan, Parry, Pratt, and Shankar, but the calls of these critics have not had enough effect on critical practice.

3. It is just this sort of argument that leads Larrain to claim that the easy dismissal of dependency theory as "outdated" glosses over the many aspects of the critique that identified problems with the global economy that remain unresolved (207–11).

4. In addition to the Arab authors already discussed, an African critique of unequal development and colonial historiography was propounded in the 1970s

and 1980s by historians including Colin Leys, Claude Ake, and Timothy Shaw. Also see Rodney, *Speaks* 65–69. Of course, as I point out in chapter 1, the key text is Rodney's 1972 study, *How Europe Underdeveloped Africa*.

5. Asfour's essay collection *Zaman al-Roaya* (Time of the Novel) represents one of the more important recent critical statements on the Arabic novel in its local context. While Asfour's critical approach is distinct from that of many of the other Arab critics I have cited, his account is broadly commensurate with this chapter's general association between genre and geohistorical location. For Asfour, the Arabic novel is connected to Arabic material realities in several ways, including its expression of urbanization in the postcolonial Arab world; its representation of the peasant reality of rural Arab life; and its resistance to the smothering hegemony of poetry among Arab traditionalists, *salafi* thought among Islamists, and the blind exercise of patriarchal authority.

6. The familiar examples include Taha Husayn's *Adib* (*A Man of Letters*) (1936), Tawfiq al-Hakim's *'Usfur min al-sharq* (*Bird of the East*) (1940), and Yahya Haqqi's *Qindil Umm Hashim* (*The Lamp of Um Hashim*) (1944). See Hassan's discussion of this backdrop to Salih's novel, which includes helpful summaries of several of *Season's* Arabic-language predecessors (84–86).

7. Note that al-Bahrawy, in a brief theoretical essay whose few examples come mostly from the early emergent period of the Arabic novel, singles out *Season of Migration* as a novel whose structure manages to combine effectively the local storytelling tradition and the genre of the European psychological novel.

8. I have chosen to contrast these postcolonial novelistic structures with the bildungsroman because this contrast seems to me clear and illustrative. I recognize that this argument must be extended to distinguish this structure from that of novels of European and American high modernism, which it more closely resembles. Furthermore, the question of modernism bears much more directly on Faulkner and his centrality here. Thus, I will take up the distinction between the postcolonial novel of revisionist historiography and modernism in chapter 4.

9. Although Gayatri Spivak's brilliant, recently published reading of Salih's novel is flawed by its view of the work as primarily responding to works in the Western tradition, such as Conrad's *Heart of Darkness,* she nevertheless understands the key to the novel as inhering in the way it addresses time and linearity. For Spivak, the Western tradition against which the novel was written is characterized

primarily by what Derrida calls "teleopoietics"—an overt concern with narrative conclusion. The Western canon has an obsession with endings, which *Season of Migration* sets out to confront directly, according to Spivak. For Spivak's discussion of *Season*, see *Death* 55–66; for teleopoiesis, see *Death* 31.

10. Hassan refers to the narrator as Meheimeed throughout the chapter on *Season* in his book-length study of Salih. "Meheimeed" is derived from tracing the same character through other stories in Salih's oeuvre. In *Season*, the narrator is never given a name, but he is directly addressed at one point in the novel as "Effendi" (85). The repeated experience of having students with no Middle Eastern cultural literacy, and no experience with Salih's other work, enter class discussion thinking the character's name is Effendi has heightened the significance of this singular sentence for me. Since an effendi is one who wears Western clothes, this further associates the narrator with a postcolonial, modern, urban, Westernized Sudan. In a sense, then, my students are correct. The narrator's Westernization has come to define him, displacing in the process the given name used in other works by Salih.

11. See Harlow's summary of Kanafani's view of obstacles to national libera-tion, specifically, the necessity "to contend with three mutually conflicting but interconnected issues and/or obstacles: 1. the reactionary local leadership; 2. the Arab regimes surrounding Palestine; and 3. the Zionist–imperialist alliance" (61). If the lack of solidarity from the Arab regimes is allegorically invoked in *Men in the Sun*, *All That's Left to You* takes up the other two obstacles as a central component of its drama.

12. Peter Gran goes even further than I would, describing modern India as an example of the "Italian road" paradigm in twentieth-century history and arguing for the use of Gramsci's reading of the Italian South to understand modern India's division between North and South (122–57).

13. Cosmopolitanism is inevitably associated with urban space, whether in the discourse of European high modernism or in the postcolonial emphasis on cities, as in Amitava Kumar's nexus among Bombay, London, and New York. The presence of exported labor in Kerala, however, gives it an interesting, anomalous local/global connection that manages to exclude national space and that may be fairly specific to new labor flows under globalization.

14. See Bose's defense of the novel against Aijaz Ahmad's questioning of Roy's

politics for an argument that incorporates the incestuous moment between Esthappen and Rahel at the end of the novel as yet another instance when an interpersonal relationship reverberates with questions of ideology.

Chapter 4. The Poetics of Peripheralization, Part 2

1. This criticism includes enlightening work by Handley, Kutzinski, Ladd, Matthews, Rámon Saldívar, and Weinstein. Of this group, Matthews and Saldívar are more invested in political economy than the others, but even critics who pay attention to the economic dynamic in *Absalom, Absalom!* (e.g., Saldívar, Godden, and Porter) focus on the Sutpen story's relationship to the linear historical narrative of American capitalism, not to the colonial economy, with its more *synchronic* form of exploitation of spatial inequalities. An overview of much recent criticism dealing with the novel's Haiti connection can be found in Matthews, "Recalling" 257–58 n.1. Such recent discussions build on a long tradition of scholarly writing connecting Faulkner and Latin American novelists. Important older studies include Mary Davis; Díaz-Diocaretz; Fayen; and Irby.

2. For important early examples of the general trend in reading "American" literature hemispherically, see Perez-Firmat; José David Saldívar; and Zamora, *Writing*. Recent studies are too numerous to mention in any detail, but the anthology of essays collected by Cohn and Smith is worth singling out as a key starting place for scholars interested in such criticism.

3. A recent important exception by See deals with the Philippines.

4. This material is examined by Hafez in an Arabic-language study that is very useful, even though it focuses primarily on formal questions and ignores the response to Faulkner in the Maghreb.

5. Siddiq's book-length study of Kanafani is the first critical work on Palestinian literature to have appeared in English. His original source for the quotation is al-Naqib (58). 'Ashur's Arabic critical biography also mentions a broadcast interview in which Kanafani cited Faulkner as a major influence on the novel (82–83).

6. García Márquez himself eventually recanted his many early statements regarding Faulkner's influence (Díaz-Diocaretz 38). Also see a similar backtracking by the Chicano novelist Rolando Hinojosa Smith (Dasenbrock and Jussawalla 269–72).

7. For a critical discussion of the role the concept of influence has played in studies connecting Faulkner and Latin American writers, see Cohn 8–12.

8. Houston A. Baker Jr., for example, begins his *Modernism and the Harlem Renaissance* with a trenchant critique of traditional definitions of modernism. This lays the foundation for his reading of the Harlem Renaissance by examining the traditional aestheticist definitions of modernism. James Joyce, alongside Yeats, has been extensively reinterpreted in terms of his project's connection with Irish postcoloniality. For an early example of such reinterpretation, see Duffy.

9. While Said's analysis has played a profound role in shaping the discourse of coloniality in Yeats, Ramazani does briefly address the formal properties of Yeats's poetry with issues of the postcolonial in mind. Ramazani's use of imaginative geography in his Yeats analysis is discussed later in this chapter.

10. Weinstein's essay is particularly helpful in its mapping of the distinctions of the categories I am discussing here, including modernism, postmodernism, and the postcolonial. Less helpful is the essay's unwillingness to theorize the postcolonial. Further, the category of unequal development is absent from the analysis, and the essay never addresses the obvious question of what allows Toni Morrison and Gabriel García Márquez to stand for postcolonial writing when they are from, respectively, Ohio and Colombia, neither of which has experienced formal colonization in nearly two centuries.

11. The important older studies of the race dynamic in Faulkner include Thadious Davis; Snead. Especially interesting here, however, are more recent studies that take up *Absalom, Absalom!* in particular, reading it with special attention to the scenes set in the Caribbean and their racial ramifications for the Sutpen story. For a list of scholars interested in connections between postcolonialism and Faulkner, see note 1, this chapter. Again, my goal here is to interrogate the potential inherent in a political-economic reenvisioning of postcolonialism for analyses of the Faulkner novel.

12. Richard Godden has addressed the socioeconomic decline of the landed gentry in recent discussions of Faulkner's South: "At least in the agricultural section, and at least until the late [nineteen-]thirties, [Southern] owners were not a bourgeoisie. The planter's concern with the maintenance of repressive social relations, as a means to a low-wage economy, marginalized those props to the bourgeois world—individual freedom and consumerism. Consequently, the planter

was a bourgeois in an impacted state of development" (129). What Godden calls an "impacted state of development" might be called a dependent state of development by a Latin American economist.

13. Sutpen several times equates going to the West Indies with becoming rich (195, 199, 201).

14. Generations of Faulkner critics have been confused by Thomas Sutpen being sent to Haiti two decades after it had gained its independence and abolished slavery. Part of the recent spike in interest in Haiti's role in the novel is centered on fascinating interpretations of this anachronism. To Godden, the text's unwillingness to end Haitian slavery and institute independence functions symbolically to reinforce the role of the Haitian Revolution as an ever-present specter haunting slave owners in the U.S. South. Kutzinski's explanation is that Faulkner actually means Cuba (65–66). Matthews compellingly argues that the novel's sporadic account of the Haitian uprising never uses the term *slave*, thus allowing the event to be read as an account of the continuing deep structure of the economic system of peonage, which endured even after formal independence ("Recalling" 252). Each of these readings suggests that this historical "error" coexists with the passage's many subtle historical verities. To those cited by the critics mentioned here, I would add the role white privilege played in facilitating material gain in Haiti's colonial economy.

15. See Rodney, *Speaks* for specific references to his debt to James (14–16, 28–29), his commitment to Marxism and historical materialism (8–10, 17–19, 27), and his interest in dependency theory (65–69).

16. I have already mentioned the work of Thadious Davis and of Snead, in addition to several recent comparativist analyses of the race question in Faulkner as seen through a Caribbean lens. For an older study that effectively presents Faulkner's nonfictional pronouncements on the race question, see Peavy. For a more recent and unique take on the race question in Faulkner, see Spillers.

17. Of the many excellent discussions of Bon's role in the novel focusing on the argument about his racial identity, see particularly the chapter on *Absalom, Absalom!* in Ladd.

18. See Jameson, *Cultural;* Lazarus.

Conclusion: The World, the Text, and Eurocentric Intellectualism

1. On this point, Spivak differs from the later, more mainstream postcolonial position expressed by Bhabha in a passage quoted and discussed in chapter 1: "What does demand further discussion is whether the 'new' languages of theoretical critique (semiotic, poststructuralist, deconstructionist and the rest) simply reflect those geopolitical divisions and their spheres of influence. Are the interests of 'Western' theory necessarily collusive with the hegemonic role of the West as a power bloc?" (20). Bhabha's response to this question is an extended and emphatic "no."

2. See, e.g., his introduction to *Culture and Imperialism*.

3. The quotation from Said reads, "Derrida's criticism moves us *into* the text, Foucault's *in* and *out.*" It is from *The World, the Text, and the Critic*.

WORKS CITED

'Abdel-Fadhil, Mahmoud. *Al-fikr al-iqtisadi al-'Arabi wa qadaya al-taharrur wal-tanmiyah wal-wahdah* [Arab Economic Thought and the Issues of Liberation, Development, and Unity]. Beirut: Center for Arabic Unity Studies, 1982.

Aboul-Ela, Hosam. "Comparative Hybridities: Latin American Intellectuals and Postcolonialists." *Rethinking Marxism* 16.3 (2004): 261–79.

Ahmad, Aijaz. *In Theory: Classes, Nations, Literatures.* New York: Verso, 1992.

Ake, Claude. *A Political Economy of Africa.* Harlow, Essex: Longman, 1981.

al-Bahrawy, Sayyid. "Al shakl al tab'a km'auq li wathifat al adab" [Derivative (or Dependent) Form as an Obstacle to the Position of Literature]. *Adab wa Naqd,* January 1982, 72–79.

Allen, Roger. *The Arabic Novel: An Historical and Critical Introduction.* Syracuse: Syracuse UP, 1982.

al-Naqib, Fadhil. "Hakadha tantahi al-qisas, hakadha tabda'" [Thus the Stories End, Thus They Begin]. *Al-Hadaf* 681, 11 July 1983, 56–62.

Alnasrawi, Abbas. *Arab Nationalism, Oil, and the Political Economy of Dependency.* New York: Greenwood, 1991.

Al-Sayyid Marsot, Afaf Lutfi. *A Short History of Modern Egypt.* New York: Cambridge UP, 1985.

'Amal, Mahdi. *Minaqashat wa Ahadith* [Discussions and Interviews]. Beirut: Dar al-Farabi, 1990.

Amin, Samir. *The Arab Nation.* Trans. Michael Pallis. London: Zed, 1978.

———. *Azmat al-mujtama' al-'Arabi* [The Crisis in Arab Society]. Cairo: Dar al-mustaqbal al-'Arabi, 1985.

———. *Eurocentrism.* Trans. Russell Moore. New York: Monthly Review P, 1989.

———. *Unequal Development: An Essay on the Social Formations of Peripheral Capitalism.* Trans. Brian Pierce. New York: Monthly Review P, 1976.

Anderson, Benedict. *Imagined Communities: Reflections on the Origin and Spread of Nationalism.* New York: Verso, 1991.

Aricó, José, ed. *Mariátegui y los orígenes del marxismo Latinoamericano.* México: Siglo Veintiuno, 1980.

Ashcroft, Bill, Gareth Griffiths, and Helen Tiffin. *The Post-colonial Studies Reader.* New York: Routledge, 1995.

Asfour, Gaber. *Zaman al-Roaya* [Time of the Novel]. Damascus: Dar al-Mada, 1999.

'Ashur, Radwa. *Al-tariq ila al-khayma al-ukhra: dirasa fi-l-'amal Ghassan Kanafani* [The Road to the Other Tent: A Study of the Works of Ghassan Kanafani]. 1977. Beirut: Dar al-Adab, 1981.

Ayers, Edward L. *The Promise of the New South: Life after Reconstruction.* New York: Oxford UP, 1992.

Baker, Houston A., Jr. *Modernism and the Harlem Renaissance.* Chicago: U of Chicago P, 1987.

Becker, Marc. *Mariátegui and Latin American Marxist Theory.* Athens: Center for International Studies, 1993.

Beebe, Maurice. "Introduction: What Modernism Was." *Journal of Modern Literature* 3 (July 1974): 1065–84.

Bellamy, Elizabeth Jane, and Sandhya Shetty. "Postcolonialism's Archive Fever." *Diacritics* 30.1 (2000): 25–48.

Beverley, John. *Subalternity and Representation: Arguments in Cultural Theory.* Durham: Duke UP, 1999.

Bhabha, Homi. *The Location of Culture.* New York: Routledge, 1994.

Bleikasten, André. "Faulkner from a European Perspective." Weinstein, *Cambridge Companion* 75–95.

Blotner, Joseph. *William Faulkner: A Biography.* New York: Random House, 1984.

Bose, Brinda. "In Desire and in Death: Eroticism as Politics in Arundhati Roy's *The God of Small Things.*" *Ariel: A Review of International English Literature* 29.2 (1998): 59–72.

Brennan, Timothy. "Postcolonial Studies between the European Wars: An Intellectual History." *Marxism, Modernity and Postcolonial Studies*. Ed. Crystal Bartolovich and Neil Lazarus. New York: Cambridge UP, 2002. 185–203.

Brooks, Cleanth. *William Faulkner: The Yoknapatawpha Country*. 1963. Baton Rouge: Louisiana State UP, 1990.

Bush, George. "Address to the Endowment for Democracy." 6 November 2003. http://www.whitehouse.gov/news/releases/2003/11/20031106-2.html.

Carlton, David L. "The Revolution from Above: The National Market and the Beginnings of Industrialization in North Carolina." *Journal of American History* 77 (September 1990): 445–75.

Carrillo, Teresa. "Cross-Border Talk: Transnational Perspectives on Labor, Race, and Sexuality." *Talking Visions: Multicultural Feminism in a Transnational Age*. Ed. Ella Shohat. Cambridge: MIT P, 1998. 391–411.

Chavarría, Jesus. *José Carlos Mariátegui and the Rise of Modern Peru 1890–1930*. Albuquerque: U of New Mexico P, 1979.

Chilcote, Ronald. "A Critical Synthesis of Dependency Literature." *Latin American Perspectives* 1.1 (1974): 4–29.

Chrisman, Laura, and Patrick Williams, eds. *Colonial Discourse and Post-colonial Theory*. New York: Columbia UP, 1994.

Cobb, James C., and William Stueck, eds. *Globalization and the American South*. Athens: U of Georgia P, 2005.

Cohen, Roger. "Iraq and Its Patrons, Growing Apart." *New York Times*, 21 December 2003.

Cohn, Deborah. *History and Memory in the Two Souths: Recent Southern and Spanish American Fiction*. Nashville: Vanderbilt UP, 1999.

Cohn, Deborah, and Jon Smith, eds. *Look Away! The U.S. South in New World Studies*. Durham: Duke UP, 2004.

Cornejo Polar, Antonio. *Escribir en el aire: Ensayo sobre la heterogeneidad socio-cultural en last literaturas andinas*. Lima: Editorial Horizonte, 1994.

Coronil, Fernando. Introduction. *Cuban Counterpoint*. By Fernando Ortiz. Durham: Duke UP, 1995. ix–lvi.

Cortázar, Julio. *Hopscotch*. Trans. Gregory Rabassa. New York: Random House, 1966.

Cvetkovich, Ann. *Mixed Feelings: Feminism, Mass Culture, and Victorian Sensationalism.* New Brunswick: Rutgers UP, 1992.

Dasenbrock, Reed W., and Feroza Jussawalla, eds. *Interviews with Writers of the Postcolonial World.* Jackson: UP of Mississippi, 1992.

Dash, J. Michael. "Martinique/Mississippi: Edouard Glissant and Relational Insularity." Cohn and Smith 94–109.

Davidson, Alistair. *Antonio Gramsci.* London: Merlin, 1977.

Davis, Mary. "The Haunted Voice: Echoes of William Faulkner in García Márquez, Fuentes, and Vargas Llosa," *World Literature Today* 59.4 (1985): 531–35.

Davis, Thadious. *Faulkner's "Negro": Art and the Southern Context.* Baton Rouge: Louisiana State UP, 1983.

De Grandis, Rita. "Incursiones en torno a hibridación." *Revista de critica literaria latinoamericana* 23.46 (1997): 37–51.

De la Campa, Román. "Hibridez posmoderna y transculturación: Política de montaje en torno a Latinoamérica." *Hispamerica* 23.69 (1994): 3–22.

———. *Latin Americanism.* Minneapolis: U of Minnesota P, 1999.

Díaz-Diocaretz, Myriam. "Faulkner's Spanish Voice/s." *Faulkner: International Perspectives.* Ed. Doreen Fowler and Ann J. Abadie. Jackson: UP of Mississippi, 1984. 30–59.

Dickens, Charles. *David Copperfield.* 1850. New York: Modern Library, 2000.

Dirlick, Aref. "The Postcolonial Aura: Third World Criticism in the Age of Global Capitalism." *Critical Inquiry* 20 (1994): 328–56.

Dorfman, Ariel, and Armand Mattelart. *How to Read Donald Duck: Imperialist Ideology in the Disney Comics.* Trans. David Kunzle. New York: International General, 1975.

Dos Santos, Theotonio. "The Structure of Dependence." *Readings in U.S. Imperialism.* Ed. K. T. Fann and Donald C. Hodges. Boston: Porter Sargent, 1971. 225–36.

———. *La teoría de la dependencia: Balance y perspectivas.* Trans. Mónica Bruckman Maynetto. México: Plaza y Janés Editores, 2002.

Duffy, Enda. *The Subaltern Ulysses.* Minneapolis: U of Minnesota P, 1994.

Easthope, Anthony. "Bhabha, Hybridity and Identity." *Textual Practice* 12.2 (1998): 341–48.

El-Saadawi, Nawal. *Memoirs from the Women's Prison.* Trans. Marilyn Booth. Berkeley: U of California P, 1994.

Faulkner, William. *Absalom, Absalom!* 1936. New York: Vintage, 1990.

———. *As I Lay Dying.* 1930. New York: Vintage, 1990.

———. *Collected Stories.* New York: Vintage, 1995.

———. *Go Down, Moses.* 1940. New York: Vintage, 1990.

———. *Snopes: The Hamlet, The Town, The Mansion.* New York: Modern Library, 1994.

———. *The Sound and the Fury.* 1929. New York, Vintage, 1990.

Fayen, Tanya T. *In Search of the Latin American Faulkner.* Lanham, MD: UP of America, 1995.

Filkins, Dexter. "Tough New Tactics by U.S. Tighten Grip on Iraq Towns." *New York Times,* 7 December 2003.

Fish, Stanley. "Interpreting the Variorum." Tompkins 164–84.

Frank, André Gunder. *Lumpenbourgeoisie: Lumpendevelopment; Dependence, Class and Politics in Latin America.* New York: Monthly Review P, 1972.

———. "Dependence Is Dead, Long Live Dependence and the Class Struggle." *Latin American Perspectives* 1.1 (1974): 87–106.

Friedman, Thomas. *The Lexus and the Olive Tree.* New York: Farrar, Strauss and Giroux, 1999.

Froelich, Peter Alan. "Faulkner and the Frontier Grotesque: *The Hamlet* as Southwestern Humor." *Faulkner in Cultural Context.* Ed. Donald M. Kartiganer and Ann J. Abadie. Jackson: UP of Mississippi, 1997. 218–40.

Frye, Northrop. *Anatomy of Criticism.* Princeton: Princeton UP, 1971.

Fuentes, Carlos. *The Death of Artemio Cruz.* Trans. Sam Hileman. New York: Farrar, Strauss and Giroux, 1964.

García Canclini, Néstor. *Hybrid Cultures: Strategies for Entering and Leaving Modernity.* 1991. Trans. Christopher L. Chiappari and Silvia L. Lopez. Minneapolis: U of Minnesota P, 1995.

———. "The Hybrid: A Conversation." *The Post-modernism Debate in Latin America.* Ed. John Beverly, Michael Arrona, and José Oviedo. Durham: Duke UP, 1995. 77–92.

———. "Memory and Innovation in the Theory of Art." *South Atlantic Quarterly* 92.3 (1993): 423–44.

———. *Transforming Modernity: Popular Culture in Mexico.* Trans. Lidia Lozano. Austin: U of Texas P, 1993.

García Márquez, Gabriel. *One Hundred Years of Solitude.* 1967. Trans. Gregory Rabassa. New York: Harper Perennial, 1992.

Gershoni, Israel, and James P. Jankowski. *Egypt, Islam, and the Arabs: The Search for Egyptian Nationhood 1900–1930.* New York: Oxford UP, 1986.

Glissant, Edouard. *Faulkner, Mississippi.* Trans. Barbara Lewis and Thomas Spear. New York: Farrar, Straus and Giroux, 1999.

Godden, Richard. *Fictions of Labor.* New York: Cambridge UP, 1997.

Gramsci, Antonio. *Selections from Political Writings 1921–1926.* Minneapolis: U of Minnesota P, 1978.

Gran, Peter. *Beyond Eurocentrism: A New View of Modern World History.* Syracuse: Syracuse UP, 1996.

Hafez, Sabry. "Tanazur al-tajarib al-hadariyah wa tafa'ul al-ru'ia al-ibda'iyah: dirasah fi ta'thir *al-Sakhib wa-l-Ghadab* 'ala al-riwayah al-'Arabiyah" [Theory of Cultural Experience and Praxis of Creative Vision: A Study of the Influence of *The Sound and the Fury* on the Arabic Novel]. *Fusul* 4.2 (1983): 215–29.

Hagedorn, Jessica. *The Dogeaters.* New York: Penguin, 1990.

Hakim, Tawfiq al-. *The Maze of Justice.* 1932. Trans. Abba Eban. London: Harvill P, 1947.

———. *Bird of the East.* 1940. Trans. R. Bayly Winder. Beirut: Khayats, 1966.

Halperín Donghi, Tulio. *The Contemporary History of Latin America.* Trans. John Charles Chasteen. Durham: Duke UP, 1993.

Handley, George. *Postslavery Literatures in the Americas.* Charlottesville: UP of Virginia, 2000.

Hannon, Charles. *Faulkner and the Discourses of Culture.* Baton Rouge: Louisiana State UP, 2005.

Haqqi, Yahya. *The Lamp of Um Hashim and Other Stories.* 1944. Trans. Denys Johnson-Davies. Cairo: AUC P, 2004.

Hardt, Michael, and Antonio Negri. *Empire.* Cambridge: Harvard UP, 2000.

Harlow, Barbara. *After Lives: Legacies of Revolutionary Writing.* New York: Verso, 1996.

Hassan, Waïl. *Tayeb Salih: Ideology and the Craft of Fiction.* Syracuse: Syracuse UP, 2003.

Haykal, Muhammad Husayn. *Zaynab.* 1914. Cairo: Muktabat al-Nahdat al-Misriyah, 1963.

Hayman, David. *Re-forming the Narrative: Toward a Mechanics of Modernist Fiction.* Ithaca: Cornell UP, 1987.

Heinzelman, Kurt. *The Economics of the Imagination.* Amherst: U of Massachusetts P, 1980.

Henry, Paget. *Caliban's Reasons: Introducing Afro-Caribbean Philosophy.* New York: Routledge, 2000.

Hourani, Albert. *Arabic Thought in the Liberal Age 1798–1939.* New York: Oxford UP, 1970.

———. *A History of the Arab Peoples.* Cambridge: Harvard UP, 1991.

Husayn, Taha. *A Man of Letters.* 1936. Trans. Mona al-Zayyat. Cairo: AUC P, 1994.

———. *The Days.* 1939. Trans. E. H. Paxton, Hilary Wayment, and Kenneth Cragg. Cairo: AUC P, 1997.

Irby, James East. *La influencia de William Faulkner en cuatro narradores hispano-americanos.* Mexico City: U Nacional Autónoma de México, 1956.

Iser, Wolfgang. "The Reading Process: A Phenomenological Approach." Tompkins 50–69.

Ismael, Tareq Y., and Rifa'at El-Sa'id. *The Communist Movement in Egypt, 1920–1988.* Syracuse: Syracuse UP, 1990.

James, C. L. R. *The Black Jacobins.* New York: Vintage, 1963.

Jameson, Fredric. *The Cultural Turn: Selected Writings on Postmodernism 1983–1998.* New York: Verso, 1998.

———. *A Singular Modernity: Essay on the Ontology of the Present.* New York: Verso, 2002.

———. "Third World Literature in the Era of Multinational Capitalism." *Social Text* 5.3 (1986): 65–88.

Jana, Reena. "Winds, Rivers and Rain: Arundhati Roy, the *Salon* Interview." 30 September 1997. http://www.salon.com/sept97/00roy2.html.

Kanafani, Ghassan. *All That's Left to You.* Trans. May Jayyussi and Jeremy Reed. Austin: U of Texas P, 1990.

———. *Men in the Sun and Other Palestinian Stories.* Trans. Hilary Kilpatrick. Boulder: Lynne Rienner, 1999.

Karem, Jeff. "On the Advantages and Disadvantages of Postcolonial Theory for Pan-American Study." *New Centennial Review* 1.3 (2001): 87–116.

Khashabah, Sami. *Tahdith Misr: Qira'ah Naqdiyah wa Mustaqbalibyah* [Modernizing Egypt: A Critical and Future-Oriented Reading]. Cairo: Mirit lil Nashr, 2002.

Klarén, Peter Flindell. *Peru: Society and Nationhood in the Andes.* New York: Oxford UP, 2000.

Kokotovic, Misha. "Hibridez y Desigualdad: García Canclini ante el Neoliberalismo" *Revista Crítica Literaria Latinoamericana* 26.52 (2000): 289–300.

Kreyling, Michael. *Inventing Southern Literature.* Jackson: U of Mississippi P, 1998.

Kumar, Amitava. *Bombay London New York.* New York: Routledge, 2002.

Kutzinski, Vera. "Borders and Bodies: The United States, America, and the Caribbean." *New Centennial Review* 1.2 (2001): 55–88.

Ladd, Barbara. *Nationalism and the Color Line in George W. Cable, Mark Twain and William Faulkner.* Baton Rouge: Louisiana State UP, 1996.

Larrain, Jorgé. *Theories of Development: Capitalism, Colonialism, and Dependency.* Cambridge: Polity P, 1989.

Lazarus, Neil. "Transnationalism and the Alleged Death of the Nation-State." Parry, Pearson, and Squires 28–48.

Leys, Colin. *The Rise and Fall of Development Theory.* London: James Currey, 1996.

Lindstrom, Naomi. "Dependency and Autonomy: The Evolution of Concepts in the Study of Latin American Literature." *Ibero-Amerikanisches Archiv* 17.2–3 (1991): 109–44.

Lutz, John. "The Texas Disease: Commodity Fetishism and Psychic Deprivation in *The Hamlet.*" *Literature, Interpretation, Theory* 13.1 (2002): 69–90.

Mahfouz, Naguib. *Midaq Alley.* Trans. Trevor Le Gassick. Cairo: AUC P, 1984.

———. *Palace Walk.* Trans. William M. Hutchins and Olive E. Kenny. New York: Doubleday, 1990.

Makdisi, Saree. "The Empire Renarrated: *Season of Migration to the North* and the Reinvention of the Present." Chrisman and Williams 535–50.

Malti-Douglas, Fedwa. "Re-orienting Orientalism." *Virginia Quarterly Review* 55.4 (1979): 724–33.

Marentes, Luis. *José Vasconcelos and the Writing of the Mexican Revolution.* New York: Twayne, 2000.

Mariátegui, José Carlos. *Seven Interpretive Essays on Peruvian Reality.* 1928. Trans. Marjorie Urquidi. Austin: U of Texas P, 1971.

———. *The Heroic and Creative Meaning of Socialism.* Ed. and trans. Michael Pearlman. Atlantic Highlands: Humanities P, 1996.

Martí, José. *Nuestra América.* México: Secretaría de Educación Publica, 1945.

Martin, Wallace. *Recent Theories of Narrative.* Ithaca: Cornell UP, 1986.

Marx, Karl. *The Eighteenth Brumaire of Louis Bonaparte.* Trans. C. P. Dutt. New York: International Publishers, 1935.

Matthews, John T. "*As I Lay Dying* in the Machine Age." *Boundary* 2 (Spring 1992): 69–94.

———. "Recalling the West Indies: From Yoknapatawpha to Haiti and Back." *American Literary History* 16.2 (2004): 238–62.

———. "Many Mansions: Faulkner's Cold War Conflicts." Forthcoming.

McClintock, Ann. "The Angel of Progress: Pitfalls of the Term 'Post-colonialism.'" *Social Text* 10.1 (1992): 1–15.

McCloskey, Deirdre. *The Rhetoric of Economics.* Madison: U of Wisconsin P, 1998.

Melis, Antonio. "Mariátegui, el primer marxista de América." *Mariátegui y los orígenes del marxismo Latinoamericano.* Ed. José Aricó. México: Siglo Veintiuno, 1980. 201–25.

Melville, Herman. *Moby Dick.* 1850. New York: Penguin, 1994.

Merrim, Stephanie. "Wonder and the Wounds of Southern Histories." Cohn and Smith 311–32.

Mignolo, Walter. *Local Histories/Global Designs: Coloniality, Subaltern Knowledges, and Border Thinking.* Princeton: Princeton UP, 2001.

Millgate, Michael. *William Faulkner.* New York: Grove, 1961.

Minter, David. *William Faulkner: His Life and Work.* Baltimore: Johns Hopkins UP, 1980.

Miyoshi, Masao. "Sites of Resistance in the Global Economy." Parry, Pearson, and Squires 49–63.

Moore-Gilbert, Bart. *Postcolonial Theory: Contexts, Practices, Politics.* New York: Verso, 1997.

Moretti, Franco. *The Way of the World: The* Bildungsroman *in European Culture.* New York: Verso, 2000.

Murphy, Patrick. "Contrasting Perspectives: Cultural Studies in Latin America and the United States: A Conversation with Nestor García Canclini." *Cultural Studies* 11.2 (1997): 78–88.

Nair, K. Ramachandran. "The Impact of the WTO on Kerala's Economy." *Kerala's Economic Development: Issues and Problems.* Ed. B. A. Prakash. Thousand Oaks: Sage Publications, 1999. 365–81.

Ngugi wa Thiong'o. *Decolonising the Mind: The Politics of Language in African Literature.* Portsmouth, NH: Heinemann, 1986.

Nichol, Frances Louisa. "Flem Snopes's Knack for Verisimilitude in Faulkner's Snopes Trilogy." *Mississippi Quarterly* 50.3 (1997): 493–506.

O'Connor, Alan. "Consumers and Citizens: On Néstor García Canclini." *Pretexts: Literary and Cultural Studies* 12.1 (2003): 103–20.

O'Donnell, Patrick. "Faulkner and Postmodernism." Weinstein, *Cambridge Companion* 31–50.

Ortiz, Fernando. *Cuban Counterpoint: Tobacco and Sugar.* Trans. Harriet de Onis. Durham: Duke UP, 1995.

Ownby, Ted. "The Snopes Trilogy and the Emergence of Consumer Culture." *Faulkner and Ideology.* Ed. Ann Abadie and Donald Kartiganer. Jackson: U of Mississippi P, 1995. 95–128.

Palma, Gabriel. "Dependency: A Formal Theory of Underdevelopment or a Methodology for the Analysis of Concrete Situations of Underdevelopment?" *World Development* 6.7–8 (1978): 881–924.

Parry, Benita. "Problems in Current Theories of Colonial Discourse." *Oxford Literary Review* 9.1–2 (1987): 27–58.

Parry, Benita, Keith Ansell Pearson, and Judith Squires, eds. *Cultural Readings of Imperialism: Edward Said and the Gravity of History.* New York: St. Martin's, 1997.

Peavy, Charles. *Go Slow Now: Faulkner and the Race Question.* Eugene: U of Oregon P, 1971.

Perez-Firmat, Gustavo, ed. *Do the Americas Have a Common Literature?* Durham: Duke UP, 1990.

Porter, Carolyn. "*Absalom, Absalom!* (Un)Making the Father." Weinstein, *Cambridge Companion* 168–96.

———. *Seeing and Being: The Plight of the Participant Observer in Emerson, James, Adams, and Faulkner.* Middletown: Wesleyan UP, 1981.

Powers, Lyall. "The Structure of *Go Down, Moses.*" *Readings on William Faulkner.* Ed. Clarice Swisher. San Diego: Greenhaven, 1998. 159–67.

Pratt, Mary Louise. "Edward Said's *Culture and Imperialism.*" *Social Text* 12.3 (1994): 2–10.

Quijano, Aníbal. *Dominación y Cultura: Lo Cholo y el Conflicto Cultural en el Perú.* Lima: Mosca Azul, 1980.

———. *Introducción a Mariátegui.* México: Ediciones Era, 1981.

Quinones, Ricardo J. *Mapping Literary Modernism: Time and Development.* Princeton: Princeton UP, 1985.

Rama, Angel. "Processes of Transculturation in Latin American Narrative." *Journal of Latin American Cultural Studies* 6.2 (1997): 155–71.

———. *Transculturación narrativa en América Latina.* Mexico: Siglo Veintiuno, 1982.

Ramazani, Jahan. *The Hybrid Muse: Postcolonial Poetry in English.* Chicago: U of Chicago P, 2001.

Ransome, Paul. *Antonio Gramsci: A New Introduction.* Hertfordshire, UK: Harvester Wheatsheaf, 1992.

Reed, Joseph, Jr. *Faulkner's Narrative.* New Haven: Yale UP, 1973.

Robinson, Owen. "Interested Parties and Theorems to Prove: Narrative and Identity in Faulkner's Snopes Trilogy." *Southern Literary Journal* 36.1 (2003): 58–73.

Rodinson, Maxime. *Europe and the Mystique of Islam.* Trans. Roger Veinus. New York: I. B. Tauris, 2003.

Rodney, Walter. *How Europe Underdeveloped Africa.* Washington, DC: Howard UP, 1982.

———. *Walter Rodney Speaks: The Making of an African Intellectual.* Trenton, NJ: Africa World, 1990.

Rodó, José Enrique. *Ariel.* 1900. Trans. M. Peden. Austin: U of Texas P, 1988.

Romine, Scott. "Things Falling Apart: The Postcolonial Condition of *Red Rock* and *The Leopard's Spots.*" Cohn and Smith 175–200.

Rostow, W. W. *The Stages of Economic Growth.* New York: Cambridge UP, 1960.

Roy, Arundhati. *The God of Small Things.* New York: HarperCollins, 1997.

Rulfo, Juan. *Pedro Páramo.* Trans. Margaret Sayers Peden. New York: Grove, 1994.

Rushdie, Salman. *Midnight's Children.* 1981. New York: Vintage, 1995.

Said, Edward W. *Culture and Imperialism.* New York: Knopf, 1993.

———. *Orientalism.* New York: Vintage, 1979.

———. *Reflections on Exile.* Cambridge: Harvard UP, 2000.

———. *The World, the Text, and the Critic.* Cambridge: Harvard UP, 1983.

Saldívar, José David. *The Dialectics of Our America: Genealogy, Cultural Critique, and Literary History.* Durham: Duke UP, 1991.

Saldívar, Rámon. "Looking for a Master Plan: Faulkner, Paredes, and the Colonial and Postcolonial Subject." Weinstein, *Cambridge Companion* 96–120.

Salih, Tayeb. *Season of Migration to the North.* Trans. Denys Johnson-Davies. Boulder: Lynne Reiner, 1997.

Sayigh, Yusuf. *Elusive Development: From Dependence to Self-Reliance in the Arab World.* New York: Routledge, 1991.

See, Sarita. "Southern Postcoloniality and the Improbability of Filipino-American Postcoloniality: Faulkner's *Absalom, Absalom!* and Hagedorn's *Dogeaters.*" *Mississippi Quarterly* 57.1 (2003): 41–54.

Shankar, S. *Textual Traffic.* Albany: State U of New York P, 2001.

Shaw, Timothy. *Africa and the International Political System.* Washington: UP of America, 1982.

Sheahan, John. *Patterns of Development in Latin America: Poverty, Repression, and Economic Strategy.* Princeton: Princeton UP, 1987.

Shehata, Samer. "In the Basha's House: The Organizational Culture of Egyptian Public-Sector Enterprise." *International Journal of Middle Eastern Studies* 35.1 (2003): 103–32.

Shell, Marc. *The Economy of Literature.* Baltimore: Johns Hopkins UP, 1978.

Siddiq, Muhammad. *Man Is a Cause: Political Consciousness and the Fiction of Ghassan Kanafani.* Seattle: U of Washington P, 1984.

Singal, Daniel J. *The War Within: From Victorian to Modernist Thought in the South, 1919–1945.* Chapel Hill: U of North Carolina P, 1982.

Skinfill, Mauri. "Reconstructing Class in Faulkner's Late Novels: *The Hamlet* and the Discovery of Capital." *Studies in American Fiction* 24.2 (1996): 151–69.

Snead, James. *Figures of Division: William Faulkner's Major Novels.* New York: Methuen, 1986.

Sommer, Doris. "Irresistible Romance: The Foundational Fictions of Latin America." *Nation and Narration.* Ed. Homi K. Bhabha. New York: Routledge, 1980. 71–98.

Spillers, Hortense. "Faulkner Adds Up: Reading *Absalom, Absalom!* and *The Sound and the Fury.*" *Faulkner in America.* Ed. Joseph Urgo and Ann Abadie. Jackson: U of Mississippi P, 2001. 24–44.

Spivak, Gayatri. "Can the Subaltern Speak?" Chrisman and Williams 66–111.

———. *The Death of a Discipline.* New York: Columbia UP, 2003.

Stiglitz, Joseph. *Globalization and Its Discontents.* New York: Norton, 2002.

Tomlinson, John. *Cultural Imperialism.* London: Pinter, 1991.

Tompkins, Jane P., ed. *Reader-Response Criticism: From Formalism to Post-structuralism.* Baltimore: Johns Hopkins UP, 1980.

Trigo, Abril. "On Transculturation: Toward a Political Economy of Culture in the Periphery." Trans. Christine McIntyre. *Studies in Latin American Popular Culture* 15 (1996): 99–117.

Twelve Southerners. *I'll Take My Stand: The South and the Agrarian Tradition.* Baton Rouge: Louisiana State UP, 1958.

Varna, Rashmi. "Developing Fictions: The Tribal in the New Indian Writing in English." *World Bank Literature.* Ed. Amitava Kumar. Minneapolis: U of Minnesota P, 2000. 216–33.

Vargas Llosa, Mario. *The War of the End of the World.* Trans. Helen Lane. New York: Avon, 1985.

Vasconcelos, José. *La raza cosmica.* Mexico City: Espasa-Calpe Mexicana, 1992.

Veron, René. *Real Markets and Environmental Change in Kerala, India.* Brookfield, VT: Ashgate Publishing, 1999.

Vitalis, Robert. *When Capitalists Collide.* Berkeley: U of California P, 1995.

Wadlington, Warwick. As I Lay Dying: *Stories Out of Stories.* New York: Twayne, 1992.

Wallestein, Immanuel. *World Systems Analysis: An Introduction.* Durham: Duke UP, 2004.

Weinstein, Philip, ed. *The Cambridge Companion to William Faulkner.* New York: Cambridge UP, 1995.

———. "Can't Matter/Must Matter: Setting Up the Loom in Faulknerian and Postcolonial Fiction." Cohn and Smith 335–82.

Williams, Louise B. *Modernism and the Ideology of History: Literature, Politics, and the Past.* New York: Cambridge UP, 2002.

Williams, Robert. *States and Social Evolution: Coffee and the Rise of National Governments in Central America.* Chapel Hill: U of North Carolina P, 1994.

Willis, Susan. "Aesthetics of the Rural Slum: Contradictions and Dependency in 'The Bear.'" *Social Text* 1.3 (1979): 82–103.

Woodman, Harold. "The Political Economy of the New South: Retrospects and Prospects." *Journal of Southern History* 67.4 (2001): 789–810.

Woodward, C. Vann. *Origins of the New South 1877–1913.* Baton Rouge: Louisiana State UP, 1951.

————. *Thinking Back: The Perils of Writing History.* Baton Rouge: Louisiana State UP, 1986.

Wright, Gavin. *Old South, New South: Revolutions in the Southern Economy since the Civil War.* New York: Basic Books, 1986.

Wyatt-Brown, Bertram. *Southern Honor.* New York: Oxford UP, 1982.

Young, Robert J. C. *Colonial Desire: Hybridity, Theory, Culture and Race.* New York: Routledge, 1995.

————. *Postcolonialism: An Historical Introduction.* Malden, MA: Blackwell, 2001.

Young, Thomas Daniel. "The Agrarians." *The History of Southern Literature.* Ed. Louis D. Rubin, et al. Baton Rouge: Louisiana State UP, 1985. 429–35.

Yudice, George. "From Hybridity to Policy: For a Purposeful Cultural Studies." Introduction. *Consumers and Citizens: Globalization and Multicultural Conflicts.* By Nestor García Canclini. Trans. George Yudice. Minneapolis: U of Minnesota P, 2001. ix–xxxviii.

Zaalouk, Malak. *Power, Class and Foreign Capital in Egypt: The Rise of the New Bourgeoisie.* London: Zed Books, 1989.

Zamora, Lois Parkinson. *The Usable Past: The Imagination of History in Recent Fiction of the Americas.* New York: Cambridge UP, 1997.

————. *Writing the Apocalypse: Historical Vision in Contemporary U.S. And Latin American Fiction.* Cambridge: Cambridge UP, 1989.

INDEX

David Copperfield (Dickens), 101, 108–9, 113, 123
Days of Dust (Barakat), 109
De la Campa, Román, 50
Death of Artemio Cruz, The (Fuentes), 108–9, 113, 123
decolonization: in Arab world, 44–45; in Latin America, 33
deconstruction, 170
Deleuze, Gilles, 21, 168–69
dependency theory: Africa and, 42; Arab world and, 42–49, 181n7; and colonialism, 161; and culture, 49–52; and Faulkner, 143; historiography of, 17, 34; hybridity and, 54; influence of, 41–42; Latin America and, 40–42, 49–50; literature and, 107–8; Mariátegui and, 16, 25, 34, 39–42, 51–52, 75; Marxist critique of, 172; and narrative, 134; origins of, 39–40; principles of, 40–41; Rostow critiqued by, 105
Derrida, Jacques, 21, 64, 65, 152, 168, 170, 171, 184n9
Desai, Anita, Clear Light of Day, 133
Dickens, Charles, David Copperfield, 101, 108–9, 113, 123
Diez Gutiérrez, Pedro, 74
Dogeaters, The (Hagedorn), 164
Don Quijote (Cervantes), 163
Donghi, Halperín, 39
Dos Santos, Theotonio, 40
dualism, in Arab society, 66, 110–11
Dubois, W. E. B., 155

Easthope, Anthony, 63–64, 66
Eco, Umberto, The Name of the Rose, 55
economic development: in Egypt, 45, 79–81; in Latin America, 73–76; stage model of, 41, 104–5
economy. See colonial economy; political economy
Egypt: arrests of critics in, 181n4; and colonialism, 13–14; comprador class in, 77–82, 181n6; dualism in, 66, 110–11; economic development in, 45, 79–81; intellectual history in, 43–44; U.S. and, 78–82
Eighteenth Brumaire of Louis Bonaparte, The (Marx), 169
Eisenhower, Dwight D., 10, 78
Empire (Hardt and Negri), 26
episodic narrative structure, 109, 112
essentialism, 12, 102

Eurocentrism: Amin on, 47–48; and Arab world, 46–47; in comparative literary studies, 12; and culturalist bias, 26–27; dependency theory critical of, 41; and economic development, 105; globalization and, 18; in historiography, 17, 34, 135; and intellectual history, 171–72; and intellectualism, 18–19, 162–71, 173; Mariátegui tradition versus, 25; in postcolonial theory, 11–12
Eurocentrism (Amin), 47–48

Faiz, Faiz Ahmad, 139
Fanon, Frantz, 158, 180n29
Faulkner, Mississippi (Glissant), 36, 154
Faulkner, William: Absalom, Absalom!, 3, 6, 130, 140–58; and American hegemony, 172; Arab writing and, 131–32; "The Bear," 88, 147; and colonialism, 2, 6; comprador class in fiction of, 84–96; and dependency theory, 143; and economics, 5–6, 7; and Global South, 130–35, 172; Go Down, Moses, 156–57; The Hamlet, 84–87, 89, 91–97, 125; historical attitude of, 7–8, 18, 35, 140–41; and Hollywood, 4–5; As I Lay Dying, 86, 97, 125; ideology of form in, 134, 140; and Indian writing, 132–33; influence of, 14, 130–34, 186n6; and Latin American writers, 130, 132, 134; literary criticism on, 2–3, 15; The Mansion, 84, 88–89, 94–95, 97–98; Mariátegui tradition and, 14–15, 37–38, 172; and modernism, 2–3, 136–37, 139–40, 151; point of view in, 96–98, 101; as postmaster, 5–6; and race, 154–57; "A Rose for Emily," 6–9, 97; The Sound and the Fury, 93, 131, 133, 142, 157; and South, 3–9, 154–55; and Southern intellectuals, 34–38; and spatial politics, 3–6, 89–90; The Town, 84, 87–90, 94–95, 97; and White House dinner, 2–3; Woodward and, 37–38
Ford, Ford Madox, 18, 137, 138
Foucault, Michel, 21, 24, 65, 168–69, 170
France, 10, 14, 78
Frank, André Gunder, 49, 73–75, 98
freedom, non-Westerners and, 165–66
Freud, Sigmund, 65
Friedman, Thomas, 18
Froelich, Peter Alan, 86
Frye, Northrup, 104, 113, 151

5094303   Lill

SA